GARDENWALKS SERIES

GARDENWALKS

IN CALIFORNIA

Beautiful Gardens from San Diego to Mendocino

ALICE JOYCE

INSIDERS' GUIDE®

GUILFORD, CONNECTICUT
AN IMPRINT OF THE GLOBE PEQUOT PRESS

The prices, rates, and hours listed in this guidebook were confirmed at press time. We recommend, however, that you call establishments to obtain current information before traveling.

To buy books in quantity for corporate use or incentives, call **(800) 962–0973, ext. 4551,** or e-mail **premiums@GlobePequot.com.**

INSIDERS' GUIDE®

Text design by Diane Gleba Hall
Illustrations and maps by Ted Enik
Maps © The Globe Pequot Press

Library of Congress Cataloging-in-Publication Data
Joyce, Alice, 1946-
Gardenwalks in California / Alice Joyce—1st ed.
p. cm. — (Insiders' guide) (Gardenwalks series)
Includes index.
ISBN 0-7627-3666-6
1. Gardens—California—Guidebooks. 2. California—Guidebooks. I. Title.
II. Series. III. Series: Gardenwalks series
SB466.U65C235 2005
712'.09794—dc22   2004060814

Manufactured in the United States of America
First Edition/First Printing

Contents

Gardenwalks from Los Angeles to San Diego

Acknowledgments

WRITING MY FIRST BOOK, *West Coast Gardenwalks*, opened up a world of change. Even before the book was published, my husband, Tom, and I embarked on a head-spinning move cross-country. I began planting a garden from scratch during the El Niño rains of 1998–99, while completing the book's final rewrite from our new home in Northern California.

In teaming up with The Globe Pequot Press for *Gardenwalks in California,* I have expanded on the original material to include recently rejuvenated gardens and others that have since appeared on the horticultural landscape.

There is so much to learn from each of the gardens I visit, or revisit. It gives me great pleasure to reconnect with gardening cohorts throughout the state, and it's equally gratifying to forge new associations.

I regret not being able to list everyone by name, but I sincerely thank the horticulturists and designers, garden directors, and dedicated staff who have shared their enthusiasm and love of plants with me. Thank you for bringing to light all aspects of making a garden and for taking time to assist my efforts to provide accurate information.

A special note of thanks to Hazel White, a gifted colleague.

To Tom and Sean, your love and support provide the ballast that allows me to sail forward on this wondrous journey.

Introduction

*G*ARDENWALKS IN CALIFORNIA takes its cue from *West Coast Gardenwalks*, a guidebook that came about as a result of my quest to discover gardens where plants reign and the art of garden design flourishes. Public landscapes, private retreats, commercial nurseries, suppliers of garden-oriented paraphernalia—all interested me as I became ever more enthusiastic (actually, quite dotty) about cultivating the tiny parcel of urban property to the front and rear of my former home in Chicago.

My husband, Tom, and I were lured by the sensory pleasures of beautiful gardens. Our all-too-brief vacations revolved more and more around visits to botanical gardens and arboretums, to specialty growers of rare plants, and to well-stocked shops purveying fine garden tools, supplies, and unusual products for gardening buffs.

We spent countless hours in used bookstores, where I perused musty old garden tomes and botanical illustrations. Tom, a patient man who enjoys bird-watching and revels in examining the myriad insects one encounters in garden settings, generally stalked different aisles, examining antiquated medical books or field guides listing the exotic fauna of whatever region we happened to be visiting.

But before embarking on each of our journeys, I would commence my search for a guidebook—one that would contain a wealth of information on an extensive range of garden locales, together with notable resources of particular appeal to someone like myself who suffers quite contentedly from gardening fever.

Since I could never find the type of gardener's travel guide I was looking for, I decided to write one myself.

I couldn't know at the time that the project would open doors to a life I could only have imagined.

Today I enjoy tending a lush sanctuary in our backyard. This year-round habitat garden is enlivened by bees, butterflies, and the incessant whir of hummingbirds feasting on the vivid blooms of salvias and cupheas and phygelius.

The Garden Walks column I write for the *San Francisco Chronicle* propels me to seek out gardens near and far, and I continue to discover convivial landscapes from the Bay Area to the North Coast to Southern California. Recent travels to explore gardens in France and England have reinforced my appreciation of and appetite for the diverse gardenscapes of North America's West Coast.

Peruse the garden entries in this book and you'll find California's major public gardens as well as private dominions and specialty plant nurseries. I've also included a chapter on garden lodgings; another chapter, "Choosing an Outing," that lists gardens by theme or type; an idiosyncratic selection of resources for gardeners; and a glossary of garden terms.

A note about specialty nurseries: Garden travelers might be overwhelmed by the multitude of nurseries encountered while exploring the area. Rather than attempt to provide a comprehensive listing, I've included in the gardenwalk write-ups a range of specialty nurseries carrying distinctive plant genera. Looking for a rare native species? Perhaps you're in pursuit of antique roses or uncommon medicinal herbs. Be sure to visit some of these exciting enterprises located within easy driving distance of major cities or in close proximity to highways.

I encourage you to find opportunities to talk with the spirited entrepreneurs responsible for overseeing day-to-day nursery operations. During my travels, chatting about plants never fails to prove enlightening. You, too, can take advantage of such occasions to learn as much as possible about unfamiliar varieties that will frequently be a cut above ordinary nursery stock. It's inspirational to meet dedicated horticulturists who earn their living promoting the plants they most cherish. And these conversations can foster new ways of thinking about gardening, setting into motion ideas for renewing or revamping the plantings in your own garden back home.

Winery gardens: Northern California's spectacular wine country—Napa, Sonoma, and Mendocino Counties—draws travelers from around the world. Unfortunately, many vineyard gardens are not open to public viewing and can only be enjoyed by individuals lucky enough to gain special entree. There are, however, a number of must-see landscapes planned primarily for the pleasure of winery visitors.

Walking the grounds of these gardens, the visitor can observe how winery owners have engaged in an aesthetic conspiracy with landscape designers. The best of their imaginative handiwork produces exhilarating design schemes linking the natural terrain with elements of hardscaping and inventive plantings.

One should not miss the alluring panoramas and intimate vistas, impeccably maintained formal gardens, and eccentrically designed areas of lush informality of the wine country.

One thing to keep in mind: It's important to call ahead to confirm seasonal business hours and to obtain detailed directions. In many cases, gardens or plant nurseries are open to the public on designated days or may be visited by appointment only. Business hours may be limited during winter, or a garden or nursery may be closed for the season.

Of course, the qualities I find most alluring about a given garden setting may not necessarily delight every garden traveler. Still, I trust that the material compiled here will provide guidance in choosing places that will appeal to your own inclinations.

All the information in these pages has been carefully checked, but please note that a garden's open hours, admission fees, etc., are always subject to change. In the case of bed-and-breakfast inns and garden-oriented businesses, ownership can change along with pricing, types of accommodations, and particular offerings. So whether planning a short jaunt or lengthy vacation, phone first before setting out to assure your sojourn is a pleasant one.

Finally, I'd like to hear about your garden adventures: the high points, as well as any plans that may not have turned out as expected. Send an e-mail to westcoastgrdnwalks@yahoo.com, or write to me c/o The Globe Pequot Press, P.O. Box 480, Guilford, CT 06437–0480. Let me know what gardens or activities you found most appealing. From one garden lover to another, here's wishing you the best of times on your gardenwalks!

Thoughts on Garden Styles

*O*FTEN I'm asked to name my favorite garden or coaxed to reveal the type of garden I prefer. In truth, I embrace the exceptional variety of garden sanctuaries and encompassing landscapes I have come to know, because each in its own way stimulates my imagination and wakens my senses. Here are some of the garden styles you'll come across on your California gardenwalks.

ARBORETUMS

ARBORETUMS are peaceful places where the mind is soothed. Wander through copses of old-growth trees and you appreciate simple pleasures, like observing the light that filters through the leaves. Deciduous trees manifest seasonal shifts, putting us directly in touch with eternal cycles of the natural world. Throughout the year, we are rewarded as trees leaf out, display autumn color, or signal the advent of winter with the rustle of fallen leaves underfoot. Even

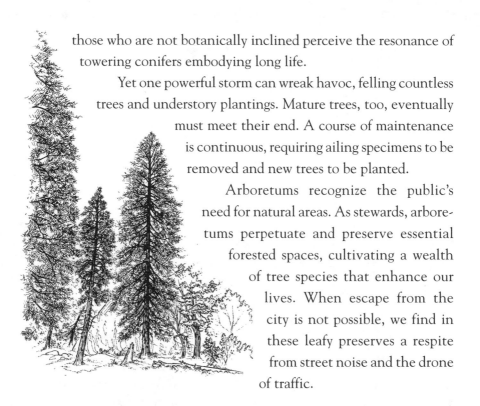

those who are not botanically inclined perceive the resonance of towering conifers embodying long life.

Yet one powerful storm can wreak havoc, felling countless trees and understory plantings. Mature trees, too, eventually must meet their end. A course of maintenance is continuous, requiring ailing specimens to be removed and new trees to be planted.

Arboretums recognize the public's need for natural areas. As stewards, arboretums perpetuate and preserve essential forested spaces, cultivating a wealth of tree species that enhance our lives. When escape from the city is not possible, we find in these leafy preserves a respite from street noise and the drone of traffic.

BOTANICAL GARDENS

A UNIQUE STATE of awareness unfolds once we set about exploring the realms of a botanical garden. Here we enter a gateway that brings us in touch with cultivated flora from the far corners of the earth.

The botanical garden is a place of beauty and learning, allowing us to become familiar with unusual, eye-catching species, labeled to help identify the plants. Educational signage further guides us, providing lessons in geography and giving relevant details about botanical families and relationships between plants.

Coherent communities of plants are set out to provide maximum interest and impact, so that we might wander from a lavish bed overflowing with dahlias to artfully arranged acres of New Zealand specimens.

The range of plants is as wide as the distance between continents. Naturalistic alliances of flora extend over rolling terrain open to the sky or enliven shady paths running through a jungle of strange, flowering trees.

Native plant displays enlighten garden visitors and conservation-minded green thumbs alike. On-site sales are the special province of garden propagators and volunteers, who encourage home gardeners to acquire native shrubs, perennials, a young sapling, or rare ephemeral woodland bulbs. Oftentimes, these species are perfectly suited to the conditions in our own backyards, resulting in naturalized plantings that carry on the garden's message.

CONSERVATORY GARDENS

In marked contrast, we are transported to another realm entirely when in the presence of exotic plants grown sequestered within a conservatory or glasshouse.

Conservatory exhibitions provide complete sensory experiences, luring us along corridors dense with moisture and laden with

fragrance. Extravagant floral displays offer a thrilling break from reality, especially when the atmosphere outdoors is bleak or cold. A stroll beneath tropical palm trees sets the stage for a languid interlude from everyday cares.

In a cloud forest habitat we come upon species threatened in the wild: The vampire orchid mesmerizes with its dusky, veined sepals and thin tails. Observing plant life in the discrete space of a beautifully constructed glasshouse, we enjoy a departure from all that is familiar. Seize the chance to immerse yourself in arrays of flora exemplified by lush, oversize foliage, bizarre plant forms, even malodorous blooms appealing to flies alone, and discover a milieu that exists beyond the borders of your own hometown.

SUCCULENT GARDENS
PRICKLY CACTI, epiphytes that draw nourishment from the air, and

other such tender succulents often make up conservatory displays; however, they can constitute outdoor exhibits in mild regions.

At the Huntington Botanical Gardens, for instance, we luxuriate in the the Desert Garden's magnificent landscape, imagining ourselves far away as we study plants from Madagascar, Latin America, and the mountains of Europe or North Africa.

Ruth Bancroft's succulent garden in Northern California transports us to such an otherworldly atmosphere of provocative plants that push the horticultural envelope, so to speak. Some of these plants appreciate a fabric shield to protect them from the intense rays of the summer sun. In winter, plastic tunnels guard other kindred groupings from freezes.

Succulent gardens also give rise to splendid winter exhibitions. Who would expect this season of slumbering plants to yield aloes aglow with thousands of tubular flowers in fiery tones of coral, tangerine, ruby red, and lemon yellow?

Plant architecture is another lesson to glean. The greenery we normally encounter in a garden is not present. Instead we encounter assertive aloes armed with red teeth playing off rotund cacti; or sharp-tipped, lancelike leaves of yuccas set off by the blushed-mauve, fleshy foliage of echeverias.

Design artistry and gardening prowess come together in a succulent garden to demonstrate the staggering scope of plant forms and patterned leaves. We find quite another sort of sanctuary in these sculptural installations of living plant material.

FORMAL GARDENS
THE PRESERVATION of formal estates like Filoli allows us to experience a refined atmosphere associated with gardens and eras long

past. Here we come to understand garden design as it is linked to the rich history and the art of Italian and French landscaping.

The great natural beauty and lyrical vistas of Filoli's setting enlarge upon the grandeur of the property's restored English Georgian revival mansion. The building's elegant interiors cast their spell, while the landscape offers unparalleled aesthetic enjoyment. We get caught up in lovely seasonal flowering displays and are deeply affected by the beauty of the hardscaping, the ornamentation, the design's harmonious sense of balance and symmetry.

Together the various elements make reference to the idealized gardens of the Renaissance. The history of Western gardens unfolds in the placement of urns and sculptures, stone terraces embellished by large-scale water features, and perfectly proportioned garden rooms articulated by clipped, emerald green hedges.

Emotions come into play as we pass from one garden room to the next hidden space. Mystery and excitement are palpable, and we wonder what horticultural creation or surprising view awaits around the next corner.

Between the keen geometry of the cultivated layout and the wild scene beyond, we indulge in the beauty while grasping the essence of the formal estate garden.

ASIAN GARDENS

THOUSANDS OF YEARS of garden making and plant cultivation contribute to the recorded history of Chinese gardens.

A governing principle is man's oneness with the universe. And while it would be possible to write a treatise on symbolism in the Chinese garden, it is significant, nonetheless, to note the potent imagery and imposing character of specific components: Ancient tree stumps function as monuments. Mountainous reconstructions of rockwork, too, serve to imitate or recapture natural scenery. Distinctive specimen rocks command our attention as individual sculptures, each possessing its own illusive features. The rustic qualities of stone stairways join garden space to rural setting.

Architecturally the Chinese garden is stunning. Its pavilions and pagodas are surrounded by lakes. Colonnades and temple buildings are set within courtyards. All stand out due to finely crafted embellishments. Wood carvings and clay roof tiles appear, as do vibrant paint color and applications of gilt. Ornamental pathways are paved skillfully with small stones, rendered to evoke waves or peacock feathers. Walls that sequester the buildings display the myriad shapes of windows and doors, outlining entrances to the hallowed space, or luring one to gaze upon a particular framed view.

A venerable tree is always accorded honor and treated as a centerpiece, while flowering displays are conspicuous for their naturalism. Rather than orderly, contained plantings, the siting of magnolias, azaleas and rhododendrons, tree peonies, cherries, and camellias appears spontaneous.

In the Japanese garden, subtlety and an essential tranquillity are keynotes.

The garden is a sacred realm. The design tradition looks to the natural world for inspiration, and within the design aesthetic interpretation comes into play through symbolic elements revolving around the representation of mountains, sea and islands, forests, and streams.

The hand of the designer shapes the space to reflect philosophical and religious constructs, thereby setting the stage for a meditative experience.

Zen Buddhist gardens incorporate arrangements of rocks and raked gravel to refer to mountain vistas, waterfalls, and rivers. Elements may allude to multilayered allegories as a way of imparting Zen fundamentals. The Japanese tea garden is a place of spiritual passage, exemplifying beliefs associated with tea ceremony.

Spacious stroll gardens are idealized landscapes, where a lofty artistry is achieved over time. All the senses are engaged as we experience evanescent blooms, the careful shaping of plant specimens, mossy expanses, and handmade fences, all ushering in lovely aspects of color, form, and spatial harmony. To punctuate the space, sculpted stone water basins and lanterns appear. Precarious stepping-stones and arching bridges draw us to explore the meandering shape of a pond with vivid koi and, farther forward, the evocative scenery.

MODERNIST GARDENS

MODERNIST GARDENS redefine traditional approaches to designing space. Simplicity is a powerful influence. Environmental issues or ecological concerns may come into play, or metaphor and allusion might prevail.

Is it a garden if there are no plants? The visions of talented landscape architects and designers are made manifest through innovative materials used in startling ways. Artificial devices may demand that we recognize a different paradigm: Can bright plastic elements be a substitute for greenery?

Conceptual underpinnings challenge our basic assumptions about the nature/notion of a garden. In each unique garden space at Sonoma's Cornerstone Festival of Gardens, we are required to contemplate individual interpretations of the garden theme. Leave your shoes behind as you walk through Andy Cao's creation: Feel the ground plane reconfigured to dip and rise; listen to the aural component that stirs one's emotions. Extrapolate from the festival's garden installations, and you begin to envision concepts that drive contemporary designers who are engaged in creating innovative twenty-first-century gardens.

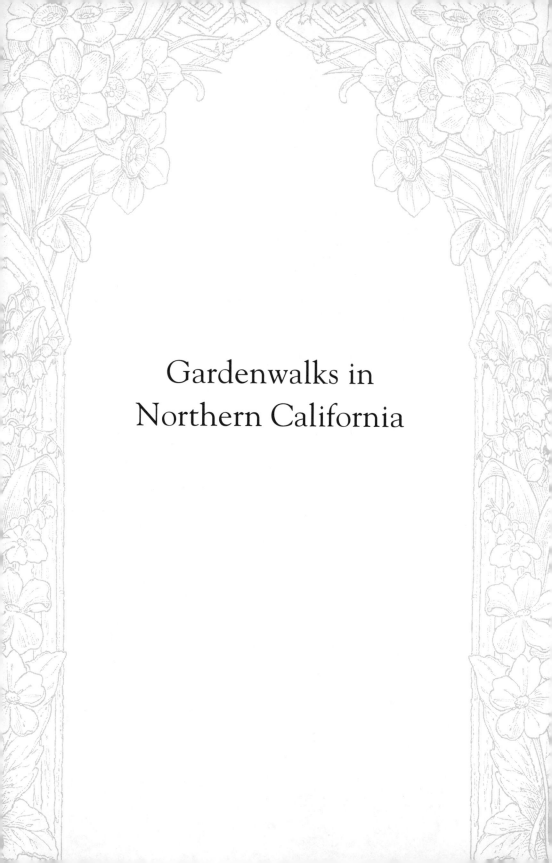

Gardenwalks in
Northern California

North Coast Gardenwalks

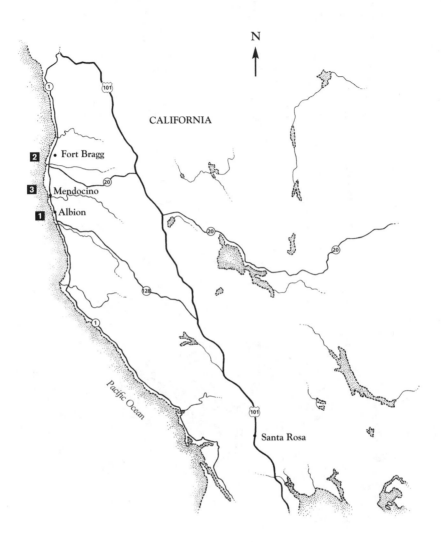

N

CALIFORNIA

Fort Bragg

Mendocino

Albion

Pacific Ocean

Santa Rosa

1. Albion: Digging Dog Nursery
2. Fort Bragg: Mendocino Coast
   Botanical Gardens
3. Mendocino: Cafe Beaujolais
   Garden

1. Digging Dog Nursery

P.O. Box 471, **Albion,** CA 95410; (707) 937–1130;
www.diggingdog.com

*G*ARDENERS along the North Coast, particularly, seem to have discovered just how satisfying it can be to orchestrate attractive plantings with heaths and heathers: versatile, acid-loving, evergreen performers. At Digging Dog Nursery in Albion, you'll find a lovely array among the offerings. Observe these plants' distinctive mounding forms and their small textural leaves, which range from silver and gold to bronze and chartreuse, all set off by cheerful little flowers of white, pink, or purple.

Heaths and heathers are but a sampling of the praiseworthy ornamental grasses and perennials, vines, trees, and shrubs that the nursery carries. Digging Dog proprietors Gary Ratway and Deborah Whigham have selected their plants for such qualities as easy care, lengthy bloom, and plenty of visual interest throughout the year. And their wonderful gardening style has attracted an appreciative customer base.

Admired for his work at the Mendocino Coast Botanical Gardens, as well as for his design at the Matanzas Creek Winery, Ratway brings an astute flair to companion plantings. Consider the Digging Dog catalog a rich resource: When engaged in garden planning, read over and reflect upon the many promising plant associations suggested in the catalog's pages.

Visitors to Digging Dog can enjoy a new demonstration garden that is being established at the nursery's southern edge, with its mix of shrubs and perennials. At the north edge of the garden, above a rock wall, a beech hedge hides a secret garden bordered by a grassy path.

✿ **Admission:** Free.

Garden open: By appointment; nursery closed Sunday and Monday.

Further information: As a retail customer, you are invited to phone to set up an appointment for a visit. If you'd like to order plants by mail, request a beautifully illustrated catalog for $3.00.

Directions: Located about four hours north of the Golden Gate Bridge, Albion is just south of the coastal village of Mendocino. If you like a slow, scenic drive, take California Coast Highway 1 north from San Francisco.

2. Mendocino Coast Botanical Gardens

18220 North California Coast Highway 1, **Fort Bragg**, CA 95437; (707) 964-4352; www.gardenbythesea.org

*E*RNEST SCHOEFER was a retired nurseryman with a mission! Founder of the Mendocino Coast Botanical Gardens, Schoefer purchased the land that would become the botanical gardens in 1961. Along with his wife, Betty, he built trails and cleared areas for plantings. Admission at the time was $1.00, but additional revenue from a gift shop and retail nursery helped Schoefer realize his vision.

Using grants received from the California State Coastal Conservancy, the Mendocino Coast Recreation and Park Department purchased the entire property in 1992. Today countless volunteers and a fairly small staff work tirelessly to maintain the grounds of this outstanding North Coast botanical domain. Presided over by a board of directors, the gardens depend upon admission and membership fees, donations, and sales revenues from their nursery and store.

The Mendocino Coast Botanical Gardens' forty-seven acres are configured to form a plant lover's dreamscape. Given the region's mild, rainy conditions in winter, and cool, fog-drenched summers, the gardens boast impressive collections of rhododendron hybrids. Visitors can admire more than twenty plant collections, including camellias and dahlias, both hybrid and species fuchsias, heathers, and Pacifica irises.

Especially thrilling are the spectacular ocean vistas revealed as one follows along the garden's Coastal Bluff Trail. Craggy bluffs reach as far as the eye can see, descending to a sparkling cobalt sea that pounds ceaselessly against rough, rocky outcroppings. As grand as the views might be, don't become so absorbed that you venture to the cliff's edge. Known to be unstable, the terrain mandates caution.

In September, the dahlia garden puts on quite a show, with deep borders displaying countless varieties of showy blooms. Also in September, a brilliant panoply of deciduous trees and coniferous specimens provides striking contrasts of color, texture, and form. November through January, the gardens are ablaze with the arresting color of Japanese maples, while ocean views thrill visitors with sightings of migrating gray whales on their way southward. Protected by a forest of native pine, the gardens are awe inspiring throughout the year.

Having a picnic on the grounds of the Mendocino Coast Botanical Gardens can be a pleasure in itself. You'll find plenty of benches where you can relax and enjoy the splendid plantings to full effect. The Cliff House, located just off the Coastal Bluff Trail, provides a sheltered spot from which you can enjoy the Pacific in all its glory.

The gardens' gift store features an intriguing array of garden-related paraphernalia. I brought back a bulbous, hand-held watering container made of rubber, with interchangeable tips for either a fine spray or a very light spritzing. Plants culled from the gardens' nursery stock are offered for sale, so that you can take home interesting specimens to plant in your own garden.

❀ **Admission:** Fee.

Garden open: March through October: daily 9:00 A.M. to 5:00 P.M., November through February: daily 9:00 A.M. to 4:00 P.M. Closed Thanksgiving, Christmas, and the Saturday following Labor Day in September. Garden store and nursery have the same open hours.

Further information: Visit the Web site to find out about special events, and to see "What's blooming right now!" Restrooms and main trails to the ocean are wheelchair accessible.

Directions: If you can avoid commuter traffic, the gardens are approximately three hours north of San Francisco and the Golden Gate Bridge. Take U.S. Highway 101 north, then go west on California Highway 128 to CA Coast Hwy. 1. The gardens are located on the west (ocean) side of CA Coast Hwy. 1, 2 miles south of Fort Bragg or 7 miles north of Mendocino.

3. Cafe Beaujolais Garden

961 Ukiah Street, P.O. Box 1236, **Mendocino,** CA 95460;
(707) 937–5614; www.cafebeaujolais.com

*C*AFE BEAUJOLAIS combines a charming ambience with great victuals. Amid a picture-perfect Mendocino setting, superb dinners at the cafe are embellished with organically grown produce and freshly baked bread delivered straight from the wood-fired oven of the Brickery next door.

Take a seat in the restaurant's atrium, and in addition to savoring fine cuisine, you'll enjoy looking out on a wonderfully landscaped garden that overflows with spectacular rarities and ingenious plant combinations. Renowned among garden lovers, the Cafe Beaujolais garden was designed with skill and panache by horticultural consultant and landscape designer Jaen Treesinger.

Investigate the vibrant mélange of unusual plants found in the one-acre domain, and you'll see that Treesinger's passion for plant collecting is unsurpassable. Treesinger once received a grant from the California Horticultural Society, a special honor acknowledging her work in researching and testing plant varieties. She has repeatedly pushed the boundaries of how far north a plant will grow.

The garden here features some 2,000 plants complemented by strategically placed sculptures. Long-blooming antique roses, ornamental grasses, and a dynamic silver border create a rich tapestry of distinctive foliage set off by lush blooms. Explore the Sunken Garden, featuring evocative remnants of an old brick wall from Mendocino's early days.

Stroll through the garden and you'll see how Treesinger integrates drought-tolerant shrubs with an incredible selection of herbs, perennials, and flowers, which are used for cut bouquets and for edible ends. Jaen Treesinger refers to her vivacious gardening style as "the abandoned villa look." Her plant palette includes a wealth of species from Australia, South Africa, and New Zealand and specimens indigenous to the Pacific Northwest, and a visit to the garden offers green thumbs an opportunity to glean innovative planting ideas.

❁ **Admission:** Free.

Garden open: Anytime.

Further information: Most of the garden is wheelchair accessible from the side street entrance near the Brickery.

Directions: The garden is located 150 miles north of San Francisco; approximately a four-and-a-half-hour drive from the Golden Gate Bridge to coastal Mendocino. Take U.S. 101 north, then follow signs west to Mendocino. Or plan a leisurely drive up the coast on scenic CA Coast Hwy. 1.

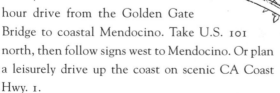

Winery Gardenwalks

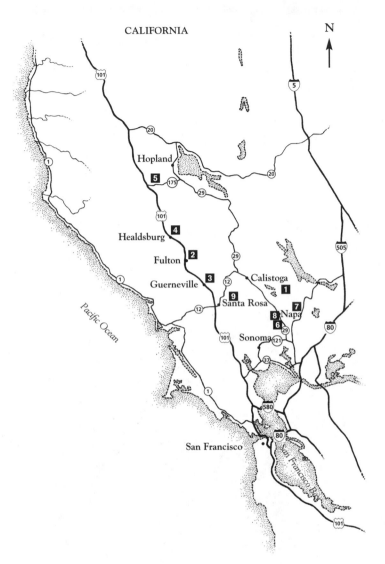

CALIFORNIA

N

1. Calistoga: Schramsberg
   Vineyards & Cellars
2. Fulton: Kendall-Jackson
   Wine Center
3. Guerneville: Korbel
   Champagne Cellars
4. Healdsburg: Ferrari-Carano
   Vineyards and Winery
5. Hopland: The Garden at
   Fetzer Vineyards

6. Napa: Artesa Winery
7. Napa: Copia, the American
   Center for Wine, Food &
   the Arts
8. Napa: The Hess Collection
   Winery
9. Santa Rosa: Matanzas Creek
   Winery Estate Gardens

1. Schramsberg Vineyards & Cellars

1400 Schramsberg Road, **Calistoga,** CA 94515; (707) 942–4558;
www.schramsberg.com

*Y*OU MAY CHOOSE to visit Schramsberg during any season of
the year, but stop by the vineyards' gardens in early April and
you'll witness the extravagant bloom of a sensational Lady Banks
rose! Although familiar with the buttery yellow, profusely flowering rose pictured in countless gardening books, I was enraptured
when I saw the legendary climber growing at Schramsberg. (*NOTE:*
The common name, Lady Banks, rightfully belongs to *Rosa banksiae
banksiae*, a rose with double white flowers. Nearly as often, I have
seen it used in reference to the two yellow species of *R. banksiae*.)

At this radiant Napa Valley estate, connoisseurs of sparkling
wines luxuriate in sampling some of the most elegant *méthode cham-
penoise* wines created this side of the Atlantic. Founders Jack and
Jamie Davies made a commitment to produce champagne-style wines
in 1965. Today, Schramsberg Vineyards is renowned for having
refined the art of wine making, creating fine wines imbued not only
with sparkle but also with great flair. At the same time, Schramsberg
has become a destination for all who enjoy great gardens.

The Lady Banks rose scaling the heights of the estate's lovely
Victorian home is just one of many horticultural delights you'll
enjoy on a self-guided tour of Schramsberg. A visit to the vineyard
must surely include roaming the beautifully planted, wonderfully
designed landscape surrounding the Schramsberg house.

Garden visitors applaud the discerning style and aesthetic
sensibilities that led Jack and Jamie Davies to renew the glorious
gardens that had graced the expansive 200-acre property during the

first golden age at Schramsberg. Back in 1862, German émigré Jacob Schram was a pioneering vintner who planted hillside vineyards and created a belowground complex of cellars in the compliant volcanic rock, turning Schramsberg into one of the finest wineries in the Napa Valley.

In the latter part of the nineteenth century, Schram had an impressive home built for himself and his wife, Annie, and the grounds covered with the lush plantings associated with the grand fashion of Victorian gardens. The Schrams entertained the likes of Robert Louis Stevenson, who chronicled the winery's idyllic setting in *Silverado Squatters*. The entire Schramsberg estate was declared a California Historical Landmark in 1957.

Today, the Schramsberg Winery garden enchants visitors with the exquisite fragrances of hedges, ground covers, and a host of aromatic trees. Creeping thymes, lavenders, and sages are among the herbs that grow vigorously here, lending their delicate blossoms to a generous exhibition of mock oranges and star jasmine, roses, and spicebushes.

Commence your gardenwalk along the path leading from the visitor reception area toward the impeccably maintained house. Here stands a venerable apple tree and, just beyond, a more recently planted black oak. These trees add character to the bounteous landscape.

Approaching the house, you'll pass a California bay laurel, a Japanese maple, and a southern magnolia that typify taller elements in the garden's design. Situated on gently hilly terrain, the house has an amazing veranda, with clematis scrambling up its pillars and roses ornamenting the fine wooden columns and gingerbread trim.

Turn away from the house and gaze on the view of Schramsberg's expansive grounds. Like stately sentries, towering fan palms keep watch over free-flowing asymmetrical islands replete with flowers and foliage.

Continue your promenade to the corner of the house, and beyond the Lady Banks rose at the end of the walkway, you'll see a dense array of Douglas fir, olive, and madrone.

In the spring, the gardens at Schramsberg are aglow with flowering dogwoods, azaleas, camellias, and Japanese quince. One large rectangular space is devoted to fruitless mulberries, reined in along two sides by flower beds, and moored at one corner by a big-leaf maple. Include Schramsberg on your itinerary and experience the charming spell cast by the gardens.

❀ **Admission:** Free.

Garden open: Daily 10:00 A.M. to 4:00 P.M.; closed Thanksgiving, Christmas, and New Year's Day.

Further information: The gardens are open without a reservation; a self-guided garden tour map is available in the visitor center. Tours are by reservation only and tastings are available for a $20 fee; phone (707) 942–4558. The gardens are mostly wheelchair accessible.

Directions: Calistoga is approximately one-and-a-half hours north of San Francisco.

2. Kendall-Jackson Wine Center

5007 Fulton Road, **Fulton,** CA 95439; (707) 571–8100; www.kj.com

A LOVELY GARDEN of perennial plants designed by British horticulturist Adrian Bloom awaits visitors to the Kendall-Jackson Wine Center near Santa Rosa.

Genial and soft-spoken, Bloom once hosted the *Victory Garden* series on PBS, where he offered viewers the vicarious pleasure of accompanying him through great gardens of Europe and beyond.

To experience the garden Bloom designed for Kendall-Jackson, amble first through the winery's varied landscape. Pass through the formal parterre garden fronting the main château, and continue around to the side of the building. Here a viticulture display encompasses a demonstration vineyard highlighting twenty-six grape varieties from chardonnay to Viognier. An inviting gazebo provides a spot to relax and enjoy a picnic.

A signpost across the adjacent driveway heralds the Blooms of Bressingham garden, its deep borders filled with lyrical drifts of plants, melding together in what Bloom has called "macro and micro views."

Overall, the garden plan revolves on artful combinations of conifers, flowering perennials, ornamental grasses, and shrubs, reflecting the refined sensibility of Adrian Bloom's gardening style. The garden also showcases perennial plants introduced by Bloom's father, renowned plantsman Alan Bloom, together with varieties brought forward in recent years by the family's business based in Norfolk, England.

In England, Bressingham serves as a destination that draws visitors to extensive gardens created over many decades by Alan Bloom and to Adrian Bloom's own Foggy Bottom, a six-acre garden.

At Kendall-Jackson, Adrian Bloom lets plantings overflow the edging to soften the pathways, while the tall, vertical shapes of evergreen Italian cypresses (*Cupressus sempervirens* 'Stricta') draw the eye and add structure. Positioned in an asymmetric order on either side of the pathway, the conifers take the eye through like connecting points, calling attention to the surrounding plant combinations.

The design plan's sight line from the château to a pergola to steps leading into the garden results in a beguiling vista. Closer in, plant tableaux come into focus wherever one stops for a moment to observe. Walking along the grassy surface of the garden's curving central pathway, you will notice plant groupings linked by contrasts in foliage and flower color, texture, and form.

The purple-toned leaves of *Heuchera* 'Bressingham Bronze' play off the blue-violet flowers of long-blooming *Geranium* 'Rozanne'. Low, mounding *Anthemis* 'Susanna Mitchell' offers complementary fernlike leaves and a summerlong production of creamy white daisies accented by primrose centers.

A bushy plant smothered in red flowers, *Coreopsis* 'Limerock Ruby' boasts abundant daisylike blooms each with a bright yellow center and petals like velvet. Bloom allies it with the silver-filigree leaves of *Artemisia* 'Powis Castle', and he calls upon textural specimens to complete the vignette—the fine foliage of bronze New Zealand sedge and *Panicum* 'Prairie Skies', a pale blue switchgrass of upright bearing.

Bloom also arranges white Shasta daisies with exotic *Aster lateriflorus* 'Prince', adorned with black-purple foliage, and *Kniphofia* 'Little Maid', a red-hot poker whose slender spikes belie its common name—the alluring pale green buds transform to creamy yellow flowers, fading to ivory.

Rare specimens appear, like *Heliopsis* 'Lorraine Sunshine', possessing variegated white foliage veined with green.

Britain's National Plant Collection of miscanthus grows at Bressingham, and Bloom is expert at using the showy grasses to masterful effects. In the middle of a bed, a miscanthus towers above other plants. And on the other side of the garden, a singular specimen of miscanthus animates the corner of the path, its cascading flower heads swaying in the breeze.

A configuration of espaliered apple trees embraces three sides of the Blooms of Bressingham garden, marking its perimeter and the entryway to the Kendall-Jackson organic culinary gardens.

The culinary garden area is designed in symmetry with stately walnut trees: Its geometric layout benefits from the assurance and balance the old trees confer.

Stroll through the aisles of the wine sensory gardens and you'll discover arrays of produce representing flavors and aromas of foods that correlate with qualities found in red and white wines.

An international quartet of gardens celebrates the cuisines of

France, Italy, Asia, and South America, with a wealth of herbs, fruits, and vegetables.

And in expansive trial gardens, the mounded rows yield heirloom vegetables grown for observation and seed saving.

✿ **Admission:** Free.

Garden open: Daily 10:00 A.M. to 5:00 P.M.; closed Thanksgiving, Christmas, and Easter.

Further information: Garden tours take place daily at 11:00 A.M., 1:00 P.M., and 3:00 P.M., if the weather permits. A gift shop is located in the château. Check the Web site for a calendar of events. The acclaimed Tomato Festival is held in September; tickets for the celebration can be obtained online. Wheelchair accessibility is limited, with broader pathways at the entrance to the gardens.

Directions: Located just north of Santa Rosa, the winery is approximately one hour from San Francisco. Visit the Web site to see a map or for detailed directions.

3. Korbel Champagne Cellars

13250 River Road, **Guerneville,** CA 95446; (707) 824–7000; www.korbel.com

THE KORBEL FAMILY first began planting the gardens around the family's summer home in the late nineteenth century. Today, the comfortable Victorian house, with a commodious wraparound porch, is surrounded by picturesque gardens that continue to fascinate visitors to the Korbel Champagne Cellars.

Towering redwoods, rolling hills, and the coastal mists form the magic landscape. The impressive 1886 redbrick winery building and the adjacent, ivy-draped Brandy Tower, with its soaring peaked crown, are architectural treasures that lend a stalwart presence to the Korbel property.

In the 1880s the Korbel brothers—Joseph, Anton, and Francis—played the legendary roles of founding fathers. Adolf Heck purchased the Korbel enterprise in 1954, and after his death in 1984, his son, Gary Heck, became CEO and chairman of the board.

The current management shows its concern for the timeless beauty of the surrounding Russian River landscape by recycling and reusing materials associated with the winery.

Given Korbel's environmental stance, I wasn't surprised to find within the ranks of the Heck family an ardent lover of gardens— Valerie Heck, Gary's sister. Widely applauded for her role in guiding the rejuvenation of Korbel's old-fashioned cottage-style garden, Valerie was instrumental in selecting horticulturist Phillip Robinson, whose design work transformed the garden.

The Korbel Garden fulfills Valerie's childhood dream and offers visitors a fine example of the type of garden usually seen only in Britain. When he was engaged in restoring the garden, Phillip Robinson adeptly cut through overgrowth to uncover the original layout, accomplishing a splendid re-creation that preserved some of the original varieties used by the Korbels.

Robinson's exuberant way with plants added dimensions to Korbel's lovely setting. Anchored by coastal redwood trees more than one hundred years old, the garden's winding paths explode in spring with yearly plantings of countless bulbs. Fuchsias, begonias, and charming Chinese lanterns with their bell-like flowers are among the more tender species used to add lively touches of color.

Moreover, the gardens at Korbel are full to bursting with herbs, interplanted with perennials to provide textural accents year-round. A bevy of traditional ground covers and flowers are standouts, from free-flowering phlox to hosta with its distinctive foliage and perfumed spikes. Romantic grapevine and Virginia creeper add further lushness. Walkways overflow with bergenia and helichrysum, alstromeria, amethyst agapanthus, and a host of unusual selections.

Tovara virginiana 'Painter's Palette' lights up shady spots with its creamy variegated leaves. In late summer, above a dense growth of brightly adorned stems, the hardy perennial sprays the air with extravagant panicles covered in tiny red beadlike flowers.

A rich sense of history permeates the Korbel Garden tour, as the guides point out both a bench and a birdbath that have been there for more than one hundred years. On my first stroll here, I noticed a fetching volunteer that grew up from the base of a rock retaining wall. Although similar in leaf form to its North American relative (*Stylophorum diphyllum*), the plant was, in fact, greater celandine (*Chelidonium majus*), an English species. Enjoying great popularity these days with avid gardeners, old-fashioned celandine with its cheerful yellow flowers stopped me in my tracks. It would have been easy to mistake this species for the one growing in a raised shade bed in my Chicago garden, were it not for the telltale narrow seedpods that are so different from the American species' rotund, bristly, dangling pods.

Robinson selected many vigorous specimens of shrubs, hydrangeas and daphnes among them. Undoubtedly the shining stars of the Korbel tour, the antique shrub roses enchant with their fragrant scent and the beguiling hues of their multipetaled blooms.

While Korbel Champagne Cellars and Winery attract busloads of wine-country vagabonds interested in sampling varieties of sparkling wines, the Korbel Garden's spectacular roses draw their own fair share of visitors. More than 250 varieties of antique roses are displayed here in a layout reminiscent of long-ago gardens. Specimens include outstanding examples of climbing 'Souvenir de la Malmaison', 'Old Blush', and a stunning polyantha rose, 'La Marne', perfectly pink in coloration. The showy floribunda 'Picasso' and *Rosa* 'Perle d'Or' work their magic, too.

Teas, chinas, and noisettes are abundantly represented along the Tea Walk, on the south side of the garden, facing the old winery. Nearly the entire arrangement here can be identified as the original design indicated in a map from 1896. Directly in front of the house, with its ornate railing that seems to stretch forever, the crisply clipped Japanese boxwood hedges function as curvilinear elements, adding a subtle formality to the clusters of bushes they serve to frame.

Should you find yourself lingering while the tour proceeds, observe a tangle of clematis scrambling through fragrant viburnum, or pause at the gazebo to take your fill of the floral bouquet.

Amidst an irresistible framework, the Korbel Garden exalts garden wanderers with an evocative blend of heirloom plants and new varieties, flanked by established trees of unadorned nobility.

❀ **Admission:** Free.

Garden open: Seasonally, May through October, during tours.

Further information: Three tours of the Korbel Garden are offered Tuesday through Sunday at 11:00 A.M., 1:00 P.M., and 3:00 P.M. Reservations or appointments are not usually required for the tours, but it's best to phone for up-to-date information. You can also visit the wine shop and tasting room, gift shop, and the Korbel delicatessen year-round except major holidays.

Directions: Traveling north from San Francisco on U.S. Highway 101, take the River Road exit just past downtown Santa Rosa and turn left (westbound) onto River Road. Go west on River Road for approximately 13 miles. Turn into the winery parking lot on the right-hand

side. The winery is located about one-and-a-half hours from the
Golden Gate Bridge.

4. Ferrari-Carano Vineyards and Winery

8761 Dry Creek Road, P.O. Box 1549, **Healdsburg,** CA 95448;
(707) 433–6700, (800) 831–0381; www.ferrari-carano.com

*U*PON FIRST approaching the gardens at Ferrari-Carano Vineyards and Winery, visitors are overwhelmed by great masses of
cheerful annuals, bedded out in exuberant displays. Take a moment
to enjoy these riotous plantings of salvias, marigolds, zinnias, and
begonias accenting the entranceway to the irresistible Villa Fiore.
This fine Italianate edifice, with exquisitely tinted stucco walls,
commanding stone columns, and a deep-toned Roman tile roof,
houses the winery's handsome tasting room and gift shop.

When you exit the building, you'll think you've landed in one
of the grand European gardens of the Renaissance. Arguably the
Ferrari-Carano Vineyards and Winery can claim one of the most
photogenic gardens Northern California has to offer. Wherever you
choose to wander within these five acres of formal gardens, a host
of arresting tableaux appear. Ferrari-Carano's endless pleasures
include charming water features, orderly parterres surrounded by
meticulous lawns, and a fine rose garden. Formidable boulders provide counterpoints to deep emerald copses and stand out against the
spiky mounds of audacious grasses.

Farther afield, follow the pale undulating curves of a concrete
walkway until you arrive at the gentle arch of a wooden bridge.
Cross over the meandering stream, which links one garden area to
another, and continue exploring. Everywhere the distinctive sound
of moving water produces a tranquil effect. Almost magically, the
moment one begins to think about taking a rest, quiet places of
reflection and repose emerge, such as rustic gazebos and arbors har-
boring attractive benches. Sheltered from the sun, these appealing

resting places provide fine vantage points from which one can bask in the flowers and foliage. Take note of the rare Portuguese cork trees, too, when you're admiring the crape myrtles, bays, and pines.

Bound to enchant garden lovers with its grand sense of style and the sumptuous spaciousness of its gardens, the Ferrari-Carano Vineyards and Winery deserves an unhurried visitation.

❀ **Admission:** Free.
Garden open: Daily 10:00 A.M. to 5:00 P.M. The Villa Fiore tasting room and gift shop is open 10:00 A.M. to 5:00 P.M.
Further information: Most garden paths are wheelchair accessible.
Directions: The Healdsburg location is approximately 75 miles, or one hour and fifteen minutes, north of San Francisco in Sonoma County's Dry Creek Valley.

5. The Garden at Fetzer Vineyards

Valley Oaks, 13601 East Side Road, **Hopland**, CA 95449;
(707) 744–7600, (800) 846–8637; www.fetzer.com

*F*ETZER VINEYARDS is widely known for its organic wines, but gardening buffs increasingly sing the praises of the Garden at Fetzer Vineyards. This wonderful five-acre garden is worthy of a special side trip, even if Mendocino County does not happen to be on your itinerary.

Organically grown grapes used in the production of Valley Oaks wines are but one facet of the garden, which has been recognized as one of the nation's premier kitchen gardens. Call ahead to schedule a tour, or be spontaneous and enjoy a self-guided stroll through the gardens. Either way, get ready to celebrate an inventive, deliciously appealing mélange of plants, represented in row upon row of culinary and ornamental varieties. The soil they are cultivated in has been enriched with the pomace remains of the grapes used in the wine-making process.

A breathtaking selection of herbs and flowers are interspersed with shrubs and fruit trees, vegetables, and berries. Edibles of all sorts are grown pesticide, fungicide, and herbicide free at the garden. Notice the signs placed around in various beds, indicating that visitors are invited to "please taste" a cornucopia of savory fruits, including blackberries, grapes, plums, basils, and a rainbow of cherry tomatoes.

Follow the self-guided tour map and take in the refined, aesthetically designed grounds of a garden that underscores good gardening practices.

This densely planted, all-organic garden counts many heirloom varieties among its diverse assortment of plants. Highlights include arrangements of obliquely angled espaliered apple trees, epitomizing the garden's savvy style. In addition to being visually striking, these trees produce copious amounts of fruit.

An extensive herb garden contains lemon verbena, chocolate mint, and licorice-sweet anise hyssop, as well as lemon and lime thyme and other fragrant herbs.

Commingling culinary plants with ornamentals might be quite the rage these days, but the garden here has long demonstrated the beauty of this type of planting. The ecological benefits of growing diverse species and ever so many flowers are illustrated by the number of beneficial insects drawn to these environs.

An incredible bounty is produced for the human species and for the garden's coexisting fauna (hummingbirds and butterflies, in particular). Beds of English lavenders and amaranths are among the more striking ornamentals planted. Although historically amaranth was cultivated for its grain seed, such standout varieties as elephant head amaranth serve to wow the garden's visitors.

Pass under the archways adorning the garden's paths, and you'll be smitten by a parade of gourds, delicious muscat grapes, and abundant flowering vines.

Seek out the Mediterranean walk, boasting borders of herbs and natives distinguished by gray foliage. On warm afternoons you'll be struck by the plants' resinous scents.

The Hot Border garners raves, with its panoply of orange and red flowers playing off the burgundy foliage of cannas, smoke bush, and plum trees. In the Habitat Border, a bounty of flowers and foliage provides multiseasonal food for bevies of insects, birds, and butterflies.

A beautiful addition to the Valley Oaks landscape is a new formal garden, with a rose and wisteria-draped gazebo, English flower border, and Italianate wall. Even more recently, the Greek garden came on the scene. Likened to mythical Olympus, its focal point is a circular arbor of pollarded sycamores planted with muscat grapes. Stone benches, a winding path, and the gurgle of fountains help to create drama here.

But a visit would not be complete without a promenade to the pavilion overlooking Lake Fume. Built in 1987, the building is the site of culinary demonstrations and cooking classes. Windows cover three-quarters of the walls, providing entrancing vignettes of swans gliding gracefully across the water's surface. A deck wraps around the building's perimeter, luring visitors on foggy mornings as well as sunny afternoons. Looking across the mirrorlike expanse, one can observe the landscape's gentle rise and stately trees punctuating the encircling sky.

Amidst this impeccable setting, where ancient oak trees reign over the ninety-five-acre Valley Oaks Ranch, Fetzer's reception building now boasts a gourmet delicatessen, featuring fresh pastries, soups and salads, and other delectable picnic fare. Not surprisingly, produce from the garden is used in many deli dishes.

The Mendocino vicinity offers a number of delightful destinations for garden lovers, so if possible, plan to stay a few days in the area and you'll not be disappointed.

✿ **Admission:** Free.

Garden open: Daily 9:00 A.M. to 5:00 P.M.

Further information: Phone (800) 846–8637, ext. 604, for information on tours and tastings. You can book a particular garden tour ahead of time, sign up when you arrive at the vineyard, or elect to tour the gardens on your own, referring to a self-guided tour map. Visit the Web site to learn about classes, food extravaganzas, and special events. The folks at Fetzer had an inspired idea when they made bed-and-breakfast lodgings available to winery visitors. Consult the listing in the "Garden Lodgings" chapter for details on Fetzer's Bed & Breakfast Inn, ensconced among the vineyards. Garden paths are a bit rough, but it's possible to drive down to the garden and park to gain wheelchair access.

Directions: From San Francisco proceed north on U.S. 101 to the town of Hopland, approximately two hours after crossing the Golden Gate Bridge. Fetzer Vineyards Valley Oaks Ranch is located ¾ mile east of Hopland on California Highway 175.

6. Artesa Winery

1345 Henry Road, **Napa**, CA 94559; (707) 224–1668;
www.artesawinery.com

*A*RTESA produces fine wines in one of Napa Valley's most dramatic settings—the Carneros region. Situated atop a knoll, Artesa's architecturally intriguing winery is amazing to behold. This masterpiece of design features a building with smoky quartz windows and remarkable, slanted grass-blanketed walls planted with native grasses. Luminously contemporary, the low, broad structure of Artesa appears to merge uninterruptedly with the summit's horizontal expanse of lawn. The building and landscaping fit seamlessly into the heavenly Carneros countryside.

A host of water features—the glistening watercourse, exquisite fountains, and courtyard with its sensational reflecting pool—add to the setting's memorable impact. At Artesa, the terrace is perfectly situated; you can sip wine, admire the stunning views, and enjoy the winery's blissful surroundings.

✿ **Admission:** Free.

Garden open: Daily 10:00 A.M. to 5:00 P.M.

Further information: Enjoy the visitor center, with wine tasting in the minimalist decor of the tasting room, along with art exhibits and historical displays in the Carneros Center and Codorniu wine-making museum. Although the front entrance features a grand stairway, an elevator and wheelchair entrance are available for guests' use.

Directions: From San Francisco, take U.S. 101 north. Exit onto California Highway 37. Turn left onto California Highway 121. Follow CA 121 for 12 miles. Turn left onto Old Sonoma Road and quickly left again onto Dealy Lane. Dealy becomes Henry Road. Artesa will be on your left on a hill. It's located 40 miles northeast of San Francisco.

7. Copia, the American Center for Wine, Food & the Arts

500 First Street, **Napa,** CA 94559; (707) 259–1600,
(888) 51–COPIA; www.copia.org

*T*HREE-AND-A-HALF acres of organic gardens unfold invitingly before the contemporary facade of Copia, Napa's 80,000-square-foot "temple" welcoming all who wish to savor, study, and extol the pleasures of wine, food, and the arts.

Drawing design inspiration from Villandry, a French château in the Loire Valley famed for its *jardin potager* (a patterned kitchen garden), Copia occupies a site on the banks of the Napa River, where it looks out over a formal arrangement of garden compartments composed of 50-by-50-foot squares, planted in an intriguing sequence of themes and styles.

Copia's expansive horizontal architecture finds an agreeable counterbalance in the crisp geometry of the landscaping and long rectangular canal flanking the approach to the building. The watercourse, running alongside the garden's periphery, follows a diagonal path, repeated by an allée of poplar trees and a lavender garden that intensifies the entryway's sensory impact.

Named for the goddess of abundance, Copia opened in November 2001 and has been buzzing ever since with performances, exhibitions, and a full calendar of programs.

Gardening workshops emphasize cultivation of the soil, with hands-on classes presented by guest instructors and the curator of gardens, Jeff Dawson.

Dawson says he wants people to come to the garden and leave with more knowledge than when they walked in. Generous walkways manifest that educational thrust. Extending out from the building, they encourage visitors to investigate a garden framework replete with herbs, vegetables, and fruits.

The thirty-five or so gardens include the Berry and Nut Grove;

Beneficial Insect Habitat; and apple, pluot, citrus, and apricot orchards.

In late summer, mounded plantings of sunflowers enliven the Edible Presentation Gardens, filled with a bounty of produce the residents chefs can use as needed. Arbors festooned with grapes exemplify the symbiosis of decorative and productive qualities inherent in design elements appearing throughout the gardens.

Seated on the dining terrace outside Julia's Kitchen (the restaurant honoring Julia Child), one catches entrancing whiffs of catmint, chamomile, and lemon verbena from the Herb Garden. Bay laurel trees grow in containers, punctuating the four corners of this aromatic oasis.

The terrace floor consists of stone paving, while an adjacent olive grove made up of eighty-year-old imported Sevillano olive trees imparts a nobility to the surroundings.

An Italian-American Garden is a permanent exhibit, pointing out contributions of Italian Americans in viticulture and to the very fabric of the region. The garden pays homage also to the Italian-American family that once lived on and farmed the Copia property.

Plants in the garden are staked with giant reeds harvested from along the river. Italian immigrants may well have culled the same material in years past to create supports for pole beans.

In the garden plan, beautiful stone walls serve as a unifying aspect. And large stone planters are placed to offset angles within compartments, with commodious steel planters providing contrast. Together, the hefty vessels accentuate garden junctures and focus attention on a host of specimen trees wreathed in fragrant foliage: dwarf Meyer lemons and figs, black cherries and satsuma plums.

Replanted seasonally, the Cultural Garden looks to Mexico for inspiration. Growing here are avocados, cactus, beans, and a cornucopia of peppers. In the future, it will be transformed into an Asian garden, then changed once again.

Peaking in September, the Red Wine and White Wine Gardens are designed to advance insights into food and wine pairings. An array of plants represents flavors and aromas associated with white wines like chardonnay and sauvignon blanc or reds like zinfandel or Sangiovese. Foods that pair well with those flavors and aromas are also represented.

A relationship between flavor and color has been found to exist, so in the Red Wine Garden there are darker-colored foods— like red and purple tomatoes, eggplants, and radicchio—that seem to go best with a dark wine.

In the White Wine Garden, golden beets, yellow sweet peppers, and golden chard appear, with a bounty of citrus fruits, apples, pears, and nectarines.

Another space highlights the Seed Savers Garden, associated with the Seed Savers Exchange. This organization protects endangered heirloom garden seeds from extinction, and its members from around the country send seeds to Copia. 'Sleeping Beauty' melon and Ethiopian lentil are planted in this part of the garden, along with 'Purple Dragon' and 'Belgian White' carrots and rare chilies. When September comes, the seed is harvested.

Located across First Street near the Garden Pavilion in the South Garden, a Vegetable Trial Garden features a dozen varieties of new tomatoes hybridized by garden curator Jeff Dawson. Selected over a period of eight years from natural hybrids, there's a succulent yellow variety with red stripes that looks as if it's painted by hand. Dubbed 'Copia', its seed will be saved and made available through the gift shop.

Avid gardeners tout Copia's gardens by word of mouth. Arrange to visit and take a tour with one of the master gardeners who volunteer as docents. See for yourself what all the buzz is about!

✻ **Admission:** Fee.

Garden open: Wednesday through Monday 10:00 A.M. to 5:00 P.M.;

closed Tuesday. Closed Thanksgiving, Christmas, and New Year's Day. Cornucopia Gift Shop is open during regular hours.

Further information: Check the Web site for a calendar of garden events. You must have a special ticket to visit Copia during the annual Mustard Festival held in March; call for details. Tickets to Copia may be purchased online or by phoning (707) 259–1600. Call Julia's Kitchen at (707) 265–5700 to make a reservation for lunch or dinner. Call the American Market Cafe at (707) 265–5701 to confirm lunch hours; coffee service is 10:00 A.M. to 5:00 P.M. Fully wheelchair accessible.

Directions: Copia is located in downtown Napa, about one hour north of San Francisco and Oakland International Airports. Check the Web site for detailed driving directions.

8. The Hess Collection Winery

4411 Redwood Road, P.O. Box 4140, **Napa,** CA 94558;
(707) 255–1144, (877) 707–4377; www.hesscollection.com

FINE CHARDONNAY and cabernet sauvignon wines may be synonymous with the Hess Collection. Garden lovers, however, are first enthralled by the winery's outdoor environment, designed by the internationally acclaimed landscape architect Peter Walker. Before entering the charming stone buildings of this outstanding Napa Valley winery, survey the formidable wisteria-draped arbor, the rectilinear pond, and the sculpture garden.

For art aficionados, the Hess Collection Winery offers galleries filled with Donald Hess's amazing compilation of contemporary paintings and sculptures by such masters as Frank Stella, Robert Motherwell, Francis Bacon, Magdalena Abakanowicz, and Georg Baselitz.

From the third floor of the visitor center, you'll enjoy a spectacular view of Mount Veeder and the winery's vineyards.

❀ **Admission:** Free.

Garden open: Daily 10:00 A.M. to 4:00 P.M. Visitor center is open daily 10:00 A.M. to 4:00 P.M.

Further information: You can also enjoy the visitor center, a self-guided tour, or a wine tasting (fee). The concrete walkway and decomposed granite paths are wheelchair accessible.

Directions: The winery is approximately one hour and fifteen minutes north of San Francisco. Proceed north on California Highway 29 past the town of Napa, turn left at Redwood Road, traveling west about 6 miles to the winery.

9. Matanzas Creek Winery Estate Gardens

6097 Bennett Valley Road, **Santa Rosa,** CA 95404; (800) 590–6464; www.matanzascreek.com

*S*ONOMA COUNTY'S trove of beautiful wineries represents a veritable Eden to garden lovers. Experience the combination of elegant naturalism and robust verdure found at the Matanzas Creek Winery Estate Gardens and you may understand how it came to be my personal favorite.

Situated amid hilly terrain and washed over in luminous hues, Matanzas Creek is an exquisite treasure yet to be discovered. In this sublime setting, majestic native oaks tower over extravagant plantings in a landscape that might well be unsurpassed by any other vineyard regularly open to the public.

Not so long ago, founders Sandra and Bill MacIver first envisioned the Matanzas Creek garden. Growing up in New Orleans, Sandra was inspired by the Longue Vue House and Gardens, her grandparents'—the Stern family's—nationally acclaimed estate. Reigning over Longue Vue's tantalizing landscape was her grandmother, doyenne Edith Rosenwald Stern. It comes as no surprise that the Matanzas Creek garden is dedicated to Edith, as undoubtedly she planted the seed for the MacIvers' garden of the future.

Landscaping at Matanzas Creek was undertaken in 1990. Apparently, the fine climate and conditions outside Santa Rosa have worked their magic, and Matanzas Creek has already attained a radiant grandeur. Ask anyone who has had the good fortune to venture down Bennett Valley Road and they'll tell you of the lavender fields thriving at this stunning Sonoma winery.

It's difficult not to be swept away by the heady aroma of lavender that greets you during a summer visit to Matanzas Creek. Aside from France's Provence region, where else might you encounter the scent emanating from 4,500 intoxicating plants?

Growing on staggered terraces delineated by charming rock walls, the splendidly cultivated lavender includes 'Grosso' and 'Provence' varieties. The lavender's hues and textures create compelling diagonal patterns, leading you on a gradual ascent up the steps of a central path toward the main building, which houses the tasting room and gift shop.

Appearing at once anchored to the land and gently integrated with the gardens surrounding it, the visitor center offers a wealth of estate-grown lavender products for purchase. Among these are sachet, potpourri, and lavender wands; sticks for grilling and fireplace bundles; and gift baskets, soaps, and bath oil. Award-winning Matanzas Creek wines are savored by wine lovers in the tasting room.

As you leave the building, descend the stairway and look to the left. The precise angles and planes of the rectangular Water Garden provide a refreshing contrast to the lavish plantings contained within it. Papyrus (*Cyperus papyrus*), with its airy terminals, and giant scouring rush, a handsome California native that resembles bamboo, are two choice specimens.

Continue strolling through the grounds and you'll enjoy artful drifts of swaying grasses like the tall purple moor grass, which produces blooming spikes from June through December, softening hillsides and walkways alike. In the summer, masses of perennials thrive under Sonoma's bright skies. Flamboyant specimens like the giant sea kale (*Crambe cordifolia*) shoot flowering stalks high above mounds of generous cabbagelike leaves.

The resplendent plantings at Matanzas Creek are the work of gifted landscape designer Gary Ratway, known for his contributions to the restoration of the Mendocino Coast Botanical Gardens. In addition to their stunning compositions filled with grasses and pungent herbs, the gardens feature outstanding selections of ornamental vines, shrubs, and unusual trees. Plantings of *Parrotia persica* 'Select' (a deciduous tree from Persia) grace the lavender field on all sides with medleys of amethyst and lemon-lime leaves in spring, shifting to shimmering golds and reds in the fall.

Eloquently described in the winery's garden tour booklet, the governing philosophy at Matanzas Creek is one of "designing to reduce design." This approach is readily apparent throughout the entire grounds, but perhaps the most striking examples are boulders that weigh 21,000 pounds. Set in place near a stairway, these massive forms look as if they have been there forever. With the rocks' crevices planted as if by the hand of nature, these boulders function as conspicuous reminders of a unique garden environment. It's a blissful paradise in keeping with the spectacular setting.

❀ **Admission:** Free.

Garden open: Daily 10:00 A.M. to 4:30 P.M.

Further information: You can purchase a copy of the garden tour booklet in the tasting room. Visit the Web site or phone to learn more about a gala event held yearly in June at Matanzas Creek. The Lavender Harvest Party features wine tastings, fine cuisine, and jazz. You must purchase tickets to this very popular soiree well in advance, as attendance is limited.

Directions: The winery is located approximately one hour and fifteen minutes north of San Francisco.

North Bay Gardenwalks

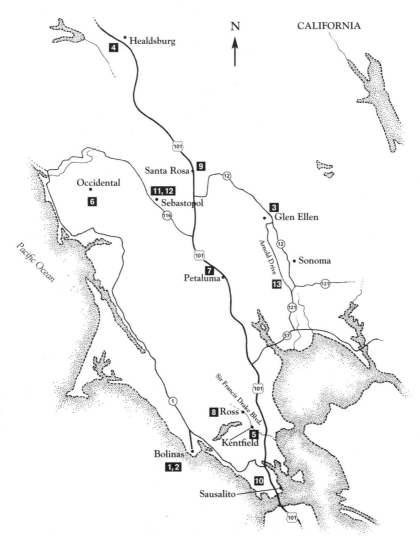

N

CALIFORNIA

• Healdsburg

4

101

Santa Rosa

9

Occidental

12

6

11, 12

• Sebastopol

3

116

• Glen Ellen

Arnold Drive

12

101

• Sonoma

Pacific Ocean

Petaluma

7

13

121

121

37

Sir Francis Drake Blvd.

101

1

8 Ross•

5

Kentfield

Bolinas•

1, 2

10

Sausalito

101

1. Bolinas: Las Baulines Nursery
2. Bolinas: Marin-Bolinas
   Botanical Gardens
3. Glen Ellen: Quarryhill
   Botanical Garden
4. Healdsburg: Russian River
   Rose Company
5. Kentfield: Geraniaceae
   Nursery and Gardens
6. Occidental: Occidental
   Arts and Ecology Center
7. Petaluma: Garden Valley Ranch

8. Ross: Marin Art and
   Garden Center
9. Santa Rosa: Luther Burbank
   Home & Gardens
10. Sausalito: The Garden at
    Green Gulch
11. Sebastopol:
    California Carnivores
12. Sebastopol: Sonoma
    Horticultural Nursery
13. Sonoma: Cornerstone Festival
    of Gardens

1. Las Baulines Nursery

150 Olema Bolinas Road (Star Route), **Bolinas,** CA 94924;
(415) 868–0808

*V*ISIT PICTURESQUE Bolinas for a stopover at this laid-back
nursery, where fetching flowering plants consort with deer-
proof, native, and acclimatized species for the coastal climate. In the
nursery store, I picked up a bottle of Porter's Lotion, a refreshing
emollient skin-care product that blends witch hazel, glycerin, camphor, rosemary oil, and other ingredients. Porter's has been made in
Montana for more than sixty years, but gardeners everywhere have
adopted this balm for its soothing properties.

❀ **Admission:** Free.

Garden open: Phone to confirm
seasonal hours of operation.

Further information: Citizens
of Bolinas like to remove the
road signs that help direct travelers to their pleasant haven, so
you may want to phone before-
hand for further information.
Restroom facilities are limited
and not wheelchair accessible.

Directions: The nursery is about
forty-five minutes north of San Francisco and the Golden Gate Bridge.
Take U.S. Highway 101 to the very scenic, winding California Coast
Highway 1; go past Stinson Beach, north along the Bolinas Lagoon,
past the sign for Audubon Canyon Ranch, and look for the turnoff to
the town of Bolinas (ask for guidance from someone local, if necessary).

2. Marin-Bolinas Botanical Gardens

250 Mesa Road, P.O. Box 650, **Bolinas**, CA 94924; (415) 388–5017; www.mbbgardens.com

*A*N ENDURING wonder for the world of plants accompanies Dr. Herman Schwartz whenever he ambles among the rare succulents in the Marin-Bolinas Botanical Gardens. An avid plantsman who delights in sharing the plants he has collected on annual journeys through Africa, the Americas, and Madagascar, octogenarian Schwartz finds the Bolinas setting to be one of the few innocent places left. "A form of heaven," he dubs "Schwartz's Folly."

How Schwartz amassed the vast array of uncommon species now growing in outdoor gardens and greenhouses is a tale that began when Schwartz was a youngster and his mother died in an automobile accident.

As a ward of the Hebrew Orphan Asylum, Schwartz found a guiding light in the resident librarian, who recognized the boy's curiosity for plants and animals. After earning a scholarship to Cornell University and a medical degree from Harvard, Schwartz was working as chief of oncology at a San Francisco hospital. At this point, fate intervened when a patient presented him with a gift of ten succulent plants.

Schwartz's seemingly boundless passion for succulents resulted. The Bolinas property was purchased in 1978, and decades later it's an unparalleled showcase for aloes and euphorbias, in particular, along with cacti, agaves, and crassulas that thrive in arid conditions.

Countless species from south of the equator are on view: plants that flower in winter wherever they grow. Here in Bolinas, they put on a brilliant spectacle when they begin blooming in November. The display is dazzling as thousands of flowers cover the plants. Aglow in wintertime, the main outdoor garden boasts hardy aloes enlivened by towering spikes and candelabra-like inflorescences emerging from densely planted mounds.

Aloe maculata exhibits patterning on its leaves along with a thorny profile. Yet another species grows on short, stout stems, with pale green leaves flushed pink and orange, their edges armed in red thorns.

Walking along the grassy paths winding through rock-rimmed raised beds, you'll see a rich variety of plants jostling together. Marked by characteristic swollen, fleshy leaves or stems, their architecture ranges from stemless rosettes and odd hairy globes to shrubby specimens like ice blue *Dudleya virens*, its plump, linear leaves colored ruby at the tips.

Schwartz built the property's first greenhouse while he was still practicing medicine. At that time everything was in pots and on benches, but a stroll through the aisles today reveals an environment teeming with tender specimens.

You'll notice a bevy of photographs, articles, and botanical prints lining the greenhouse walls: a representative chronicle of Schwartz's intrepid travels.

Schwartz is perhaps most widely known for the uncommon euphorbias in his collections, and many remain very rare in cultivation. On a visit you'll discover tall columnar plants reaching skyward, diminutive species, and sprawling specimens—some spiny, others spineless—in the Euphorbia House, constructed two years ago. Isolated in its own space, *Euphorbia magnicapsula* plays a prominent role, its human-size form rising from the ground plane like a dancer with arms outstretched.

The botanical gardens' site takes in fourteen acres overall, with expansion plans calling for the building of a new greenhouse to highlight aloes.

Outdoors, a Children's Meadow encompasses a cornucopia of carefully selected, colorful plants that do not contain any irritating sap. This garden space is meant to create a ready source of cuttings and small plants that children can take home with them. Here youngsters are encouraged to appreciate the wonders of the plant world, and an active outreach program attracts groups of school-children who enjoy tours of the gardens.

※ **Admission:** Free; donations appreciated from groups.
Garden open: Saturday and by appointment.
Further information: Outdoor education groups and schools can contact Shirley Morrison, director of education and community relations, at (415) 383–0362.
Directions: From San Francisco take U.S. 101 across the Golden Gate Bridge. The gardens are located approximately thirty minutes north of the city. Before visiting, call for detailed directions.

3. Quarryhill Botanical Garden

P.O. Box 232, **Glen Ellen**, CA 95442; (707) 996–3802 (tours), (707) 996–3166 (office); www.quarryhillbg.org

*R*ARE AND ENDANGERED Asian species thrive in the naturalistic setting of Quarryhill Botanical Garden, located squarely within Sonoma County's bucolic Valley of the Moon.

Spanning some sixty acres, Quarryhill was originally the weekend home of benefactor and founder Jane Davenport Jansen. Today, one-third of the terrain supports a unique woodland environment devoted to collections of plants from the temperate regions of China, Japan, and the Himalayas. More than 90 percent of the flora is grown from wild-collected, scientifically documented seed, so the collections hold a significant place throughout North America.

On a docent-led tour, you'll discover a twenty-acre cultivated space, displaying a wealth of mature trees and shrubs, ground-covering roses, and masses of lilies. An important mission of the garden is conservation, but visitors also see how beautiful the plants are. Most surprising is how quickly the plantings have taken shape, as nothing was planted before 1990.

A sturdy arbor partly encircled by a dry rock wall marks the gathering point for a tour. The wooden structure is the only formal element in the garden plan, and it stands out amid a rolling landscape of densely planted hillsides, large pools formed by a winter stream, and smaller ponds created from old quarries that endow the property with its name.

The arbor's beguiling shroud of vines provides welcome shade, with tangles of clematis, clambering wild grape, and evergreen *Holboellia coriacea,* with glossy, lance-shaped leaflets and intensely fragrant white flowers in spring.

Docents call attention to a vigorous wild rose growing outside the low rock wall. If you're a rose fancier, you might recognize evergreen *Rosa chinensis* var. *spontanea,* native to Sichuan, China. One of the parents of modern hybrid tea and floribunda roses, the rose had not been seen for nearly one hundred years, when the director of Quarryhill found it in 1988 while on a seed-collecting expedition.

Notice how the garden's uncommon specimens are planted close together, as they would grow in the wild. Emerging alongside the paths that traverse the hills, you'll find many plants with labels to identify the genus, species, and origin.

Roses begin blooming in March, and rhododendrons reach peak bloom in April. During May, a fine representation of dogwoods lends exuberance to the setting, as the emerging inflorescences ornament the surroundings. One of the few evergreen dogwoods, *Cornus capitata,* is a wonder: Commonly known as Himalayan strawberry tree or Bentham's cornel, the tree wears a fetching cloak of creamy yellow bracts in June, followed by huge red fruits with warty protuberances.

Continuing all through spring and summer and into the fall, collections of lilies from China and Japan offer colorful effects and scented displays.

Together with irises that bloom in May, the lily exhibition begins with the elegant white trumpet flowers of tall *Lilium leucanthum.*

In June and July, different species produce showy trumpets ranging from orange to pink to a soft shade of purple. The so-called turk's caps of *Lilium duchartrei* provide a visual counterpoint, characterized by white overhanging flowers composed of reflexed petals spotted red.

Holding forth in August, tiger lilies climb 6 feet high, and *Lilium speciosum*, with quantities of lavish pink flowers, oftentimes grows even taller.

So many plants are endangered these days or on the edge of extinction, and a dwindling biodiversity of all species creates cause for concern. Yet Quarryhill is creating a reservoir of information about plants in the wild and in cultivation.

After an enlightening tour of the garden, you'll reach the final high point: a mound of rocks adorned with Tibetan Buddhist prayer flags. From this overlook, gaze out at a spectacular view of the landscape's amazing contours. You'll have an indelible memory to carry home.

Admission: Fee; free for members.

Garden open: March through October; visits by appointment only.

Further information: Visit the Web site for a tour schedule or for information on workshops at the garden. Botanical study tours take place on the third Saturday of each month from March through October; call (707) 996–3802 for reservations. Wheelchair accessibility is limited.

Directions: The garden is about a one-hour drive north of San Francisco on California Highway 12 (Sonoma Highway) and just northeast of Glen Ellen.

4. Russian River Rose Company

1685 Magnolia Drive, **Healdsburg,** CA 95448; (707) 433–7455;
www.russian-river-rose.com

*T*O YIELD a mere two ounces of distilled rose oil, Jan and
Michael Tolmasoff harvest more than a half ton of rose
blooms from their Healdsburg gardens—that's about 130,000
intensely fragrant flowers.

The Russian River Rose Company gardens first sprouted in
1980, when Jan Tolmasoff used money from a Christmas gift to buy
roses to adorn their vineyard's row ends. That chance beginning led
to the current collection of more than 600 rose varieties, fanning
out in lavish beds along the street and vibrant arrays surrounding
the Tolmasoffs' home.

You'll discover here a historical arrangement, starting with
species roses like Lady Banks rose and *Rosa californica*, a California
native. These wild roses grow under the trees across Magnolia Drive,
as shown on a walking-tour map of the gardens.

Antique roses of European and Middle Eastern descent grow
on the opposite side, where the tour starts. Mainly once-bloomers,
these hardy gallicas, albas, and centifolias are valued for their resist-
ance to disease, and they broadcast a remarkable bouquet of fragrance in the spring.

The beautifully formed flowers of bourbon roses and heavenly
scented hybrid perpetuals and China roses grow along the front of
the house. Although susceptible to cold, this group delivers a
glorious, summerlong bloom. 'Slater's Crimson China', for one, blossoms here. Its lineage traces back to 1792, when it was first introduced in the United Kingdom. Its claim to fame is as a stud rose
responsible for crosses with roses from Europe. This distinctive
parentage resulted in the so-called modern roses, endowed with the
ability to flower in flushes throughout the season.

The Butterfly Garden encircling the house's turret embodies the Tolmasoffs' desire for a more natural feeling in their gardens. A combination of annuals, perennials, and roses braid together color, form, and texture. The relaxed planting features irises and calendulas as spring highlights. Summertime allies include verbena, cosmos, pincushion flower, echinacea, and statice, outlined in a border planting of miniature, own-root roses. Stunning 'Black Jade' is red-black, and 'Brass Ring' is a lovely apricot-copper mix.

Immediately opposite in the White Garden, only the best of this gossamer class are allowed to remain. One standout, 'Jardins de Bagatelle', is a creamy ivory rose blushed pink in bud. A fully double classic hybrid tea, it opens in a lovely swirl.

Nearby, you'll see the Miniature Rose Hall of Fame section, celebrating the American Rose Society selections. As a group, these are adorable and hardy. The intriguingly named 'Green Ice' premiered in 1971. Of all roses, its color is closest to a true green.

An entry arch supports a number of shade-tolerant roses; among them are hybrid musks.

Another area is devoted to tea roses. While tender teas must be grown under glass in other regions, many thrive in Northern California. One of the most beautiful is 'Etoile de Lyon', producing a constant show of ivory blooms on a nice round bush form.

An assembly of hybrid teas and floribundas include 'La France', from 1867, the first hybrid tea variety.

Some of the earliest varieties, perhaps unfamiliar even to rose fanciers, grow at Russian River Rose Company. 'Talisman', for one, is said to be available at only one or two nurseries worldwide.

The "painted" look of roses bred by McGredy in New Zealand will capture your attention, with a bevy of unusual colors and petals displaying white on the reverse and an airbrushed effect on top. A flamboyant example, 'Old Master', is a blend of pink-orange to red to lavender.

Heavy with fragrance, an allée leading through the vineyard to the perfume rose field is the most beguiling element of the garden design. Articulated by a series of seven arches 12 feet high and wide, the allée will entice you to experience a treat for the senses beneath its canopy of climbing and pillar roses. Each arch has a different theme. The first supports old ramblers that have naturalized in the village of Mendocino. Lavender-purple 'Veilchenblau' is propagated at the Tolmasoffs' nursery.

The earliest bloom to adorn the allée appears on the climbing tea rose, 'Souvenir de Madame Leonie Viennot', with masses of primrose yellow flowers boasting copper shading.

The perfume rose field presents a unique spectacle consisting of hundreds of specimens of 'Kazanlik' (*Rosa damascena triginti-petala*), an ancient Bulgarian damask rose, along with plantings of 'Rose de Rescht' and 'Ulrich Brunner'.

During the annual perfume rose oil harvest tours, participants can watch Michael Tolmasoff demonstrate the use of a Prohibition-era still with copper distillation kettles to make rose water and rose oil from overflowing buckets of flowers freshly picked from the perfume field. Michael produces a unique eau de toilette, Rose Embrace, sold only in fall because the rose oil must first age.

In these redolent gardens, the queen of flowers anchors the radiant surroundings.

❀ **Admission:** Free during special open days; fee for perfume rose oil harvest tours; donation requested for some events.

Garden open: Call to confirm seasonal hours and special event times; also open by appointment.

Further information: Call or check the Web site for display garden and nursery open hours. Special events and a schedule of perfume rose oil harvest tours are posted on the Web site. Reservations are required for harvest tours and they fill quickly; fee charged. To reserve, call the number above.

Directions: Take U.S. 101 to the Central Healdsburg exit. Turn left at the second light (Westside Road). Go under the freeway, then turn left onto Kinley and right onto Magnolia. Proceed ¾ mile to 1685 Magnolia.

5. Geraniaceae Nursery and Gardens

122 Hillcrest Avenue, **Kentfield,** CA 94904; (415) 461–4168; www.geraniaceae.com

GERANIACEAE NURSERY AND GARDENS is a treasured secret among ardent Bay Area gardeners and designers. The botanical designation—*geraniaceae*—conveys the nursery's specialty—a host of plants in the geranium family. A keen plantswoman and popular speaker on the gardening scene, Robin Parer is the force behind this gemlike enterprise that celebrates the beauty and relevance of hardy geraniums.

Tucked away in Marin County, Geraniaceae occupies a one-acre site originally consisting primarily of steep clay slopes. The property's present transformation is altogether remarkable. Even before you enter the long, sloping driveway, the plantings growing streetside sound an alert: This is obviously not your typical suburban domicile.

Parer takes advantage of a small stream running beside the road to cultivate uncommon species that prosper in wet conditions. A South African rarity with a stately vertical bearing, *Chondropetalum tectorum* plays off a row of dwarf weeping birches that are being encouraged to grow in a horizontal linked form.

Lining one side of the driveway, a broad thicket of deer-resistant, flowering grevilleas provides an excellent harbor for beneficial insects, birds, and other wildlife. One recent evening I visited near dusk and encountered a cacophonous cotillion of hummingbirds darting about and sipping nectar while vying for dominance. Stout bumblebees enjoy this bounteous habitat, too, arguably matching ounce for ounce the weight of each individual hummer!

A landscape ablaze with architectural plants is showcased on the driveway's opposite perimeter. The startling floral hues and dramatic foliage of cannas mingle with the immense deep purple arrow-shaped leaves of a taro (*Colocasia* 'Black Magic'), giving rise to a distinctly tropical backdrop. In the foreground a carpet of yellow-splashed butterbur catches the light, while the tall inflorescences of a cyperus and the subtly striped blond canes of 'Alphonse Karr' bamboo serve as statuesque anchors mooring the design.

Myriad pots are placed about the approach to the front gate to accommodate a wealth of textural specimens. These containers focus attention on burnished grasses, elegant Japanese maples with dissected leaves, strappy bronze phormiums, and the glossy rosettes of outstanding succulents.

Not common English ivy but a luminous bower of 'Sulphur Queen' adorns the garden's entryway. Parer explains, "I use ivies as a way to bring sunlight into dark spaces." The climbing vine with variegated foliage aglow in shades of gold and green is one example of fine Canary Island and Persian types gracing the gardens.

Mere steps from the ivy-shrouded arbor, the Bruised and Battered Border spills over with an abundance of hot colors. Displayed in densely planted terraces to maximize the space, this exciting assemblage provides exhilarating contrasts. From the stunning chartreuse of a mock orange (*Philadelphus coronarius* 'Aureus') to the plum-colored, fernlike foliage of *Anthriscus sylvestris* 'Ravenswing', the spirited panoply fascinates visitors.

Continue walking through the garden's upper area and you'll arrive at the Venus Border, with its cool, comforting color scheme. An old crape myrtle with silken bark stands sentry, embracing a full company of romantic roses, clematis, and lilies.

After traversing the nursery's tidy rows of potted plants, descend the steps to a serene woodland setting where mature camellias reside with abutilons attired in pendulous flowers. A mulched path leads the way to a gazebo wearing a perfumed mantle of the opulent climbing rose 'Souvenir de la Malmaison'.

In this area a rare barberry also thrives. With its impressive thorns and cloak of patterned bark, the choice shrub produces abundant racemes of yellow flowers, turning a translucent pink in fall.

Nearby in the vegetable garden, an espaliered fig tree produces a linear framework of decorative branches. Parer also planted a lovely dogwood some twenty years ago, and now its flowers ornament this garden room in May. A majestic elm towers over the commendable congregation of arboreal beauties, shrubs, perennials, and countless geraniums.

An adventurous traveler, Parer frequently journeys to far-flung places to hunt for new plants. Consequently, species unavailable in cultivation often appear in her gardens.

There's certainly plenty for curious gardeners and plant enthusiasts to glean about harmonious companion plantings incorporating geranium cultivars with delightful blooms and verdant foliage. Then, too, there are tender species, like *Geranium maderense* from Madeira. The showy biennial is described by Parer as flaunting "bouquets of deep pink flowers on stems covered in sticky glandular hairs. Real plant erotica!"

With her discerning eye and insightful outlook, Parer has garnered the admiration of the West Coast's gardening professionals, and earned the respect of an international society of horticulturists. Visit the Geraniaceae gardens and you'll witness the creative sensibilities and finesse of a remarkable garden maker.

❀ **Admission:** Free.

Garden open: By appointment April 1 through October 1.

Further information: To visit the gardens, phone in advance to arrange an appointment and to obtain detailed directions. For questions about geraniums, you can call anytime.

Directions: Geraniaceae is about one-half hour north of San Francisco.

6. Occidental Arts and Ecology Center

15290 Coleman Valley Road, **Occidental,** CA 95465;
(707) 874–1557, ext. 201; www.oaec.org

*T*HE OCCIDENTAL ARTS AND ECOLOGY CENTER celebrated
its tenth anniversary recently, carrying on a tradition of
organic gardening that goes back some thirty years, making it the
ninth-oldest certified organic farm in California and one of the
country's oldest biointensive gardens.

The property's earliest incarnation was as the Farallones Insti-
tute, which opened in 1974. The Center for Seven Generations, a
privately funded enterprise, maintained the grounds during the early
1990s. And the Sowing Circle, an intentional community, acquired
the eighty-acre site in 1994.

Through all three incarnations, there's been a consistent ethic.
It is evidenced by dark, loamy garden soil that has always been hand
tilled. The soil's humus-rich consistency demonstrates the benefits
of plentiful amendment with the "black gold" of homemade compost. Moreover, no machines are used.

The bounteous gardens exhibit a simplified layout based upon
straight garden beds, a design developed during the late 1980s when
the site was a market garden.

A depleted cow pasture in days past, the center's cultivated
spaces now foster a trove of heirloom plants, making every bed an
actual seed bank. Through classes, training programs, and plant
sales, the folks here are always working to further agricultural biodiversity.

The exuberant South Garden is sloped, with a relatively hot
and still microclimate given over to heat-loving plants. Sweet peppers and 120 varieties of tomatoes mingle with perennials, annuals,
fruit trees, and herbs. Weeds appear as well, but they don't cause any
panic among the gardeners.

Although other gardeners might frown at an endless supply of self-sown volunteers, the tiny, tender greens are welcomed here as flavorful summer salad ingredients. Amaranths create a spectacle with their burgundy plumes, and at the same time, their seeds deliver a high-protein food. Seeds from one solitary plant can engender a plush ground cover of salad fixings, ready for picking soon after they emerge.

Among specimen trees, 'Panache' is a rare fig variety with variegated fruits set off by the sculpted edges of its foliage. One need only cut into a 'Golden' or 'Chioggia' beet to discover the savory promise of its patterned flesh.

A fall visit coincides with a colorful congregation of rotund pumpkins and curious gourds ready for harvesting. Brassicas are among the prevailing fare. From broccoli to cauliflower and cabbage, these vegetables state their presence in ways that rival summer's floral displays. Romanesco (sometimes called minaret) hails from Northern Italy. A cauliflower that bears similarities to broccoli, its chartreuse hue draws attention. Dressed for the holidays, fringed kale foliage is marked by conspicuous pinks and purples. 'Blue Solaise' leek, a French heirloom variety, possesses violet leaves.

The organic profile of a bench made of clay, sand, and straw appears beyond the nursery, just before one descends the fieldstone stairway leading to the larger North Garden. Built using an old English technique known as cob, the bench represents a natural, sustainable approach to construction—a topic usually featured among the class offerings.

In the North Garden, perennial borders offer a vibrant display that starts in May. One of the annual plant sales, which takes place around Mother's Day, invites visitors to enjoy edibles mixed with ornamentals. The demonstration herb beds bring to the fore culinary, medicinal, fiber, and dye plants.

An important crop in Peru and Ecuador, mashua (*Tropaeolum tuberosum*) produces a climbing vine shrouded in edible leaves, similar in appearance to the foliage of garden nasturtiums. The plant's sweet-tasting, pale yellow tubers are striped crimson. And in November and December, its crimson flowers provide hummingbirds with nectar when little else is in bloom.

Another staple crop from the Andes, oca—an oxalis—is harvested in November. Orange, yellow, or pink, its fingerling-shaped tubers taste like potatoes with sour cream.

Produce from these abundant gardens provides sustenance for Sowing Circle members, who share their harvest with students. As part of the center's courses, handcrafted meals—homemade from scratch—are provided!

Acting as a hub, the ecology center helps to spread the word on organic horticulture practices. And the center hosts special events to bring people together, like a chautauqua featuring stories, songs, and clowns. One took place in the garden's new outdoor performing space, boasting a fancifully designed redwood stage.

❁ **Admission:** Donation requested; free during plant sales.

Garden open: For scheduled tour dates and during plant sales.

Further information: Check the Web site for a schedule of garden and site tours, courses, programs, and biodiversity plant sales. Wheelchair access to the gardens is limited.

Directions: The center is 65 miles north of the Golden Gate Bridge, approximately ninety minutes from San Francisco. Detailed directions and public transit information are found on the Web site.

7. Garden Valley Ranch

498 Pepper Road, **Petaluma,** CA 94952; (707) 795–0919;
www.gardenvalley.com

*L*OCATED in a region internationally famous for the production
of fine wines and sublime vineyard-blanketed vistas, the Garden Valley Ranch operation revolves around the cultivation of glorious roses. More than 8,000 rosebushes are grown and harvested at this vibrant enterprise.

Although fire destroyed the main Victorian house on the nine-and-a-half-acre property in 1984, other historic Victorian buildings remain. A charming old belfry houses the Garden Valley Nursery shop and its enticing array of gardening tools, gifts with a floral theme, scented perennials, and rosebushes for sale to the public.

Garden Valley has one of only twenty-five national All-America Rose Selections test gardens. Celebrated rose expert and well-known garden writer Rayford Reddell is one of the judges of the All-America Rose Selections. He calls Garden Valley Ranch home. As you roam through this official test garden, you'll be able to survey unnamed varieties of hybrid teas and floribundas, miniatures, climbers, grandifloras, and landscape roses.

To explore Garden Valley's extensive grounds and stunning landscape, you'll first need to pick up a self-guided tour booklet (free with admission). Among the most enchanting of the many beautifully designed garden spaces is a serene one-acre fragrance garden. Here you'll find formal beds with aromatic flowers and foliage; a wisteria-draped pergola; an apple walk; an acid border where rhododendron are interplanted among witch hazel and lilac, magnolia and sweet olive, to name but a few specimens; and an adjoining woodland garden.

Garden Valley's pond garden is complete with frolicking koi, scented water lilies, and surrounding ornamental grasses. This water feature was actually conceived as an unique solution to supplying a water source in case of another fire. After a refreshing respite here, explore the antique and David Austin roses planted nearby.

Rose fanciers, of course, will find incomparable fields of heavenly scented roses. Garden Valley's countless rose species and cultivars present a unique opportunity for learning about almost every type of rose in cultivation today.

For a particularly inviting vantage point, find a perch within the Victorian belvedere. According to Garden Valley's tour booklet, this structure "was once a south porch on a neighboring Victorian farmhouse." Take a few moments to muse upon the beauty of the place. It's easy to imagine the setting as a wedding site, and many have chosen to take their vows here. At the same time, Garden Valley Nursery is a terrific place to pick up turkey manure, alfalfa pellets, and other indispensable supplies your roses at home will certainly appreciate.

❀ **Admission:** Fee.

Garden open: Wednesday through Sunday 10:00 A.M. to 4:00 P.M.—events permitting. Nursery hours are the same. Closed for one week between Christmas and New Year's.

Further information: Garden Valley occasionally closes for special events; phone before visiting to find out if weekend events are scheduled. A self-guided tour booklet is included with the admission fee. No fee is required to visit public areas and the nursery shop, which carries gift items, too. The Garden Valley Web site offers a terrific link to the Petaluma area. Garden paths are level; restrooms in the main building are wheelchair accessible.

Directions: Avoid commuter traffic and this Petaluma location is about forty-five minutes north of San Francisco. Take U.S. 101 to the last Petaluma exit—Old Redwood Highway/Penngrove. Turn left at the end of the exit, crossing back over the highway to the second stoplight. Turn right onto Stony Point Road; go 1½ miles, then turn left onto Pepper Road. The second parking lot is for nursery and garden visitors.

8. Marin Art and Garden Center

30 Sir Francis Drake Boulevard, P.O. Box 437, **Ross**, CA 94957;
(415) 454–5597; www.maagc.org

H IDDEN WITHIN the boundaries of Marin County, the prosperous town of Ross lies near San Anselmo, a short distance west of U.S. 101. Preserved by a consortium of community groups as a cultural oasis and horticultural haven for Marin's citizenry, the Marin Art and Garden Center occupies a wooded ten-acre site.

Buildings located on the property are dedicated to various functions: art exhibitions, theater productions, and meeting rooms for ardent garden clubs such as the Garden Society of Marin, one of the center's founding organizations. Built in 1864 and fully refurbished with a gleaming interior, balcony, and circular staircase, the picturesque Octagon House now shelters the Jose Moya del Piño Library and Ross Historical Society.

A butterfly garden and beautifully designed beds and borders bursting with ornamental grasses, perennials, and showy shrubs adorn the grounds. Yet the Marin Art and Garden Center is perhaps best known for its fine array of trees. An enormous southern magnolia is showcased, planted in 1870 by the son-in-law of the town's founding father, James Ross. Centrally located on the property, this monumental specimen presides over the landscape, truly living up to its botanical name, *Magnolia grandiflora*.

Other rarities include the dawn redwood, relative of the coast redwood (this rare deciduous tree was thought to be extinct until rediscovered growing in China in 1946); the center's giant sequoia, which exhibits a prematurely aged domed form due to its sunny position; English oak; hawthorn; Atlantic cedar and camphor; silk tree; evergreen ash; and dogwood. These are only a few of the excellent specimens found in the sylvan groves of Marin Art and Garden Center.

❀ **Admission:** Free.
Garden open: Dawn to dusk.

Further information: Most of the garden walkways are wheelchair accessible.

Directions: Ross is located about thirty-five minutes north of San Francisco. Take U.S. 101 to the San Anselmo exit; follow Sir Francis Drake Boulevard through the towns of Greenbrae and Kentfield to the Marin Art and Garden Center.

9. Luther Burbank Home & Gardens

Intersection of Santa Rosa and Sonoma Avenues, P.O. Box 1678,
Santa Rosa, CA 95402; (707) 524–5445; www.lutherburbank.org

*P*LANT BREEDER extraordinaire Luther Burbank developed, and improved upon, a wealth of plant species, leaving behind a tremendously vital legacy of fruit and nut trees, vegetables, and ornamental flowers. Many of these choice varieties are enjoyed and cultivated by modern gardeners.

Born in Massachusetts in 1849, Burbank settled in Northern California, where he pursued more than half a century of horticultural research at a six-acre garden in Santa Rosa and on an experimental farm in the town of Sebastopol. Dedicated to Burbank's accomplishments, the Luther Burbank Home & Gardens currently comprise a 1.6-acre site in central Santa Rosa. Approaching from Sonoma Avenue, visitors see an appealing stone fountain, one of the wonderful elements of this parklike setting. In 1960, at Burbank's widow's request, the gardens were redesigned. A section called the Burbank Memorial Garden, honoring Burbank's role as influential forefather of American horticulture, was completed in 1991. Warmly inviting, the garden has espaliered fruit trees displayed on curved wooden screening.

Consistent with his urge to benefit humanity, Burbank concentrated on breeding plants that would produce greater quantities of food. He even investigated such plants as spineless cacti for their potential to feed cattle in a desert environment. Burbank's research yielded myriad beneficial plants, including the 'Paradox' walnut, with its refined wood grain for use in furniture.

A recent project incorporated more plants related to Burbank's work and updated structural elements to revitalize the gardens. Pass through the main entrance of this registered national, state, and city historic landmark, and you'll enjoy a fabulous rose garden. Roses introduced by Burbank encircle a birdbath fountain, while parent varieties that were used to breed roses are growing by the fence. You'll also find richly fragrant old garden roses, along with modern roses that were developed by California hybridizers and are here placed along curving lines according to color.

Although edible plants were Burbank's specialty, his reputation flourishes as the breeder of hundreds of shrubs and flowers, including the queen of all blooming plants, the rose. The Border Garden in front of the Burbank home features lilacs, spireas, and lavish displays of annuals and perennials grown in Victorian times. Other plantings include a small orchard of fruit-bearing trees located by the carriage house and along the property's perimeter, raised demonstration beds, bird and butterfly gardens, and a medicinal herb garden.

❀ **Admission:** Free.

Garden open: Tuesday through Sunday 8:00 A.M. to dusk. The Carriage House Museum and Gift Shop is open during tour season (April through October) 10:00 A.M. to 4:00 P.M.; closed Monday.

Further information: The gardens are open to the public every day for self-guided tours. During tour season, docent-led tours of the 1875 Burbank Home, 1889 greenhouse, and a portion of the gardens are available every half hour from 10:00 A.M. until the last tour at 3:30 P.M.; audio tours of the gardens are also available; fees charged. Visit the City of Santa Rosa Web site, www.ci.santa-rosa.ca.us for information on area events and attractions. The gardens are mostly wheelchair accessible.

Directions: Follow U.S. 101 north to the downtown Santa Rosa exit; the home and garden are approximately one hour from San Francisco.

10. The Garden at Green Gulch

1601 Shoreline Highway, **Sausalito**, CA 94965; (415) 381–0253;
www.sfzc.org

*Z*EN PRACTICE meets the pursuit of organic gardening at this remarkable Marin County destination. Green Gulch admirably combines the study of Zen Buddhism with the conscientious nurturing of a farm and gardens. While many guests of the center come for meditation retreats, others visit to partake in a range of classes and special seminars on natural gardening techniques.

In addition to the land cultivated for farming (the excellent produce is sold to some fine local restaurants), the Garden at Green Gulch has lovely ornamental flower gardens that are accented with espaliered fruit trees and a circular planting of herbs. Note how the ambrosial noisette roses scramble over the arbors. A short hike across meadowland takes you through sweetly scented paths to the water's edge at Muir Beach on the Pacific Ocean. In all, Green Gulch encompasses more than one hundred acres.

"Stalking the Wild Herb" is one example of a recent class offering at Green Gulch Farm. As part of the class, visitors are invited to follow knowledgeable instructors as they explore the valley. After participants have assisted in harvesting edible herbs, they return to the kitchen to create and enjoy soup and salad prepared from the pickings.

A typical gardening seminar might span topics such as organic gardening principles and practices; plant propagation, irrigation, and integrated pest management; or design, cultivation, and fertilization of the home garden.

The highly regarded annual plant sale supplies gardening patrons with organically grown perennial flowers and shrubs; culinary, ornamental, and medicinal herbs; bamboo; old-fashioned roses; and vegetable starts.

❀ **Admission:** Free. Parking is limited; there is a parking fee between 8:45 and 10:30 A.M. on Sunday. Cars with three or more people park free.
Garden open: Daily 9:00 A.M. to 4:00 P.M.
Further information: Groups of six or more should call the office before visiting. No picnics. Visit the Web site for a schedule of garden classes. The Green Gulch nursery offers organically grown perennials, natives, culinary, and medicinal herbs. Volunteers are welcome to work in the garden Tuesday from 9:00 A.M. to noon and are invited to stay for lunch, but you must phone the office before coming in case special events preempt garden work. Phone the main office at (415) 383–3134 for information on personal retreats at Green Gulch Farm Zen Center. A stay includes three vegetarian meals made from some of Green Gulch's fresh produce. The road and lawn paths can be a little bumpy but are basically wheelchair accessible. People with difficulty walking or who need wheelchair access can be driven to the garden gate.
Directions: The garden is just north of San Francisco and the Golden Gate Bridge. Take U.S. 101 north to the exit for California Coast Highway 1, Stinson Beach/Mill Valley. Drive west 2½ miles along CA Coast Hwy. 1; go past the Panoramic Highway turnoff. Drive another 2 miles, and look for the Green Gulch sign.

11. California Carnivores

2833 Old Gravenstein Highway South, **Sebastopol,** CA 95472;
(707) 824–0433; www.californiacarnivores.com

*A*N IMPRESSIVE collection of carnivorous plants is displayed at California Carnivores, a unique plant nursery that recently relocated to Sebastopol.

The new 11,000-square-foot Cal Carnivores facility functions as a retail nursery and mail-order enterprise, offering a great selection of these wonderfully bizarre species for sale on the premises.

Boasting more than 700 varieties of insect-eating plants, Cal Carnivores is the place to learn about growing the Venus flytrap, pitcher plants, and other astonishing types of flora. Pick up a copy of owner Peter D'Amato's informative, award-winning book, *The*

Savage Garden, for helpful instructions on plant care and culture, as well as for descriptions of the intriguing characteristics of numerous varieties.

Be advised, visitors are obliged to bring their own bugs if they intend to feed the plants!

❀ **Admission:** Free.

Garden open: Thursday through Monday 10:00 A.M. to 4:00 P.M.; closed Tuesday, Wednesday, and major holidays.

Further information: Take time to smell the roses at Vintage Gardens —specialists in antique and heirloom roses—right next door. At California Carnivores, the floor is gravel but mostly wheelchair accessible.

Directions: Cal Carnivores is about forty-five minutes north of the Golden Gate Bridge. Take U.S. 101 north to the Cotati/California Highway 116 west exit. Head west on CA 116 toward Sebastopol. Go 6 miles. Turn right on Old Gravenstein Highway at the Antique Society building. Drive 1½ blocks. Cal Carnivores is on the left at Vintage Gardens.

12. Sonoma Horticultural Nursery

3970 Azalea Avenue, **Sebastopol,** CA 95472; (707) 823–6832; www.sonomahort.com

*N*OT-TO-BE-MISSED "Sonoma Hort" (as it is referred to by locals) specializes in abundant varieties of rhododendrons and azaleas as well as in shade-loving plants appropriate for the type of moist environment where "rhodies" thrive. You'll delight in the nursery's extraordinary display gardens amid an expansive seven-and-a-half-acre property where countless fine specimens are assembled.

As might be expected, the emphasis on rhododendrons at Sonoma Horticultural Nursery makes for a lavish and colorful spring season, but the breadth of companion plantings is just as impressive. A leisurely saunter along 1½ miles of footpaths rewards patrons with visions of towering foxgloves and huge flamboyant clematis flowers decorating vertical posts and pillars along the way. This retinue of complementary blooms magnifies the voluptuousness of the rhododendrons, making for an exhibition that rivals any Northern California garden you might visit.

Indelibly imprinted on my memory is one stopover very early in May during an El Niño season, when I witnessed the heart-stopping performance of a legendary dove tree (*Davidia involucrata*). Thanks in large part to proprietor Polo DeLorenzo's magic touch, these rare beauties are grown, propagated, and offered for sale at Sonoma Hort.

You'll see flourishing examples of the tree in a circular driveway adjacent to the nursery's main parking area. One incomparably handsome, mature dove tree is protected by a special ordinance. Look for the plaque that designates this tree a Sonoma County treasure—Heritage Tree #20. Originally from China, the uncommon species is also known as the handkerchief tree. Usually it is late April when dove trees parade their flowing white bracts like fluttering handkerchiefs.

Another revelation in May is the empress tree (*Paulownia tomentosa*), with its spectacular show of purple flowers resembling foxgloves. Still, by no means is spring the only season promising a fanfare. Alluring perennial plantings put on sweeping summery displays, while the delightful woodland setting boasts strapping examples of the primitive-appearing *Gunnera chilensis* and equally picturesque vegetation. Replete with beguiling vignettes, Sonoma Horticultural Nursery represents a unique sanctuary for plant lovers throughout the year.

❀ **Admission:** Free.

Garden open: March through May: daily 9:00 A.M. to 5:00 P.M. June through February: Thursday through Monday 9:00 A.M. to 5:00 P.M.

Further information: Visitors are welcome; groups of ten or more require reservations. Paths are uneven and laid with coarse shale, so people who have difficulty walking or are in wheelchairs will have a difficult time navigating the gardens.

Directions: Sonoma Hort is 60 miles north of San Francisco (approximately one hour) in the heart of the wine country. Follow U.S. 101 north, exit at Cotati, and proceed west toward Sebastopol on CA 116. Travel about 4 miles to the SECOND Hessel Road and turn left; then turn right onto McFarlane. Proceed about a mile and turn right onto Azalea Avenue.

13. Cornerstone Festival of Gardens

23570 California Highway 121 (Arnold Drive), **Sonoma,** CA 94574; (707) 933-3010; www.cornerstonegardens.com

*I*NSPIRED BY avant-garde garden festivals—Chaumont-sur-Loire in France and the Grand-Métis in Quebec, Canada—the Cornerstone Festival of Gardens was inaugurated in 2004 as a captivating venue for garden design in the United States, located in the wine country of Northern California.

President and founder Chris Hougie unveiled the festival in the heart of Sonoma Valley, calling upon distinguished landscape architect Peter Walker to develop the initial site plan for the project and upon the celebrated landscape architect Ron Lutsko to design a beautiful garden for a special events area.

Hougie selected an international roster of acclaimed landscape architects and designers to create the first wave of gallery-style gardens. A perimeter of privet hedging outlines the geometric layout of the gardens, and as the hedges mature to form 6-foot-high walls, their emerald green foliage will embrace each space.

Unlike the show gardens at most landscape shows, you can walk through these installations, allowing you to explore every nuance of each garden. Meander through the gardens, and you'll likely come away impressed by a realm where no division exists between notions of a garden and the artistry of a space enlivened by ideas.

Admittedly, I lean toward contemporary art, and many of the creators' conceptually based designs dazzled me. Pamela Burton's

Earth Walk, for instance, demonstrates an emotionally resonant physicality. At ground level, bales of straw increase one's sense of enclosure. The garden reveals a massive wedge carved out of the terrain. A central expanse of billowy grass looms like a poetic vision, and alongside the grassy swath, you follow the inclined ground plane down a mulched path to the floor of the garden, where a tranquil pool arises. Swept away by the harsh beauty and profound materiality of the exposed earth, I felt immersed in the site.

Andy Cao's creation, a Lullaby Garden, is engagingly dreamy. Shoeless, you mount a small stairway and step forward to experience directly the qualities of an undulating earth form. Covered in a blanket woven from thick monofilament, the uncharted hills are satisfyingly tactile beneath your feet. Discovering voices rising to the surface of "a dark whirlpool" is another tantalizing element that contributes to the hypnotic atmosphere.

You'll discover elements of whimsy as well as social commentary and site-specific allusions to the Sonoma landscape. From subtle Japanese minimalism to the inventive use of materials, you can expect to be surprised.

❀ **Admission:** Fee; children under the age of twelve are admitted free.
Garden open: Daily 10:00 A.M. to 5:00 P.M. except Monday, when the gardens are open noon to 4:00 P.M. Call to confirm winter closings.
Further information: The ten-acre grounds include a cafe, plant nursery, exhibits gallery, and bookstore. Call (707) 933–3010 to confirm cafe and bookstore hours. Artefact Design & Salvage, an enterprise offering a trove of botanical gifts, garden ornaments, and antique elements, is housed here, too. Call (707) 933–0660 to confirm open hours. Wheelchair accessibility may be limited within individual garden spaces, but main paths are accessible.
Directions: Cornerstone is in the Sonoma countryside, fronting California Highway 121, approximately forty-five minutes north of San Francisco's Golden Gate Bridge.

San Francisco Gardenwalks

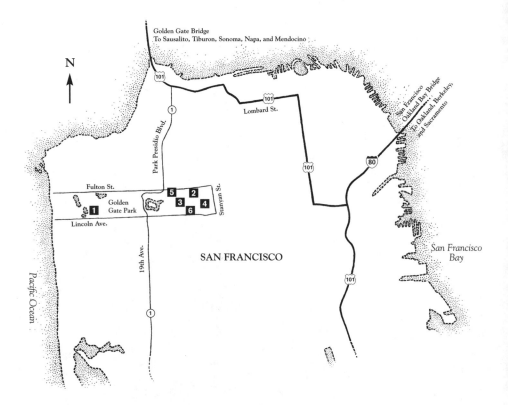

1. Golden Gate Park
2. Conservatory of Flowers, Golden
   Gate Park
3. Japanese Tea Garden, Golden
   Gate Park
4. National AIDS Memorial
   Grove, Golden Gate Park
5. Rose Garden, Golden Gate Park
6. San Francisco Botanical Garden
   at Strybing Arboretum, Golden
   Gate Park

1. Golden Gate Park

Stanyan Street west to the Pacific Ocean, and Fulton Street south to Lincoln Avenue, **San Francisco,** CA 94117; (415) 831–2700; www.frp.org

*E*NCOMPASSING more than 1,000 acres, Golden Gate Park is to San Francisco what Central Park is to New York City: a vast, welcoming refuge of greenery. To this day San Franciscans pay homage to William Hammond Hall, the man who in 1872 worked wonders with a barren landscape of desert and dunes. Historians recall how the acclaimed landscape architect Frederick Law Olmsted suggested that San Francisco would do well to find another site for such an important undertaking, saying that the land was too dismally sandy and windswept to grow trees on.

Following in Hall's footsteps, John McLaren, the park's superintendent at the turn of the twentieth century, devoted more than half a century of his own life to developing the park's impressive grounds. Famed for endowing Golden Gate Park with hundreds of uncommon species from around the globe, Scotsman McLaren is said to have planted one million trees. His gifted floriculture skills transformed the park into a landscape of rare beauty in the midst of a large metropolis.

At Golden Gate Park, you can observe a herd of American bison; indulge yourself in golf, handball, tennis, and equestrian sports; or, if it suits your fancy, operate model boats. With its beautiful lakes, horticultural treasures, first-rate museums, and miles of pathways for jogging, biking, or walking, the park will gratify most any predilection for recreational activity.

❀ **Admission:** Free.

Garden open: Daily, 6:00 A.M. to 10:00 P.M.

Further information: The Friends of Recreation and Parks Web site is a great resource, providing a map of the park and its museums. Look for useful links to a bevy of gardens at www.frp.org/links/index.html. The San Francisco Recreation and Park Department offices are in McLaren Lodge, 501 Stanyan Street. Portions of the park are wheelchair accessible.

Directions: Located in the northwest area of the city, the park is situated between the Richmond and Sunset Districts.

2. Conservatory of Flowers, Golden Gate Park

John F. Kennedy Drive at Conservatory Drive, **San Francisco,** CA 94117; (415) 666–7001; www.conservatoryofflowers.org

𝒫OISED LIKE A GEM atop the city's tourist attractions, the reopened Conservatory of Flowers is drawing out of towners and locals alike to marvel over the scope of the botanical displays and special exhibits.

Extensively rehabilitated with laminated glass and state-of-the-art systems capable of controlling temperatures or bringing on rainfall, the Victorian-era glasshouse rises grandly from its site in Golden Gate Park on a stunning approach from the valley. Symmetry and restraint distinguish the adjacent promenade and staircase, circa 1918.

During the building's eight-year closure, a committee of experts crafted a fresh vision for the institution. And despite difficulties involved in bringing plants into California, a process was undertaken to acquire select specimen plants from Florida, including some 35 feet tall! Step inside the landmark building today and you'll find plantings and exhibitions reconceived for the new millennium.

The new design puts into play five distinct spaces, capitalizing on different climate chambers. Notice the signs fashioned from glass panels and placed unobtrusively to emphasize a sense of immersion in this tropical oasis. Here you'll enjoy experiential and educational encounters.

Entering through an orientation space outfitted with informational displays that illuminate the historic context of the building and its flora, you move directly beyond into the jungly realm of the Lowland Tropics section. Situated beneath the structure's spectacular cathedral-like dome, amid all manner of exotic plant life, the sultry habitat of this central area beckons.

Immediately you see crown shafts of the sealing wax palm (*Cyrotostachys renda*), their red, green, and chartreuse segments providing a key to the common name.

Among age-old specimens, the enormous imperial philodendron dominates. Its venerable bearing warranted a temporary greenhouse of its own during the restoration. Another centenarian, *Dioon spinulossum*, hails from the Yucatan; it's a chubby Y-shaped cycad

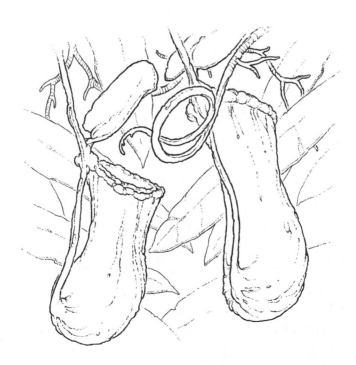

with attitude. A fine *Bismarckia* palm represents one of the Florida acquisitions.

The cooler air of the East Wing signals your passage into the Highland Tropics section, where lush tree ferns set the tone.

An unusual breed of rhododendron, Vireyas, thrive here in a sunken garden. They benefit from perfect growing conditions by producing fragrant flowers to adorn the surroundings. Grown out-doors previously, these species suffer damage or can perish during periods of extreme cold, but here they flourish.

A highlight of the conservatory is its renowned collection of pleurothallid orchids (a botanical subsection) housed here. Among the trove of rarities finding shelter are bromeliads and epiphytic orchids from higher elevations.

Masdevallia and *Dracula* orchids cling to tree sculptures and moss-covered trees. *Dracula vampira,* characterized by eerie dark blooms, is surely the most provocative member within its genus, and one that creates an alien atmosphere. An uncommon *Araucaria* species from New Caledonia, a relative of the monkey puzzle tree, also makes itself at home here.

The sensory wonderland of the Aquatic Garden emerges next, producing hypnotic effects with waterfalls, fountains, and imposing water lilies from the Amazon River. First cultivated in this country at the conservatory, *Victoria amazonica,* the Amazon water lily, boasts leaves up to 8 feet across. Floating placidly on the surface of a pond, its blossoms transform during their two-day duration from white to pink to rosy purple. You may be surprised by an Amazon lily hanging overhead, a beautifully crafted piece of art glass com-missioned specially for the space.

In the West Wing, the Potted Plants Gallery pays homage to Victorian pot culture. It's a savvy realm energized by vibrant, sea-sonal flowers in myriad containers surrounding an arbor.

A visual banquet of tactile surfaces and strong shapes awaits, complementing the floral color with the materiality of rugged stone, burnished wood, and glazed clay appearing in centuries-old troughs, tall Javanese vessels, and 1950s moderne benches. Holding center stage, a lushly planted, oversize travertine plaster container embellished with carved *putti* dates from the 1915 Panama-Pacific International Exposition.

A gallery devoted to special exhibits completes the array.

Without a doubt, the conservatory building is foremost among recent American historic preservation projects. Its beautiful facade has provided past and present residents of San Francisco with a perfect backdrop to commemorate special moments for more than a century. Thankfully, it's open to the public once again!

❀ **Admission:** Fee.

Garden open: Tuesday through Sunday 9:00 A.M. to 4:30 P.M.; closed Monday; open on major holidays.

Further information: The gift shop kiosk is located outside the main entrance. Last entry to the conservatory is at 4:30 P.M.; visitors must leave by 5:00 P.M. The conservatory is wheelchair accessible.

Directions: The conservatory is located in the eastern end of Golden Gate Park, near John F. Kennedy Drive (south) and Conservatory Drive (north, west, and east). Log on to www.conservatoryofflowers .org/visitus/index.htm for detailed directions or public transportation information.

3. Japanese Tea Garden, Golden Gate Park

Hagiwara Tea Garden Drive, **San Francisco**, CA 94117;
(415) 831–2700

*N*OT JUST FOR garden lovers, but certainly a treat for those who appreciate fine garden design, the Japanese Tea Garden is one of San Francisco's most popular tourist attractions. Mature palms line Hagiwara Tea Garden Drive, the road running between the M. H. de Young Memorial Museum and the California Academy of Science and into the garden. Graced with a quartet of fountains and row upon row of wonderfully pollarded sycamore trees, the generous plaza in front of the Academy of Science is known as the music concourse. A legacy of the California Midwinter International Exposition of 1894, the concourse facing the de Young Museum features the Spreckels Temple of Music, a bandstand with classical columns and an impressive portico.

Thought to be the oldest Japanese-style garden in the United States, Golden Gate Park's Japanese Tea Garden was constructed in 1893. The individual largely responsible for the garden's initial design and the fabrication of many of its authentic buildings was Makoto Hagiwara, a prominent Japanese landscape designer. In 1979 Hagiwara's part in the garden's unveiling during the California Midwinter International Exposition of 1894 was commemorated by a startling emerald mound of English boxwood, crowned by a peak of variegated Italian buckthorn. Known as the Mount Fuji hedge, the sculptural planting honors Hagiwara's region of birth. After you go through the garden's lovely main gates, look for it to the right of the admission booth.

Pass by the Mount Fuji hedge, following along the path until you reach the Hagiwara Gate, which is painted in a palette of harmonious yet distinctly contrasting earthy hues. The garden ornaments adorning the gateway include the full, rounded forms of ceramic vessels glazed in midnight blue, azure, and russet. Pass under the gate through to the redbrick terrace overlooking the Sunken Garden, where large koi frolic in the meandering pond. Even in January, when the deep green scenery can be enveloped in gentle mists, camellias offer their colorful blooms as an antidote to gray skies.

Continue walking and you'll meet up with a striking example of statuary placed amid clipped Monterey pines. Here a large bronze Buddha raises one hand in peaceful repose. Cross the long bridge to find stately redwoods and, in the forefront, the stunning red pagoda, built for the Japanese Exhibit of the Panama-Pacific International Exposition of 1915.

Behind the Buddhist pagoda, a modest Zen garden may be viewed from a walkway where bamboo fencing prevents visitors from disturbing its gravel river and stone waterfall.

The garden's teahouse is a popular place to rest while sipping tea and taking in the view of various garden vignettes. Be sure to stop and admire the Drum Bridge, located between the tea garden's main gate and south gate. You may wish to climb the bridge's steep curve if it's not overrun by avid photographers at the time of your visit.

Near the garden's south gate, you'll discover Waterfall Hill, the site of a collection of fine dwarf trees planted over many years by Makoto Hagiwara. His descendants, like countless Japanese Americans living in the United States during World War II, were forced to relocate, leaving behind their beloved garden, not to mention decades of dedicated service and personal history. When the Hagiwara family's home was destroyed as a result of anti-Japanese sentiments, members of the household removed the rare specimens of dwarf trees and entrusted them to a friend. Fortunately, these trees, and elemental pieces such as rocks and lanterns, were eventually sold to Dr. Hugh Fraser, whose widow, Audrey, became the collection's final owner. Upon her death, Mrs. Fraser made certain that Hagiwara's specimens of dwarf trees were returned to the tea garden.

✿ **Admission:** Fee.

Garden open: March through October: daily 8:30 A.M. to 6:00 P.M. November through February: daily 8:30 A.M. to 5:00 P.M.

Further information: Visiting the garden is free when you enter during the first or the last hour of the day. Gift shop phone: (415) 752–1171. About half of the garden paths are wheelchair accessible.

Directions: If driving, enter Golden Gate Park heading west on John F. Kennedy Drive, then watch for signs and turn left onto Hagiwara Tea Garden Drive. Call MUNI at (415) 673–6864 for public transportation information.

4. National AIDS Memorial Grove, Golden Gate Park

Intersection of Middle and Bowling Green Drives,
San Francisco, CA 94117; (415) 750–8340, (888) 294–7683;
www.aidsmemorial.org

A FORMIDABLE BOULDER of Sierra granite stands sentinel at the intersection of Middle Drive and Bowling Green Drive in Golden Gate Park, marking the main portal to the National AIDS Memorial Grove.

Rich with history, the grove's seven-and-a-half-acre site hearkens back to the earliest days of the park, when an elk paddock and seasonal lake occupied the area. By the 1920s, Jose Vicente de Laveaga provided funds to transform the environment into a welcoming dell embellished with a waterfall and fragrant rhododendrons.

Although the de Laveaga Dell fell into disrepair in the 1970s, destiny favored the forlorn site. And thanks to the efforts of a small group of individuals who first envisioned a place where people could come to find hope while remembering and grieving their loved ones, the dell has become an inviting garden once again.

Redesigned and renovated, the de Laveaga Dell terrain resembles an open-bowl shape. Today, in place of an impenetrable jungle of blackberry vines, English ivy, and elm suckers, you'll find a confluence of stately redwoods, live oaks, and California bays and a lofty canopy of aged Monterey pines and cypresses.

From the mobility access ramp leading into the grove, you can follow the walkway to the Crossroads Circle and beyond to the Fern Grotto on the western boundary. Pass the Redwood Grove on the left and Pine Crescent on the right, and a low-lying meadow washed in light appears.

The lanky demeanor of Monterey pines and cypresses emerges on the North Slope, bearing witness to the previous century. Alongside these giants—approaching the end of their life span—notice the dense, symmetrical forms of younger trees planted to eventually replace the current canopy.

Throughout the grove an abundance of native species create pleasing associations with introduced varieties of shrubs, trees, perennials, and bulbs, resulting in changing displays from one month to the next.

Close to the walkways native snowberry grows, alongside the fragrant flowers and leaves of spicebush.

Growing as a shrub or tree, both mature and recently planted specimens of *Luma apiculata* also come into view: A South American stunner that develops a smooth, cinnamon-colored bark as it ages, *L. apiculata* boasts white flowers with showy stamens off and on through summer.

Running along the floor of the dell, a dry streambed strewn with cobblestones serves as a study in contrast to diverse vegetation —tree ferns, maples and, from Mexico, *Fuchsia thymifolia*, covered in a profusion of tiny blooms aging to a deep pink.

Benches situated in quiet nooks punctuate the tranquil woodland, while at intervals boulders with small negative shapes carved into them loom large. Capturing rainwater to form tiny pools, the boulders' indentations function in the dry season as receptacles for messages or mementos from visitors.

Follow the lower walkway, tracing the length of the South Slope, and you'll discover a place for commemorative gatherings. The subdued shelter of the Circle of Friends features a flagstone terrace with names engraved in concentric circles, commemorating individuals who have died, their loved ones, and donors to the grove.

A place of spiritual nourishment to the local and global community alike, these cloistered surroundings are illuminated by the Dogwood Crescent, which offers up a froth of blossoms in March and April. A glorious massing of *Rhododendron* 'Fragrantissimum' on the hillside vividly acknowledges spring.

❀ **Admission:** Free.

> **Garden open:** Daily 6:00 A.M. to 10:00 P.M.
>
> **Further information:** Volunteers—some 125 to 200—come together to share in a spirit of hope and remembrance on garden workdays, held on the third Saturday of the month, eight times a year, March through October. Much of the grove, including the Circle of Friends, is wheelchair accessible.
>
> **Directions:** Follow signs on Nineteenth Avenue in San Francisco, turning east onto Martin Luther King Drive into the park; the AIDS Grove is located in the eastern end of Golden Gate Park, across from the tennis courts.

5. Rose Garden, Golden Gate Park

John F. Kennedy Drive on the south, Fulton Street at Park Presidio Boulevard on the north, **San Francisco**, CA 94117; (415) 831–2700; www.frp.org

A BEVY OF HYBRID TEA, floribunda, grandiflora, and miniature roses is on view in the Golden Gate Park Rose Garden, designed in 1961 by then assistant superintendent of parks Roy Hudson.

You can count upon three to four lavish bloom cycles when the garden is at its best. Mother's Day to Father's Day is a most impressive time. A fine bloom takes place also around July Fourth, and beginning around Labor Day, another lovely display continues through mid-October.

Enter the garden at Kennedy Drive, and you'll find a vivid fusion of colors appearing in two long rows of rectangular beds, marching side by side all the way to Fulton Street. These fifty or so rose beds occupy the dominant expanse of the garden plan.

In keeping with the rectilinear quality of the original space given over to the garden, Hudson's design encompasses a long straight walkway that spans the entire length of the eastern perimeter. Alongside this main path, a lattice fence draws attention to a bed displaying climbing, shrub, and old garden roses. Arrays of 'Lavender Lassie' produce lavender-pink double blooms with a flower form like an old rose.

Planted here is the elegant 'Sally Holmes', with single, soft, pale pink to white flowers, and the eglantine or sweetbriar rose (*Rosa eglanteria*). A tall-growing old rose, the eglantine rosebushes are cloaked in large red-orange hips in late summer. They thrive in the San Francisco climate, blooming twice a year rather than just once and producing another display of hips around Christmas.

Climbing roses serve as a backdrop on the garden's western boundary, where they adorn decorative latticework configured in a crescent shape. Tall yews stand sentry to the rear.

'Golden Showers' blooms continuously throughout the growing season; it's a pretty yellow rose with loosely formed flowers. Multicolored 'Joseph's Coat', 'Royal Sunset', and 'Altissimo' offer up a brilliant medley of red, orange, and gold hues, together with the yellow-orange blended 'Autumn Sunset'.

In the foreground, to counterbalance the design's angular elements, the curving line of the latticework repeats in a circular planting surrounded by the lawn.

The circle-shape bed highlights two rows of miniature roses. Rising in the center are taller roses: 'Mister Lincoln' and 'Glowing Peace'. Placed in between is a white border composed of 'Gourmet Popcorn', a big miniature that never stops blooming.

Labels make it easy to identify roses you find appealing. The garden's main source of roses comes from the All-America Rose Selections, an organization that donates the most sought-after award-winning roses each year. Thus, you can preview roses that will be available at plant nurseries the following year. A winner in the floribunda class, for instance, takes center stage. The exotic colora-

tion of 'Hot Cocoa' is truly stunning, with dusky orange petals set
off by russet tones.

Such novel new varieties stand out against the garden's abundant displays of beautifully formed, classic roses.

❁ **Admission:** Free.

Garden open: Daily during park hours, 6:00 A.M. to 10:00 P.M.

Further information: Call the San Francisco Recreation and Park
Department at the number above. The garden's main paths are paved
and wheelchair accessible.

Directions: Visit the Friends of Recreation and Parks Web site to see
a map of the park and the exact location of the Rose Garden:
www.frp.org/links/index.html.

6. San Francisco Botanical Garden at Strybing Arboretum, Golden Gate Park

Ninth Avenue at Lincoln Way, **San Francisco,** CA 94122;
(415) 661–1316; www.sfbotanicalgarden.org

A VISIT TO San Francisco would hardly be complete without
exploring the fifty-five-acre San Francisco Botanical Garden
at Strybing Arboretum located in Golden Gate Park. One of the
country's premier urban spaces, the garden at Strybing exceeded the
goals described in its mission statement: to display "plants from
around the world suited to the central coastal region of California
and the San Francisco Bay Area"; "offer a place for reflection, enjoyment, and relaxation for the public"; and provide enlightening
environmental and horticultural programs.

Established in 1870, Golden Gate Park was without an arboretum for many years, although the park's earliest superintendent,
William Hammond Hall, had included one in the drawing of the
park's master plan. Despite Hall's best intentions, it was not until
the tenure of landscape architect John McLaren that the arboretum
became a reality.

McLaren envisioned a setting on a par with the Arnold Arboretum of Harvard University, a challenging objective that would require Golden Gate Park's distinguished superintendent to raise considerable funding. In the 1890s a number of conifers were planted on the site of today's San Francisco Botanical Garden, but the lack of adequate funds made it impossible to go forward.

Fortunately, McLaren's good friend, Helene Strybing, donated a sum of money to the City of San Francisco, and on her death Mrs. Strybing bequeathed an ample gift that constituted most of her estate. Her generous legacy, which she earmarked especially for an arboretum and botanical gardens, made the development of the gardens possible in the 1930s.

Interestingly, Helene Strybing appears to have been quite a forward thinker who wanted the collections to include indigenous plants and those with medicinal applications. As planning went forward, McLaren together with Eric Walther (the director from 1937 to 1957) designed a master scheme for the gardens, with geographically designated sections of extensive communities of plants. Dedicated in 1940 as Strybing Arboretum, it has long been celebrated nationally for diverse and distinctive plantings.

Today, in what is an effective partnership between the public and private sectors, the City of San Francisco takes responsibility for staffing the gardens, while the Strybing Arboretum Society provides a community of dynamic volunteers who help preserve many species of plants and cultivate unusual varieties. Their renowned plant sales, featuring rare and highly desirable specimens, draw avid folks with green thumbs from near and far. Gardeners come to acquire the exciting offerings and, of course, to visit the gardens to glean ideas for how they might incorporate uncommon plants in their landscapes at home.

Should your visit fall during the winter months, you'll still find massings of plants that manifest surprising reminders of tropical wonderlands. The New World Cloud Forest highlights plants located in the Western Hemisphere: Spectacular salvias exhibit a range of colors from fire-engine reds and delicate pinks to the magenta blooms of *Salvia wageriana,* which unfurl to embellish the plant's long, arching limbs. Trees of various heights seek out their required quotient of light. In the area's dense understory of plants, a wealth of epiphytes thrive in little or no soil, and bromeliads run riot over tree stumps and living trees. Fuchsias, too, abound, dripping with elongated blooms that lure hummingbirds to the service of pollination.

Generally considered akin to the Mediterranean's mild climate, conditions in the greater San Francisco Bay Area rank among the West Coast's most remarkably fertile environments. San Francisco Botanical Garden at Strybing Arboretum successfully grows an incredible variety of plants from all over the globe. Although many plants originating in Asian countries have acclimated to the habitats and climates in the fifty states, the botanical garden supports one of the most significant selections of flora from Asia to be found in North America. Overall, the arboretum and gardens boast 8,000 plants from multinational pedigrees—a glorious demonstration of the accommodating milieu.

The Asian gardens, some of the most evocative settings, are filled with superb magnolias and camellias, celestial Japanese maples, and *Michelia doltsopa*, a Himalayan relative of magnolias. Conifers are also handsomely represented. Along the path not far from the Helen Crocker Library, you'll find a choice example of *Ginkgo biloba*, a broad-leaved conifer. If you cross the lawn heading south then west, you'll come upon a service road. Follow the path there to a stream, until you glimpse a grove of redwoods. Discovered in 1941 in China, these three rare *Metasequoia glyptostroboides* are particularly striking with their magnificent sienna-colored bark.

During your visit explore the popular Moon Viewing Garden,

given by the Ikebana International Society. The garden's wooden deck, oriented so that one may look out at the moon, functions sublimely as a momentary resting place where you can revel in the glimmering contrasts between the trees and shrubs.

The Old World Cloud Forest is enchanting, if not in name alone. Its Vireya rhododendrons are unusual for their capacity to rebloom in San Francisco's summers, after putting on a most impressive floral exhibition in the spring. In the Primitive Plant Garden, plants related to more ancient species are displayed. Proceed along the angular, zigzagging wooden walkway to view imposing tree ferns, horsetails, and the enormous presence of *Gunnera chilensis* from Patagonia.

If you like scented gardens, the Garden of Fragrance will lure you with its myriad aromas. The garden has braille labels designed for the visually impaired. For a wealth of ideas, perennial gardeners may want to study the handsome plantings of the Zellerbach Garden of Perennials, which was developed in 1967 and, after a redesign, reopened in 2001.

Savor the special atmosphere of this region by spending time in the arboretum's redwood grove that has been developed into the Redwood Trail. Here species of plants native to coastal redwood habitats are featured. Discover the John Muir Nature Trail and the Arthur Menzies Garden of California Native Plants, which also display the local flora.

When I reminisce on walks through the San Francisco Botanical Garden at Strybing Arboretum, my mind's eye recalls image upon image of arresting plants in harmonious arrangements. Strolling past the wildfowl pond to the adjoining boggy gardens, I rejoiced in the awe-inspiring apparition of gunnera, with its sprawling leaves and immense form. The upright coral pokers of South African aloes and sensational Cape Province kniphofias are representative of the garden's brilliant displays.

Perhaps you've heard someone say about the San Francisco Bay Area, "Just take a plant and stick it in the ground, then watch it grow . . . and grow!" A visit to these gardens proves this saying right. Although fire, drought, and frigid weather occasionally wreak havoc on the garden's tenderly nurtured horticultural treasures, this botanical garden admirably demonstrates just how blessed the region is. Before departing the gardens, amble over to the Helen Crocker Russell Library of Horticulture, located just inside the main entrance on the left. Here you may take advantage of the library's peaceful reading room to peruse extensive compilations of nursery catalogs, periodicals, and books, as well as slides and videos. There is no charge to visit.

Don't fail to explore the new three-quarter-acre entry garden inside the main gate. The exciting plantings here include vibrant combinations of plant material such as palms, cycads, bamboo species, and a variety of bananas. Hundreds of exceptional plants are featured in this lush garden, which is the work of David McCrory and Roger Raiche, a design team known as Planet Horticulture.

Just inside the main gate to the right, look for the kiosk housing the bookstore and gift shop. There you'll find a fine selection of regional titles, general gardening books, and *Pacific Horticulture* magazine, an especially stimulating read when visiting the region.

❀ **Admission:** Free, donations welcome.

Garden open: Weekdays 8:00 A.M. to 4:30 P.M., weekends and holidays 10:00 A.M. to 5:00 P.M. The bookstore is open daily 10:00 A.M. to 4:00 P.M.; closed major holidays. The library is open daily 10:00 A.M. to 4:00 P.M.; closed major holidays.

Further information: Daily docent-led walks depart from the bookstore or the Friend Gate at the north entrance; donations appreciated. For plant sale questions, phone (415) 661–3090. Major paths are paved and are wheelchair accessible.

Directions: To take public transportation to the gardens, phone (415) 673–MUNI. For detailed driving instructions, log on to the Web site.

East Bay Gardenwalks

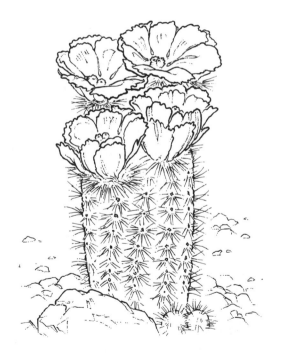

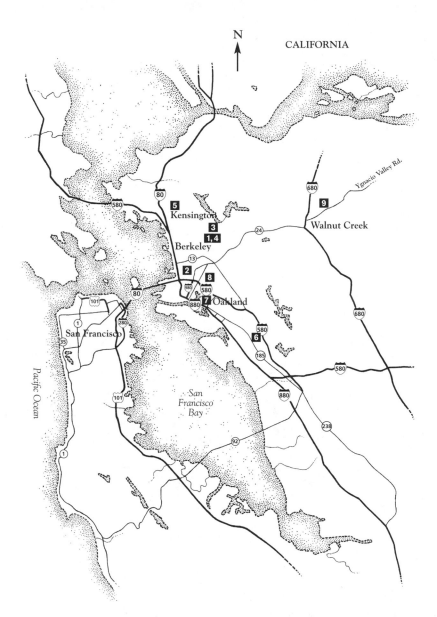

N

CALIFORNIA

Ygnacio Valley Rd.

Kensington

Walnut Creek

Berkeley

Oakland

San Francisco

Pacific Ocean

San Francisco Bay

1. Berkeley: Berkeley Rose Garden
2. Berkeley: Our Own Stuff Gallery Garden
3. Berkeley: Regional Parks Botanic Garden, Tilden Regional Park
4. Berkeley: University of California Botanical Garden

5. Kensington: Blake Garden
6. Oakland: Dunsmuir Historic Estate
7. Oakland: Lakeside Park Gardens
8. Oakland: Morcom Rose Garden
9. Walnut Creek: The Ruth Bancroft Garden

1. Berkeley Rose Garden

1201 Euclid Avenue and Bay View Place, **Berkeley,** CA 94704;
(510) 981–5150

A NATIONAL CANVASS of public rose gardens would doubt-
lessly place the Berkeley Rose Garden among the country's
most fetching settings. Boasting a dazzling structural design replete
with thousands of roses, this north Berkeley haven will satiate any
ardent rose connoisseur.

Explore the rose garden's spectacular amphitheater. Begin your
descent at street level, then stroll beneath the ample curvilinear
configuration of connecting arbors and strapping wooden pergola
that form the garden's graceful framework. Note how the fragrance
of strongly scented climbing roses is intoxicating, especially in May
around Mother's Day when blooming peaks.

Discerning garden travelers can swoop down the multitiered
amphitheater's dramatic stairways, crisscrossing comfortable horizontal walkways, to bask in the garden's lavish rose beds, arranged
to emphasize the varied colors. Berkeley's gentle climate fosters a
lengthy cycle of bloom for roses, as well as a wealth of other flowers. You can expect to enjoy early blooming varieties of roses that
flower in April, and then again throughout the summer months on
into October.

The Berkeley Rose Garden presents a veritable banquet of
delights throughout the year.

❀ **Admission:** Free.

Garden open: Daily 6:00 A.M. to 10:00 P.M.

Further information: Pathways are steep and there are many steps;
wheelchair access is limited (reached through the Codornices Park

Tunnel on the east side of Euclid). The overlook at street level is accessible.

Directions: The garden is located in northeast Berkeley, about thirty-five minutes east of downtown San Francisco via the Bay Bridge. To see a map, log on to www.ci.berkeley.ca.us/parks/parkspages/Berkeley RoseGarden.html.

2. Our Own Stuff Gallery Garden

3017 Wheeler Street, **Berkeley,** CA 94705; (510) 540–8544

W IDELY KNOWN for her carved stone works, Marcia Donahue creates sculptural pieces of rustic grace that can be found in many a West Coast garden. The artist's own wonderfully eccentric Berkeley garden is celebrated for the fantastic juxtapositions of boldly textured, audacious plantings with artwork crafted by Donahue and her partner, Mark Bulwinkle.

Donahue's Berkeley residence consists of a brown-shingled Victorian house wearing a heavy cloak of foliage. The lush outgrowth results from an imaginative grouping of trees, including a hundred-year-old cordyline, a distinctive weeping cypress, and a tall, willowy eucalyptus. Also in the front garden space, Bulwinkle's sculptures, with their active forms and richly rusted surfaces, announce the horticultural extravaganza awaiting visitors in Donahue's inner sanctum.

Traveling along a side walkway, you'll enter a sumptuous tropical garden, which is full of exceptional specimens. I was captivated by the conspicuous beauty of *Solanum quitoense*, with its luxuriant purple-veined leaves and provocative red-violet new growth. A wooden gate in the shape of a brawny hand is the muscular icon that affords entree to Donahue's high-spirited, elaborately structured rear garden.

On my initial visit, I felt a delectable sensory overload. Uniquely conceived, Donahue's urban realm is distinguished by a canopy of towering flora combined with a generous understory of rare plants. Add to this the unexpected placement of abundant ornamentation and a surprising assemblage of found objects, and you have horticultural theater at its most expressive. Mind you, all this takes place within the boundaries of an unexpectedly bantam-size realm, which measures 40 by 60 feet!

Note a collection of boisterous bowling balls. This raucous rainbow of lustrous orbs is set against the backdrop of exquisite, pale-hued bamboo varieties. Only here will you witness such an outrageous mixture of incongruous elements. Certainly the exciting examples of bamboo Donahue has gathered point to the finesse of a savvy plantswoman. But look closely, for some of these stately canes are handcrafted ceramic forms made by Marcia herself! Glazed clay totems are just one example of the surprises that await you amid the dense plantings.

You'll happen upon sculptural stone pieces, such as a full-featured face I discovered during my visit. A tiny leaf had fallen upon the sad countenance of that stone visage, taking on the appearance of a teardrop and accentuating the garden's theatrical impact. During your visit to Marcia Donahue's bewitching garden, expect to be drenched in colorful contradictions. You'll enjoy encountering the unexpected.

❀ **Admission:** Free.

Garden open: Sunday 1:00 to 5:00 P.M.

Further information: The garden takes the form of an outdoor gallery for sculpture by Mark Bulwinkle, Marcia Donahue, and Sara Tool. Phone ahead for detailed directions.

Directions: This Berkeley garden is located in the East Bay, approximately a half hour from downtown San Francisco via the Bay Bridge.

3. Regional Parks Botanic Garden, Tilden Regional Park

Wildcat Canyon Road at South Park Drive, **Berkeley,** CA 94708; (510) 841–8732; www.nativeplants.org

*E*STABLISHED WITHIN the boundaries of Berkeley's expansive Tilden Regional Park, the Regional Parks Botanic Garden presents an exciting environment in which to learn about California's flora. While discovering breathtaking views amid sometimes steep and rocky terrain, you'll find that the garden appears at once cultivated and untamed.

The Regional Parks Botanic Garden specializes in the propagation of the state's trees, shrubs, and flowers. Divided into nine distinctive sections, the garden displays the diverse flora growing in California's various geographical regions—from the desert to the Pacific rain forest.

At any time of the year, you'll find compelling plant species to study and admire in the garden's fine collections of conifers and oaks, ceanothuses, and numerous endangered plants. If it's blooming or colorful specimens you're after, you won't be disappointed. In March, the fragile beauty of trout lilies, fritillaries, trilliums, and California poppies usher in spring. The berries of the madrone, the blooms of the chaparral currant, and the leaves of deciduous oaks, dogwoods, willows, and hawthorns put on a show of striking colors throughout the fall season. Even a December visit can be a harbinger of things to come: The first manzanita blooms come out at year's end, followed by a riot of flowering manzanitas, silktassels, and currants in January.

The grounds of the Regional Parks Botanic Garden captivate visitors with their natural beauty.

❀ **Admission:** Free.

Garden open: Daily 8:30 A.M. to 5:00 P.M.; closed Thanksgiving, Christmas, and New Year's Day.

Further information: Pick up a map of the garden at the visitor center for a self-guided tour. The Friends of the Regional Parks Botanic Garden have a comprehensive Web site, with a calendar of special events and classes. The garden terrain is steep and paths are narrow, but wheelchair accessible areas include the visitor center, which offers tours and lectures throughout the year: Call for Saturday and Sunday tour times.

Directions: The garden is located in Contra Costa County in the Berkeley Hills of the East Bay, about forty-five minutes from downtown San Francisco via the Bay Bridge. Visit the Web site for maps and detailed directions.

4. University of California Botanical Garden

200 Centennial Drive, **Berkeley,** CA 94720; (510) 643–2755; http://botanicalgarden.berkeley.edu

WITH ITS HILLY TOPOGRAPHY and sometimes steep paths, Strawberry Canyon is the perfect setting for Berkeley's University of California Botanical Garden. Stretching over thirty-four acres, the grounds' geographical arrangement of gardens displays plants from around the world.

The abundant plantings and the university's educational outreach and research make the UC Botanical Garden a thriving horticultural museum without walls. Located across Centennial Drive to the northwest of the garden entrance is the Mather Redwood Grove. Within the garden the large section devoted to California natives is full of color throughout the year: The profuse blooms of spring wildflowers are followed by bright poppies in summer, conspicuous Madia sunflowers in fall, and fetching California lilacs (ceanothus), manzanitas, and currants in winter.

In May, seek out the perfumed air of the garden of old roses. Nearby, the traditional English knot garden, which features Western herbs, is one of the most popular displays. Continue along the path, pass the herb garden's flagstone terrace and handsome stone

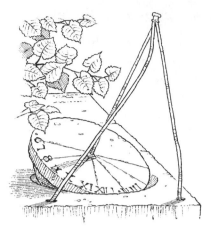

sundial, and you'll find a section devoted to Chinese medicinal herbs. In the summer season, savor the fragrance of blooming herbs. In other sections of the garden, fine collections of diverse flora from South America, the Mediterranean, and Asia are exhibited.

The Mesoamerican section pulses with the animated activity of hummingbirds as they flash and shimmer among summer's abundant flowers. The birds' ostentatious enterprise, however, is not the only thing to rivet one's attention in this garden realm. The view across the bay will enchant all who wander through here.

Indoors in the Desert and Rain Forest House, you'll find succulents and epiphytic orchids. Ferns and insect-eating plants grow in a building nearby, and tropical crops such as bananas and coffee flourish in the Tropical House.

There is always something in flower at this wonderful garden. Especially noteworthy are fragrant wintersweet (*Chimonanthus*) that bloom in January and February. March and April are ablaze with blooming rhododendrons and other spring-flowering plants. And throughout the summer and fall, until frost arrives in December, the Mexican and Central American collections are abloom.

Each time I visit, I'm grateful to the staff and faculty of years gone by, whose far-flung expeditions contributed exceptional specimens to the garden's plant collections. The horticulturists at the botanical garden have created a splendid haven—a place where we can joyfully observe the plant world in all its glory.

❀ **Admission:** Fee and parking fee; free every Thursday.

Garden open: Daily 9:00 A.M. to 5:00 P.M.; closed first Tuesday of every month, Thanksgiving Day, December 24 and 25, December 31, and January 1. The garden shop is open 10:30 A.M. to 4:30 P.M.

Further information: Call for special summer hours; visit the Web site for notice of special events and programs. The garden shop can be reached at (510) 642–3343.

Directions: The garden is in the East Bay, about forty minutes from downtown San Francisco via the Bay Bridge. Visit the Web site for detailed directions, parking information, etc.

5. Blake Garden

70 Rincon Road, **Kensington,** CA 94707; (510) 524–2449;
www.laep.ced.berkeley.edu/laep/blakegarden

*E*XQUISITE MEDITERRANEAN-TYPE gardens, a handsome elongated reflecting pool, and breathtaking views of the San Francisco Bay—all are yours to behold when you visit Blake House, the residence of the president of the University of California at Berkeley. Situated in the stunning East Bay section of Kensington near Berkeley, Blake House was given to the university by alumni and benefactors Mr. and Mrs. Anson Stiles Blake. This lovely house was built in the Mediterranean style by architect Walter Bliss in the early 1920s, and it has functioned as the president's house since 1967.

An avid horticulturist, Mrs. Blake looked to her sister Mabel Symmes, a student of landscape architecture at UC Berkeley, for expertise in planning the formal ten-acre garden. From the garden's inception in the 1920s, Mr. and Mrs. Blake encouraged the university to utilize it. Maintained today by the Department of Landscape Architecture, the Blake Garden is a valuable resource for students of the program.

The garden's sun-swept hills and terraced areas feature a remarkable collection of approximately 1,000 species and varieties. In the garden's more sylvan areas, you'll discover dawn redwoods that were started from seed. Numerous types of oak and pine grow here, along with magnolia and maple, plum, cherry, and rhododendrons and roses. There is also a rich profusion of perennials and herbs. Striking floral colors are provided by flowering maples (*Abutilon*) and angel's trumpets (*Brugmansia*), monkey flowers, rockrose, and fragrant climbers such as jasmine and Japanese wisteria.

✿ **Admission:** Free.

Garden open: Monday through Friday 8:00 A.M. to 4:30 P.M.; closed weekends and university holidays.

Further information: Tours are available to groups of ten or more if reservations have been made. A free brochure is available to visitors who visit the Web site: Look for "Materials," then download the PDF file. On the Web site you'll also discover links to many Bay Area gardens. Most of Blake Garden is accessible to wheelchairs.

Directions: Blake Garden is 4 miles north of the UC Berkeley campus, adjacent to and just north of Berkeley in the East Bay, and approximately forty-five minutes from downtown San Francisco via the Bay Bridge.

6. Dunsmuir Historic Estate

2960 Peralta Oaks Court, **Oakland,** CA 94605; (510) 615–5555; www.dunsmuir.org

A GRAND MANSION distinguished by neoclassical revival architecture is set here amid a forty-acre estate, with gardens and landscaping originally designed with the assistance of Golden Gate Park's John McLaren. Camperdown elms, bunya-bunya, hornbeam, and palm trees add to the ambience when taking a stroll through the grounds.

✿ **Admission:** Free.

Garden open: The grounds are open for walking on weekdays 10:00 A.M. to 4:00 P.M. February through December. Gift shop opens during special events and tours. Call to confirm hours.

Further information: Most weekdays you can enjoy a self-guided tour of the estate's grounds. Reservations required for docent-led tours of the Dunsmuir Mansion; fee charged (members free). Call for tour dates and times from April through September. Grounds are paved and level, making them mostly wheelchair accessible.

Directions: From San Francisco cross the Bay Bridge and continue to Interstate 580 east toward Hayward. Exit at 106th Avenue/Foothill Boulevard. Make three left turns at the three stop signs. Drive under the freeway and turn right onto Peralta Oaks Drive. Follow signs to Dunsmuir.

7. Lakeside Park Gardens

666 Bellevue Avenue, **Oakland,** CA 94610; (510) 238–7275; www.oaklandnet.com/parks

*T*HIS FIVE-ACRE Oakland site is incorporated within the Lake Merritt parkland. It features an assemblage of garden areas devoted to herbs and lilies, rhododendrons, fuchsias, and more.

Look for the sun-drenched Butterfly Garden, then move on to the sound of rushing water in a neighboring waterfall environment sheltered by pines and Atlas cedars.

Be sure to visit the lath structure, with its special moderated environment, that is home to one of the few outdoor collections of Vireya rhododendrons in the United States outside of Hawaii.

Beyond the lath house, you'll discover an audacious tableau of prickly succulents. And farther along, explore the Lakeside Park Palmetum, with palm trees from around the world.

The open-air realm of the Bonsai and Suiseki Display Garden (located inside Lakeside Park Gardens) delights bonsai lovers.

❁ **Admission:** Free.

Garden open: Monday through Friday 10:00 A.M. to 3:00 p.m., Saturday and Sunday 10:00 A.M. to 5:00 P.M. Bonsai Garden open Wednesday through Friday 11:00 A.M. to 3:00 P.M., Saturday 10:00 A.M. to 4:00 P.M., Sunday noon to 4:00 P.M.

Further information: Phone (510) 763–8409 to reach the docent shelter of the Bonsai and Suiseki Display Garden; it closes during inclement weather (rain). Main path up to and including the Bonsai Garden is accessible; limited wheelchair accessibility on the peripheral grounds.

Directions: Lakeside Park is about a half hour from San Francisco via the Bay Bridge.

8. Morcom Rose Garden

700 Jean Street **Oakland,** CA 94610; (510) 238–3187

CONSTRUCTED IN 1934 as a project of the Works Progress Administration, this gem of a garden can be found secreted in Oakland, just 1 block off Grand Avenue on Jean Street. Named for a onetime mayor of Oakland, the Morcom's original hardscape and picturesque layout designed by landscape architect Arthur Cobbledick is preserved here.

Once you are inside the classical gateway, the breadth of the garden's four-acre geometry is revealed. It's a showcase for hybrid teas—the so-called modern repeat-blooming roses that were first bred in the late nineteenth century.

Lining the entry walkway, arrays of floriferous hybrid teas follow a pattern where rich red varieties meld into a gradation of hues, becoming lighter and lighter as you approach a large pool of still water.

Positioned between the pool and the Florentine area along the garden's far western boundary is the historic Mother's Walk, where heritage roses thrive within a circular framework of tea roses, noisettes, and polyanthas that bloom twice a year.

A pleasing sense of proportion distinguishes the Morcom's Renaissance motif, structured around a dominant cross axis defined by a broad staircase leading to a raised area to the left of the pool.

Ascend the stairs, passing fountains and a cascade of rushing water, and you reach the elevated position and commanding views of the Wedding Terrace—an open-air veranda rimmed by the deep green backdrop of Italian stone pines.

Plan your visit around Mother's Day in mid-May and bask in the Morcom Rose Garden's annual crescendo of bloom.

❀ **Admission:** Free.
Garden open: Daily dawn to dusk.

Further information: Weddings often take place in the garden from May through October. The gardens can be accessed by wheelchairs, but not the restroom, which is upstairs.

Directions: The garden is about a half hour from downtown San Francisco via the Bay Bridge. Visit www.oaklandnet.com/parks/facilities and click on Rental Facilities, then click on Morcom Rose Garden to obtain detailed directions.

9. The Ruth Bancroft Garden

1500 Bancroft Road, P.O. Box 30845, **Walnut Creek,** CA 94598; (925) 944–9352; www.ruthbancroftgarden.org

*T*HE FIRST GARDEN in the United States to merit the sponsorship of the Garden Conservancy, the Ruth Bancroft Garden is a great garden in every sense of the word. The Bancroft Garden grows on land located below Mount Diablo, a parcel of what was originally a 400-acre property Hubert Bancroft set about developing in the 1880s as orchards and ranch land. Carrying on the tradition of the Bancroft family's connection to the landscape, Philip Bancroft's wife, Ruth, began the installation of the gardens in the early 1950s. Soon after gardens sprang up around their house, Mrs. Bancroft started cultivating succulents, her favorite plants, in greenhouses.

The Bancroft Garden's overall framework was created in 1972 with the assistance of designer Lester Hawkins. Mrs. Bancroft proceeded to place and plant the numerous specimens she had been collecting. She eventually devoted two-and-a-half acres to her outstanding "dry garden," where today visitors can discover a breathtaking array of unusually striking succulent plants, with their often peculiar, generally stunning forms, textural foliage, and vibrantly colored and distinctive flowers.

A sterling plantswoman, Ruth Bancroft has thoughtfully selected species and hybrid forms of succulents, emphasizing the wonderful structure of agaves, yuccas, and African aloes, as well as stunning desert cacti, euphorbias, and ice plants. Graceful pine, mesquite, and paloverde trees offer some shade for those plants that require screening from the sun. Stately Australian bottle trees, shapely palms, and *Eucalyptus pauciflora*, with its sensational peeling bark, all lend grandeur to the setting. Visitors can learn here all the fundamentals about creating a garden where water conservation is of primary concern.

The Bancroft Garden demonstrates Mrs. Bancroft's passion for and knowledge of succulents. You will find here one of the country's finest gardens of drought-tolerant species showcased in a splendidly designed landscape.

In 1993 the Ruth Bancroft Garden was incorporated as a nonprofit organization. The following summer Mrs. Bancroft deeded the garden property. The garden now operates through the support of its founder, by contributions from members, and from grants, plant sales, special events, and tour fees.

❀ **Admission:** Fee.

Garden open: By reservation only.

Further information: Dates change each year, so visit the Web site or call for a schedule of docent-led and self-guided tours. You can reserve online or by calling the Garden Hotline at (925) 210–9663. Plants propagated from the garden are offered after tours and following special events. Parking is limited. The garden paths are level and wheelchair accessible.

Directions: The Ruth Bancroft Garden is located about 28 miles east of San Francisco, about a forty-minute drive in light traffic via the Bay Bridge. From San Francisco take Interstate 680 north and exit at the Ygnacio Valley Road exit. Turn right onto Ygnacio Valley Road and follow it for 2 miles to Bancroft Road. Turn left onto Bancroft Road and the Garden is located on the right.

The Peninsula and South Bay
Gardenwalks

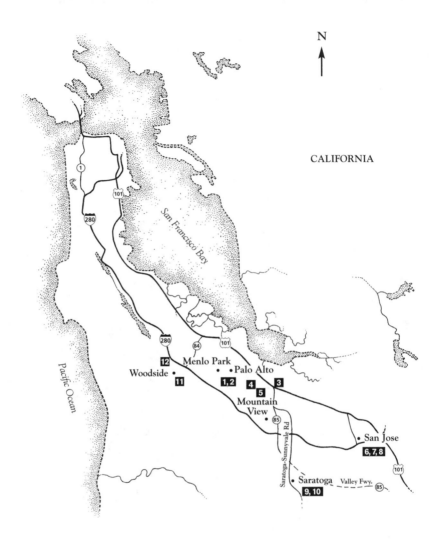

N

CALIFORNIA

1. Menlo Park: Allied Arts Guild
2. Menlo Park: Sunset Garden
3. Mountain View: Shoreline at
   Mountain View and
   Rengstorff House
4. Palo Alto: Arizona Garden at
   Stanford University
5. Palo Alto: Elizabeth F. Gamble
   Garden Center

6. San Jose: Japanese Friendship
   Garden in Kelly Park
7. San Jose: Overfelt Gardens
8. San Jose: San Jose Municipal
   Rose Garden
9. Saratoga: Hakone Gardens
10. Saratoga: Villa Montalvo
11. Woodside: Filoli
12. Woodside: Yerba Buena Nursery

1. Allied Arts Guild

75 Arbor Road at Cambridge, **Menlo Park,** CA 94025;
(650) 324–2405; www.alliedartsguild.org

*W*HEN YOU pass through the portals of the recently renovated
Allied Arts Guild's Spanish colonial–style complex, you
will see a flurry of artistic activity, similar to the energy of the arts
and crafts movement, which was taking place when the guild was
first launched in 1929.

The Allied Arts Guild was the creation of arts aficionados
Garfield and Delight Merner, who together with the foremost residents of San Francisco's peninsula communities established a superb
environment in which the arts could flourish. Here in a courtyard
setting decorated with wrought iron, and with murals and mosaics
by California artist Maxine Albro, the work of contemporary artists
and artisans is exhibited in a series of studios and art-related shops.
These enterprises specialize in unique handcrafted items such as
clothing and pottery, home furnishings, garden ornaments, and gifts.

The three-and-a-quarter-acre, sun-drenched surroundings invite garden travelers to explore the Court of Abundance, a Moorish-
design orangery with central fountain; the Garden of Delight, a
theme garden featuring blue Nile lilies, hydrangeas, and a blue-tiled
fountain; and the intoxicating Rose Allée with its stately rose
standards.

The fetching pathways, vine-shrouded rustic structures, captivating arches, and mesmerizing water features combine to furnish a
spectacular framework for the Allied Arts Guild's showcase of
Mediterranean specimens.

Run by the Woodside-Atherton Auxiliary to the Lucile Salter

Packard Children's Hospital at Stanford, an alliance benefiting the hospital, the guild provides philanthropic support for children with chronic illnesses. A commendable objective, it is one more reason to contemplate spending an afternoon at this alluring locale.

❀ **Admission:** Free.

Garden open: Monday through Saturday 10:00 A.M. to 5:00 P.M.

Further information: The historic restaurant serves lunch Monday through Saturday indoors, and from May to October on the Blue Garden patio. Phone (650) 324–2588 for restaurant reservations. Visit the Web site for information on lectures and special events throughout the year. Most pathways are wheelchair accessible.

Directions: Allied Arts Guild is approximately one hour south of San Francisco or Oakland, near Stanford Shopping Center; ten minutes from Interstate 280 and U.S. Highway 101.

2. Sunset Garden

80 Willow Road, **Menlo Park,** CA 94025; (650) 321–3600; www.sunset.com

*S*UNSET PUBLISHING CORPORATION produces informative, enlightening garden-design books and how-to manuals. *Sunset* magazine features gardening topics among a wealth of beautifully photographed and illustrated articles on design, decorating, travel, and cuisine. Sunset's various publications function as essential references for serious western gardeners and neophytes alike, whether living in Seattle or Southern California.

Headquartered in Menlo Park, the company occupies early California–style office buildings. Designed by Thomas Church, Sunset's expansive display garden integrates special areas representing various West Coast climates.

While one section acknowledges the wet, cold winters of the Pacific Northwest region, others are planted to reflect Northern California's milder climate, Central California's coastal environment, and the hot Central Valley. Another distinctive garden area celebrates the Southwest desert and Southern California, concentrating on drought-tolerant perennials, cacti, and succulent plants.

Befitting Sunset's laudable profile in the world of horticulture, the company's landscaping is impressive. Flower beds at Sunset Garden are replanted throughout the year with seasonal displays. A sweeping lawn is irrigated with well water. On this sunlit green carpet looms the commanding form of a coast live oak, with its enormous, lopsided limbs supported by steel posts. This tree alone is worth a visit to Sunset. To help maintain the venerable old tree's health, stones encircle its base to the edges of the drip line (a reminder of the live oak's intolerance of extra water once the season of wet weather has passed).

Be sure to investigate what's happening in the Test Garden, a 3,200-square-foot space where plants, garden projects, and new equipment are put to the test by Sunset staffers.

❧ **Admission:** Free.
Garden open: Monday through Friday 9:00 A.M. to 4:30 P.M.; closed holidays and for ten days or so each year in mid-May (phone for dates).
Further information: Pick up *A Walking Tour of the Sunset Gardens* pamphlet and enjoy a self-guided exploration of the gardens. The Sunset gardens are wheelchair accessible.
Directions: Menlo Park is about one hour south of San Francisco. Directions to Sunset can be found on the Web site.

3. Shoreline at Mountain View and Rengstorff House

3070 North Shoreline Boulevard, Shoreline Park, **Mountain View,** CA 94043; (650) 903–6392; www.ci.mtnview.ca.us

*H*ISTORIC Victorian Rengstorff House was moved in 1980 from its original location to the present spot in the park. Mountain View's oldest home, the now splendidly restored house is surrounded by inviting gardens, all part of the Shoreline Park recreational area. In the park you'll find hiking trails, marshland and wildlife habitats, and a saltwater lake.

❧ **Admission:** Free.

Garden open: Daily dawn to dusk. Rengstorff House tours are held Tuesday, Wednesday, and Sunday 11:00 A.M. to 5:00 P.M.

Further information: Stroll the Shoreline grounds anytime. The Rengstorff Gardens sometimes close during special events, so you may wish to call (650) 903–6088 in advance. Or visit www.r-house.org for more on Rengstorff House tours, featuring docents dressed in period clothes. Shoreline is wheelchair accessible.

Directions: Shoreline Park is 1 mile off U.S. 101 at the north end of Shoreline Boulevard.

4. Arizona Garden at Stanford University

South side of mausoleum off Quarry Road, between Campus Drive and Arboretum Road, **Palo Alto,** CA 94309; (650) 723–3050; www.stanford.edu

*T*HE RECENTLY rejuvenated Arizona Garden at Stanford University boasts a meticulously groomed, exuberant succulent theme that demonstrates the vitality of an earlier epoch in garden history.

Originally designed in the 1880s by German landscape gardener Rudolph Ulrich, the garden and the arboretum surrounding it are the only surviving elements of a far-reaching landscape plan conceived by Ulrich to adorn the grounds of a proposed new country home for Leland and Jane Stanford.

Today the Stanford family is at rest in a mausoleum located a short walk from the Cantor Center for Visual Arts. Only a few hundred feet away from the mausoleum, the Arizona Garden has reawakened after decades of neglect.

Ulrich's layout is as innovative as it is rare, with a highly formal, symmetrical design emphasizing cacti and exotic plants.

At approximately 17,000 square feet, the cactus garden, as it is commonly referred to, is wonderfully interesting year-round. Rather than flowers, myriad textures are the highlight, with blooms coloring the scene as well.

The garden's restoration followed a plan prepared by landscape designer Nancy Hardesty, resulting in a welcoming garden elevated by the bold architecture of succulent plants.

Mounded beds outlined with serpentine rock serve to showcase arrays of succulents. Overall, the beds' organic contours create an ornamental pattern, while decomposed granite paths tie the entire arrangement together.

Situated at the very heart of the garden, a central bed contains a venerable California fan palm remaining from the many palms originally planted. Around 1890 some thirty palm trees were transplanted from here to enhance the landscaping of Stanford's Inner Quadrangle.

None of the mature saguaro cacti that played notable roles in Ulrich's scheme have survived. Yet during that earlier era, their presence clearly bespoke a status garden.

The garden now features columnar cacti, *Cereus* species, as replacements for the saguaros, to capture the essential look of the original.

Among the garden's specimens, ancient yuccas and opuntias stand out. Survivors from long ago include the compelling forms of tree yuccas (*Yucca filifera*): One with a double trunk of impressive girth and height dominates the scene to the right of the center bed. On the far left, the figure of another mighty tree yucca grows in an outstretched sprawl.

Eye-catching plants that can be traced to the restoration include prickly pear and golden barrel cactus (*Echinocactus grusonii*) donated by one of the country's great gardens, Ganna Walska Lotusland in Santa Barbara.

Plants and labor have been donated by groups and individuals, including the San Francisco Succulent and Cactus Society and a cadre of volunteers who lifted and reset most of the rock work by hand.

The paths of decomposed granite create an aspect that is pleasing to the eye at the same time that they visually connect the garden beds.

A division into two main sections split down the center gives the plantings definition.

An area dedicated to the Eastern Hemisphere is distinguished by aloes, jade plants, and the like, native to Europe, Asia, and Africa. The Western Hemisphere area is home to plants of the Americas, such as cacti. Visitors may notice variations on this dual theme, where certain vintage specimens remain in their original positions.

A stroll around the garden reveals agaves in shades of blue and tawny green, pale ice blue euphorbias adorned with tiny purple flowers like hats, and the leaves of *Aloe striata* tinged pink.

In summer, look for large drifts of ice plant, producing a raucous show of yellow and pink, purple, and magenta blooms. The Santa Rita prickly pear, *Opuntia* var. *santa-rita*, exhibits its own dramatic coloration; hues that develop on its flat-jointed, bluish gray pads spotted and edged in purple can vary depending upon conditions such as temperature, light, and stress.

Near the garden's perimeter, the strange profile of the boojum tree looms. Another vigorous boojum appears in the Western Hemisphere section. Listed botanically as *Fouquieria* or *Idria columnaris*, the Baja native can be identified by its growing habit, akin to a tall candle. Characterized by thin twisting stems near the top, the boojum appears to flail like a sea creature with tentacles. Its name, *boojum*, first appeared in a fantasy world created by Lewis Carroll in *The Hunting of the Snark.*

Fittingly, the boojum is at home in the refreshed and reincarnated Arizona Garden, an animated realm where history comes alive in a winning marriage of design and horticulture.

✿ **Admission:** Free.

Garden open: Daily during daylight hours.

Further information: To learn more, log on to the direct link with Stanford's Grounds Services: http://grounds.stanford.edu/points /gardens/arizonagarden.html. Some narrow, interior pathways may be limited in terms of wheelchair accessibility.

Directions: The garden is approximately one hour south of San Francisco. A map of the campus and detailed directions can be found on the Stanford University Web site.

5. Elizabeth F. Gamble Garden

1431 Waverley Street, **Palo Alto,** CA 94301; (650) 329–1356; www.gamblegarden.org

WITH ITS MILD CLIMATE and generally sunny skies, the pleasant town of Palo Alto boasts a major university, Stanford, and a prominent community-oriented horticultural foundation, the Elizabeth F. Gamble Garden. Volunteer gardeners work with the resident horticulturist in planting and caring for both formal and working gardens. A restoration effort has beautifully recaptured the original turn-of-the-twentieth-century gardens. The garden's heirloom roses are especially striking. Its enchanting woodland garden offers a teahouse and handsome collections of viburnum and hydrangeas, camellias, and Japanese maples.

A cherry allée and a grotto are located along the garden's Churchill Avenue boundary. One of the most spectacular sights is the bewitching wisteria garden, which intermingles several varieties that display their pendulous flower clusters during April in an admirably arranged garden room.

Another springtime phenomenon found in a number of Bay Area gardens is the Lady Banks rose. At Elizabeth Gamble Garden the rose's breathtaking ascent adjacent to the parking area dazzles onlookers with a vast cover of vivacious blooms.

Demonstration and working gardens flank the right side of the entrance walkway. Featured here are annuals and perennials, an iris border and a salvia bed, a cutting garden, and espaliered fruit trees. A striking gazebo, the focal point within this section of the former Gamble estate, provides a pleasant place from which one can observe the enthusiastic involvement of the multigenerational participants and volunteers.

❀ **Admission:** Free.

Garden open: Daily dawn to dusk.

Further information: Since the center is the site of many weddings and receptions, it's best to phone before visiting to find out whether the formal gardens are taken up with a special event. Visit the informative Web site for details on classes, garden tours, and teas. Walkways are level and mostly wheelchair accessible.

Directions: The center is located 40 miles south of San Francisco. From U.S. 101, exit on Embarcadero Road West toward Stanford University for approximately 1½ miles. At the sixth stoplight, turn left onto Waverley Street. Use the parking lot on the left.

6. Japanese Friendship Garden in Kelley Park

1300 East Senter Road, **San Jose,** CA 95112; (408) 277–4191

*V*ISIT THIS multileveled, traditional Japanese stroll garden and enjoy its picturesque waterfalls and koi pond.

❀ **Admission:** Free.

Garden open: Daily 10:00 A.M. to sunset.

Further information: There are lovely spots to picnic while in Kelley Park. Portions are wheelchair accessible.

Directions: The garden is in central San Jose, between Keyes Road and Alma Avenue. Detailed directions and maps are available at www .sanjose.org.

7. Overfelt Gardens

2145 McKee Road at Educational Park Drive, **San Jose,** CA 95116;
(408) 251–3323

ILDRED OVERFELT bequeathed her property to the City of San Jose as a serene haven for nature lovers. A landscape of some thirty-three acres offers garden travelers a host of cultivated gardens and natural areas set amid lovely hilly scenery. Overfelt Gardens includes a wildlife sanctuary as well as gardens devoted to fragrance and the state's native flora. A Chinese Cultural Center features a pavilion and distinctive landscaping.

❀ **Admission:** Free.
Garden open: Daily 10:00 A.M. to sunset; closed Thanksgiving, Christmas, and New Year's Day.
Further information: Parking is available on Educational Park Drive. Portions are wheelchair accessible.
Directions: The gardens are in east San Jose. Detailed directions and maps are available at www.sanjose.org.

8. San Jose Municipal Rose Garden

Between Dana Avenue and Naglee Avenue,
San Jose, CA 95126; (408) 277–5422

PARTICULARLY ENTICING landscape encircled by redwoods, San Jose's lovely rose garden has brought joy to the community for nearly seven decades. Surrounding the garden's pool and fountain are beds that burst into bloom as early as April. In early May the garden is awash with fragrance.

❀ **Admission:** Free.
Garden open: Daily 8:00 A.M. to sunset.
Further information: Portions of the garden are wheelchair accessible.
Directions: The rose garden is located just outside downtown San Jose. Visit www.sanjose.org for detailed directions and maps.

9. Hakone Gardens

21000 Big Basin Way, **Saratoga**, CA 95070; (408) 741–4994;
www.hakone.com

*M*AGNIFICENT black-stemmed, golden, and Japanese timber bamboo varieties are represented in a two-acre Bamboo Park, first incorporated into Saratoga's beautiful Hakone Gardens in 1987.

The summer residence of the Stine family, Hakone Gardens was established as a Japanese-style retreat in the early part of the twentieth century. In the 1930s a subsequent owner, Maj. C. L. Tilden, built the gardens' main gate. Restoration work under the auspices of the City of Saratoga began in 1966, and today Hakone Gardens is praised for its estimable plantings and authentic design.

As early as January and February, visitors are treated to the entrancing blooms of flowering plum trees, camellias and azaleas, daphnes and violets. A sublime asymmetry contributes to Hakone's splendid terrain, where a sensitive balance is achieved between the varying dimensional forms and shallow shapes of the garden's design. Unlike the inherent regularity found in a formal Western garden plan, here no specific focal point or center is sought after. From the veranda of the Upper House, perched on the Moon Viewing Hill, you can observe waterfalls, the serpentine pathways of the hill and Pond Garden, and the mossy inclines of the Tea Garden. In the contemplative Zen Garden, patterns are created by bold stone shapes and raked gravel.

Among the gardens' imposing trees, Hinoki cypress, valley oak, Japanese red pine, and California laurel lend a quiet grandeur to the scene. A congregation of flowering cherries puts forth abundant blossoms, while Japanese maples contribute richly hued foliage and elegant forms.

The Bamboo Garden's central section—Kizuna-en—has fascinating woven fences that exemplify the binding of international friendships between the sister cities of Saratoga in the United States and Muko-shi in Japan. Be sure to pick up the informative printed brochure offered by the Japan Bamboo Society of Saratoga. It will help you understand the garden's symbolism as well as learn more about the types and habits of bamboo plants.

❀ **Admission:** Free; fee for parking (except members and Saratoga residents).

Garden open: Weekdays 10:00 A.M. to 5:00 P.M., weekends 11:00 A.M. to 5:00 P.M.; closed Christmas and New Year's Day. The gift shop is open the same hours.

Further information: Guided tours are given April through September on weekends between 1:00 and 4:00 P.M. Go online to the Web site's calendar to learn about festivals, classes, and workshops throughout the year, or write the Hakone Foundation, P.O. Box 2324, Saratoga, CA 95070.

Directions: Hakone is approximately one-and-a-half hours south of San Francisco, right outside of Saratoga Village.

10. Villa Montalvo

15400 Montalvo Road, **Saratoga,** CA 95071; (408) 961–5800; www.villamontalvo.org

*N*AMED FOR Garcia Ordoñez de Montalvo, a Spanish writer of the sixteenth century said to be responsible for naming California, Villa Montalvo exudes a rich historical presence in the midst of serene, pastoral surroundings. Situated near San Jose, at the base of the Santa Cruz Mountains, the villa is a fine example of Mediterranean design. On the property are also a guesthouse containing artist residency apartments and an octagonal Carriage House and Art Gallery.

Built by James Duval Phelan in 1912, Villa Montalvo is currently home to a joyous flurry of artistic, musical, and literary activity. Support for Villa Montalvo is gleaned from members' donations, corporate sponsorship, rental of facilities, special fund-raising events, and volunteers from the community. Encompassing 175 acres, the bucolic estate contains magnificent natural woodlands of oaks, redwoods, firs, and eucalyptus and miles of nature and hiking trails of varying difficulty. Spectacular views await hikers who pursue the fairly steep Lookout Trail to its final destination.

Reaching out to the community at large, Villa Montalvo offers readings, visual arts exhibitions mounted in a handsome gallery space, and a notable performing arts season that draws an appreciative audience from throughout the Bay Area to its lovely outdoor amphitheater. Concerts are held outside in the Garden Theatre and also on the expansive Front Lawn, inside the Carriage House Theatre, and at the Fox Theatre nearby.

Thrice mayor of San Francisco and a United States senator, Phelan reveled in the arts and enjoyed hosting talented friends and providing them with places to work and a stimulating intellectual climate. He shared the tranquil beauty of his estate with many of his day's most celebrated writers and thespians. Phelan's legacy continues to this day with Villa Montalvo's thriving artist residency program of international renown.

A timeless gardenscape graces Villa Montalvo's main building, where the picturesque design features classical statuary and manicured emerald lawns. Curving hedges trace discreet walkways, while low, mounded rock walls embrace fragrant lavender plantings. Visit in spring and be mesmerized by the villa's divine pergola lavishly draped in wisteria.

Explore the sprawling lawn and garden areas laid out to the front of Villa Montalvo and you'll arrive at a breathtaking vista, the Love Temple. Take a pause and contemplate this tiny, jewel-like pavilion, set among towering trees.

Whatever season you choose to visit, Montalvo will enchant you with Saratoga's forests' bracing bouquet, at once fresh and fragrant.

❀ **Admission:** Free.

Garden open: April through September: Monday through Friday 8:00

A.M. to 7:00 P.M., Saturday, Sunday, and holidays 9:00 A.M. to 7:00 P.M. October through March: Monday through Friday 8:00 A.M. to 5:00 P.M., Saturday, Sunday, and holidays 9:00 A.M. to 5:00 P.M.

Further information: The public parkland and gardens may be closed due to special events or poor weather; always call ahead to confirm open hours. Pick up a map of hiking trails and the gardens at Montalvo's box office and administrative offices. Parking, restrooms, and limited pathways are wheelchair accessible. Visit the Web site for current information on park activities.

Directions: Villa Montalvo is approximately one-and-a-half hours south of San Francisco. Approach Villa Montalvo from the Saratoga–Los Gatos Road (California Highway 9).

11. Filoli

Cañada Road, **Woodside,** CA 94062; (650) 364–8300; www.filoli.org

*O*NE OF THE country's most breathtaking estates, the impeccably maintained, lavishly planted formal gardens of Filoli should not be missed on your San Francisco Bay Area itinerary.

As described in one of Filoli's brochures, the motto "Fight, Love, Live" was drawn from William B. Bourn II's personal philosophy that one should "fight for a just cause, love your fellow man, live a good life." It was Bourn who bestowed the acronym, Filoli, upon his beloved country property south of San Francisco.

Owner of the Empire Mine, Bourn became enraptured in the early 1900s by the landscape near another of his businesses, the Spring Valley Water Company, because it reminded him of Ireland's Lakes of Killarney. After purchasing a substantial piece of land, Bourn selected architect Willis Polk to design an elegant English Georgian revival mansion. Landscape designer Bruce Porter together with Isabella Worn were instrumental in planning and planting the sublime sixteen-acre gardens styled after grand European landscapes.

Mr. and Mrs. Bourn moved into their magnificent new home

in 1917, where they both passed away nearly twenty years later in 1936. The following year, the estate became home to the Roths, who subsequently bequeathed Filoli to the National Trust for Historic Preservation.

Exuding a tremendous joie de vivre, the Filoli mansion and elaborate gardens present an intoxicating feast for the senses. Filoli's garden plan unfolds in a series of beautifully lush, walled garden rooms, with terraces and lawns, parterres, and magnificent pools. The mansion itself features a U-shaped floor plan with two axes and a long hallway paralleling the valley beyond. The garden's overall design with its north–south axis repeats the line of the mansion's transverse hall.

A grove of olive trees lines the front drive. Just north of the house, blue Atlas cedars impart a sylvan grace, and coast live oaks stand in ancient splendor. In the spring Filoli's entry courtyard is fragrant with the scent of magnolias and bolstered by the alluring forms of Japanese maples. Everywhere one can see how the wonderful plan of the house and gardens celebrates the natural vegetation and vistas surrounding the estate.

The renowned Yew Allée exemplifies Filoli's grandeur. Unquestionably, it is these Irish yews, which were so close to William Bourn's heart, that impress all who come here. At Filoli more than 200 of these yews are grown, all started from cuttings taken from William Bourn's daughter and son-in-law's home in Ireland, Muckross House. Along with yews, espaliered apple and pear trees lead to the High Place, a lovely open-air theater facing south, where ancient columns form an inspiring backdrop.

Filoli opens its gates in early spring, when the mansion's clematis and wisteria-draped portico and terrace balustrades bid a riotous welcome. In February, March, and April, the grounds teem with gala exhibitions of tulips and daffodils, azaleas, camellias, wildflowers, and blooming shrubs. Late spring brings forth glimmering dogwood and 'Sunburst' honey locust, flowering cherries, and glowing laburnums.

Where the outlines of reflecting pools, lawns, parterres, and brick paths frame perfectly complementary shapes, you will find another exceptional garden room: the Sunken Garden. Dramatic in scale, the Sunken Garden's design is a balancing act between meticulously groomed hedges, soaring trees, containers in profuse bloom, and classic ornamentation in the form of petite, cast-lead water maidens. From here you can gaze at the vast hilly terrain visible in the distance.

In the knot gardens at Filoli, Celtic patterns are woven with emerald germander, violet-hued Japanese barberry, soft lavender, and silvery santolina, with its perky yellow flowers.

Designed by Arthur Brown Jr., Filoli's teahouse serves as an integral part of the estate's distinctive brick enclosure—the Walled Garden. Italian Renaissance in style, the Walled Garden holds a central place among Filoli's gardens. This partitioned realm encompasses three garden rooms, each one characterized by its own indelibly romantic ambience.

In the Walled Garden, you'll find the Wedding Place and its fifteenth-century red-marble Venetian fountain; the Dutch Garden, with rare New Zealand black beech trees and fine latticework; and a dazzling floral scene, the Chartres Cathedral Garden. Here, replicating a stained-glass window, are boxwood borders, English holly hedges, and flower beds filled with annuals and standard roses.

The property surrounding the estate is a haven of undeveloped woods and fields that can be explored on hikes with Filoli's nature docents. Filoli's Woodside microclimate, 25 miles or so south of San Francisco, is a nearly ideal environment for a garden of this caliber. Because William Bourn so appreciated this land, the vision of Bruce Porter and Isabella Worn was focused upon the sumptuous gardens visitors enjoy to this day. Interestingly, Isabella Worn remained involved in the plantings until the age of eighty-one. Together with Filoli's owner and benefactor, Mrs. William P. Roth, the two lovingly nurtured the estate's gardens for decades, carrying on in the spirit of Bourn himself.

The glorious house and landscape of Filoli are now preserved and maintained in their estimable present-day condition under the auspices of the National Trust for Historic Preservation, Filoli Center, and the Friends of Filoli, a congregation of avid volunteers.

❁ **Admission:** Fee.

Garden open: Tuesday through Saturday from mid-February to the end of October, 10:00 A.M. to 3:30 P.M., last admission at 2:30 P.M. Closed Sunday, Monday and all federal holidays. Garden Shop is open 10:00 A.M. to 3:30 P.M.; Quail's Nest Cafe is open 9:30 A.M. to 3:30 P.M.

Further information: Docent-led tours are available by reservation; phone the tour office at (650) 364–8300, ext. 507. Self-guided tours are offered Tuesday through Saturday from 10:00 A.M. with last admission at 2:30 P.M.; no reservations but fee is required. Visit the Web site to learn about special seasonal events and nature hikes. Fioli is wheelchair accessible.

Directions: Fioli is approximately 25 miles south of San Francisco and north of San Jose; 12 miles southwest of San Francisco International Airport.

12. Yerba Buena Nursery

19500 Skyline Boulevard, **Woodside,** CA 94062; (650) 851–1668; www.yerbabuenanursery.com

SPECIALIZING IN California native plants and ferns, Yerba Buena was founded by Gerda Isenberg in 1960, a true pioneer and proselytizer of the beauty and usefulness of natives. Current owner Kathy Crane carries on Isenberg's tradition of growing and propagating native species, and she has also added all sorts of exciting plants to the nursery's forty acres. Kathy's admirable, high-energy personality makes visiting Yerba Buena something special.

The nursery's Gerda Isenberg Native Plant Garden features welcoming information cards, allowing visitors to identify plant origins (regions spanning California's shoreline to the Sierra range) and garden uses. Lath houses, greenhouses, and venerable old buildings grace the Yerba Buena property, while the garden shop and the Tea Terrace offer respite from trekking about the beautiful Woodside landscape.

With more than 600 species represented, Yerba Buena is the perfect setting to learn about California's communities of resilient native plants. The helpful nursery staff will answer questions and provide explanations.

✿ **Admission:** Free.

Garden open: Nursery and garden shop are open Tuesday through Sunday 9:00 A.M. to 5:00 P.M.; closed Monday. The Tea Terrace is open Saturday and Sunday. Call to confirm hours.

Further information: Nursery customers and groups of fewer than six people are welcome to enjoy self-guided tours. Visit the Web site for news of special events, and dates when traditional high tea is served; reservations required and fee charged. No buses are allowed. Portions of the nursery are wheelchair accessible.

Directions: Yerba Buena is situated in the coastal hills above Woodside, approximately one hour and fifteen minutes south of San Francisco. It is within easy reach from the Filoli Estate, and not far from the Saratoga area, in case you're planning a visit to Villa Montalvo and Hakone Gardens. Detailed directions and a map can be found on the Web site.

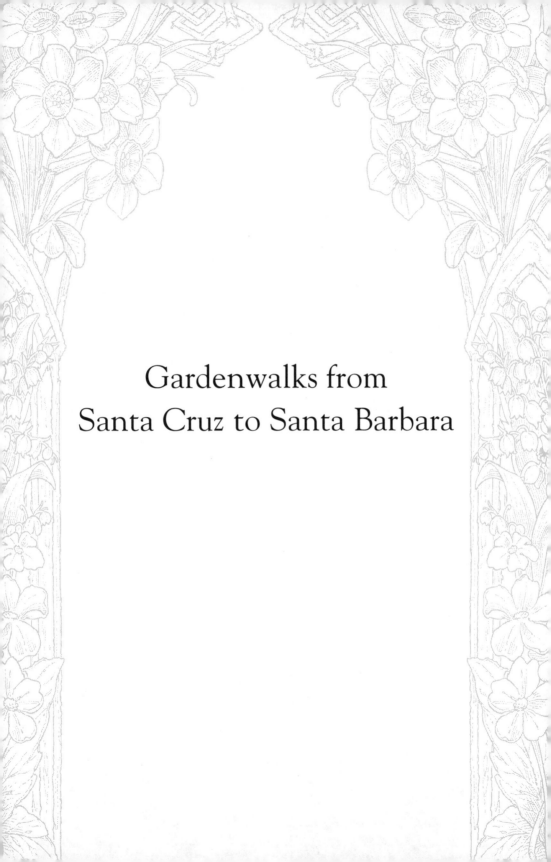

Gardenwalks from
Santa Cruz to Santa Barbara

Central Coast Gardenwalks

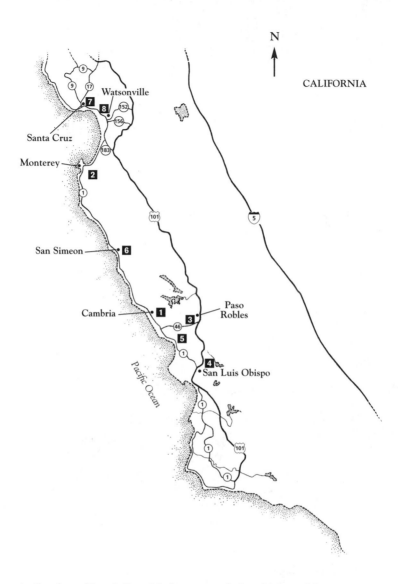

N

CALIFORNIA

1. Cambria: Heart's Ease Herb
   Shop & Gardens
2. Monterey: Monterey State
   Historic Park and Adobe Gardens
3. Paso Robles: Sycamore Farms
4. San Luis Obispo: Dallidet Adobe
5. San Luis Obispo: San Luis
   Obispo Botanical Garden, El
   Chorro Regional Park

6. San Simeon: Hearst
   Castle Gardens
7. Santa Cruz: Arboretum at the
   University of California, Santa
   Cruz
8. Watsonville: Sierra Azul
   Nursery & Gardens

1. Heart's Ease Herb Shop & Gardens

4101 Burton Drive, **Cambria,** CA 93428; (805) 927–5224, (800) 266–4372

*F*OUNDED BY garden writer and illustrator Sharon Lovejoy, Heart's Ease Herb Shop and its adjacent gardens are currently owned and operated by Susan Pendergast. Susan admirably carries on the traditions and educational goals of this delightful enterprise.

Located in the village of Cambria on California's Central Coast, the Heart's Ease Herb Shop is housed in an original Victorian cottage on the town's main historic street. Well known to devotees of herb culture and crafts, Heart's Ease stocks a bounty of herbal gift items along with gardening implements and a number of books for gardeners and nature lovers. The shop also carries products and preparations made from both dried and fresh herbs.

Alongside the charming blue building, you'll find the Heart's Ease Nursery. Here new plant stock is propagated from cuttings taken from the gardens' own mother plants, or procured from local growers of rare herbs and perennials. Then the stock is either sold or planted in the gardens. Featured are California natives, cottage-garden flowers, and herbs.

The Heart's Ease Garden was successfully recouped from parking lots when the property was purchased by Sharon Lovejoy. On the lilliputian site, you can explore traditional theme gardens: the Bee Garden and Grey Garden, a tiny Knot Garden, a Culinary and Tot's Garden. The garden beds were designed and planted more than fifteen years ago.

Heart's Ease offers a stimulating environment where kids can learn about the natural world. There's a worm bin to fascinate young visitors, and the Peter Rabbit Garden encourages future gardeners.

Annual events include both a faerie festival and a rosemary festival. To commemorate these celebrations, Sharon Lovejoy wrote and illustrated booklets that continue to be sold at the shop. With their melding of fantasy, plant lore, and hands-on projects, the booklets thrill youngsters and intrigue older readers.

If you are planning a tour of the Central Coast region or a visit to Hearst Castle and its gardens, don't fail to stop at the delightful Heart's Ease Garden in nearby Cambria.

❀ **Admission:** Free.

Garden open: Daily 10:00 A.M. to dusk; closed Christmas Day.

Further information: Call to confirm seasonal hours for the Heart's Ease shop. Portions are wheelchair accessible.

Directions: Located approximately four hours from San Francisco or Los Angeles. Take California Highway 46 west from U.S. Highway 101. Cambria is on California Coast Highway 1 (Pacific Coast Highway), just south of Hearst Castle in San Simeon.

2. Monterey State Historic Park and Adobe Gardens

20 Custom House Plaza, **Monterey,** CA 93940; (831) 649–7118; www.parks.ca.gov

*P*ICK UP A COPY of the "Monterey Walking Path of History" map at the visitor center downtown or other venues throughout the city, then wander through the restored adobes that are part of the Monterey State Historic Park, enjoying a self-guided tour of the city's unique gardens. The Custom House Garden, for one, features lovely succulent plantings and, as a bonus, a fine view of the harbor. Or participate in a guided tour of Old Monterey, gaining insight into the significance and history of the area.

❀ **Admission:** Self-guided tours are free.

Garden open: Daily 10:00 A.M. to 4:00 P.M.; closed Thanksgiving, Christmas, and New Year's Day.

Further information: Specific times and days vary for seasonal guided tours of the adobe gardens and historic houses; call the office number above in advance for information. State Park Walking Tours begin at the Pacific House Museum in the Custom House Plaza; staffing changes can cause tours to cancel, so call to confirm. Or visit the state park Web site, where you can also learn about special events when many of the adobe gardens are open to the public. To schedule a Historic Garden Tour for a group, call (831) 649–7109; fee charged. Wheelchair accessibility varies: The Stanton Visitor Center/Maritime Museum and the gardens of Pacific House, Custom House, Larkin House, and much of the Cooper-Molera Adobe complex are generally accessible. To schedule a tour of these gardens, call the Historic Garden League at (831) 649–3364; fee charged.

Directions: Monterey is located on the Pacific coast 115 miles south of San Francisco. Maps and directions for the Monterey Peninsula area can be viewed on www.mty.com or www.monterey.com.

3. Sycamore Farms

2485 Highway 46 West, **Paso Robles,** CA 93446; (805) 238–5288, (800) 576–5288; www.sycamorefarms.com

A BASIL FESTIVAL and a Mozart concert are just a few of the events sponsored by the Shomlers' two-acre Sycamore Farms. The farm has a large display garden devoted to culinary and medicinal herbs. Aromatic herbs such as sage and thyme, rosemary, lavender, and Mediterranean bay grow contentedly here. An extensive retail nursery features hundreds of varieties of potted herbs. Many varieties of fresh-cut herbs are available throughout the year.

Overall the property encompasses forty acres of rolling and terraced hills. In addition to the herb farm, there is a large irrigation pond and a thirty-acre vineyard where Viognier and Syrah grapes are grown and harvested for the Bonny Doon Winery of

Santa Cruz. A tasting room on the premises features Bonny Doon wines. A gift and garden shop is located in the barn building. Two seasons of classes and workshops instruct participants in the many uses for herbs, with an emphasis on reviving lost arts such as creating natural dyes. There always seems to be something to sample and savor for visitors who stop by to purchase plants or to pick up tips on growing and cultivating herbs.

Visit the Sycamore Farms Web site and enjoy their entertaining gazette. It covers events, provides recipes, and offers a trove of interesting articles, such as a recent one titled "Ancient Herbalism," which discussed the importance of herbs in societies as diverse as ancient Greece, Rome, and the New World. Look for links to area wine festivals, too.

In the *Sycamore Gazette*, you'll also find out what's happening at the farm, from the installation of new garden areas to ideas for specific theme gardens. For example, for a butterfly herb garden, the gazette recommends planting catmint, butterfly bush, golden butterfly bush, licorice-mint hyssop, and bee balm.

❀ **Admission:** Free.

Garden open: Daily 10:00 A.M. to 5:00 P.M; closed Easter, Thanksgiving, Christmas, and New Year's Day. Hours are limited on July 4, December 24, and December 31.

Further information: Tours are offered for a small fee; phone ahead to reserve. Grounds and paths are partially wheelchair accessible, but the staff will assist guests by bringing in any plants one wishes to see if someone has difficulty with the gravel paths.

Directions: Sycamore Farms is approximately 30 miles north of San Luis Obispo; 3 miles west of U.S. 101 on CA 46 west (leading to Cambria and Hearst Castle).

4. Dallidet Adobe

1185 Pacific Street near Santa Rosa Street, **San Luis Obispo**, CA 93401; (805) 543–6762; www.slochs.org/dallidet

*V*ISIT A vivacious garden surrounding the historical (circa 1850) adobe dwelling of French vintner Pierre Hyppolite Dallidet, bequeathed to the historical society by his descendant Paul Dallidet.

❀ **Admission:** Free.
Garden open: Sunday 1:00 to 4:00 P.M. from Memorial Day to Labor Day. San Luis Obispo County Historical Society is open 10:00 A.M. to 4:00 P.M.; closed Monday and Tuesday.
Further information: Visit the historical society at 696 Monterey Street or call (805)543–0638 for more details. The Pacific side entrance into the gardens and the Toro Street side are both wheelchair accessible.
Directions: From U.S. 101, take the Marsh Street exit going east; turn right onto Santa Rosa Street and left onto Pacific Street to the cul-de-sac.

5. San Luis Obispo Botanical Garden, El Chorro Regional Park

California Coast Highway 1, P.O. Box 4957, **San Luis Obispo**, CA 93403; (805) 546–3501; www.slobg.org

*T*HE SAN LUIS OBISPO BOTANICAL GARDEN is in its "preview garden" stage, with plans for a new education center to feature a straw-bale design. The two-acre site suggests wonderful things to come in future years. Overall, 150 acres have been slated for the development of a world-class botanical garden, which will highlight plants from five Mediterranean climate zones of the world.

❀ **Admission:** Free, donations welcomed; parking fee.
Garden open: Daily during daylight hours in conjunction with El Chorro Regional Park.
Further information: You'll find the preview garden across CA Coast Hwy. 1 from Cuesta College. Visit the Web site to get updates on the garden's progress and to find out about special Saturday at the Garden

seasonal events, taking place on the second Saturday of each month from April through November, 1:00 to 4:00 P.M. Most paths are wheelchair accessible, but upper trails (a small portion of the garden) are not easy to navigate.

Directions: Located on CA Coast Hwy. 1, between San Luis Obispo and Morro Bay, about 7 miles from the ocean and halfway between Los Angeles and San Francisco. Visit the Web site to view a map.

6. Hearst Castle Gardens

Hearst San Simeon State Historical Monument,
750 Hearst Castle Road, **San Simeon,** CA 93452;
(800) 444–4445; www.hearstcastle.com

*T*HE HEIR TO an immense fortune, newspaper tycoon and art collector William Randolph Hearst is perhaps best remembered for creating one of the world's foremost private estates. Christened La Cuesta Encantada ("The Enchanted Hill") by Hearst, the palatial estate generally referred to as Hearst Castle, or San Simeon, endures as one of our nation's best-known landmarks.

Among private estates Hearst Castle is arguably unequaled in grandeur. Its extravagant architecture has at times been labeled excessive by past critics. However, Hearst Castle is now being re-examined by historians who see it in the appropriate context of the era in which it was created—America's Gilded Age. Since 1958 San Simeon has been a California Historical Monument operated and maintained by the California State Parks. Perched atop a lofty knoll in the Santa Lucia Mountains of California's Central Coast, the estate actually comprises 165 rooms and 127 acres of gardens, terraces, and pools. Astounding dimensions and eclectic design reflecting Italian, Spanish, and Moorish traditions are hallmarks of Casa Grande, the main building, and the property's equally dramatic guesthouses. These so-called cottages, named Casa del Mar, Casa del Monte, and Casa del Sol, pay homage to the sea, the mountains, and the sun.

Esteemed San Francisco Bay Area architect Julia Morgan worked with Hearst for nearly three decades of never-ending construction and landscaping to realize this extravagant dream. Specialized craftsmen and innumerable laborers toiled from 1919 until 1947, building as well as continually evolving Hearst's fascinating Mediterranean revival estate.

Still bedazzling visitors today are Hearst's vast collections of venerable art; stunning antique furnishings from Spain, Italy, and France; commissioned works such as ornate, decorative ceilings; and the castle's exalted grounds. Planning a visit involves selecting one of five separate tours that focus on various areas in the castle, grounds, and cottages. Tour 4 is of special interest to garden lovers. Presented from April through October, it gives an overview of San Simeon's landscape along with selected highlights of the estate. All tours offer views of two remarkable swimming pools: the outdoor marble-and-tile Neptune Pool, and the exquisitely designed indoor Roman Pool, with its luminescent Venetian glass tiles and accent tiles of opulent gold leaf.

On Tour 4, when you view the magnificent esplanade, terraces, and elaborate walkways, the guides explain how W. R. Hearst placed particular emphasis on planning and planting the gardens of La Cuesta Encantada. Unquestionably, Hearst believed the landscape was of equal importance to the estate's majestic exteriors and sumptuous interior decor.

Although Julia Morgan devised the garden's planting plans, various distinguished landscape architects and designers were also called upon. Horticultural authorities and advisers involved in San Simeon's landscaping include Bruce Porter, who suggested ideas for layouts and plantings, and Isabella Worn, who contributed ideas for stylish color schemes. William Randolph Hearst, of course, requested his personal preferences for flowers as well as for specific shrubs and trees.

Historical documents indicate reams of correspondence between Hearst and Morgan concerning issues involving the gardens of his hilltop sanctuary. Before any planting of the estate's fabulous gardens could go forward, tons of topsoil had to be imported to the site's rocky hilltop. Because Hearst wanted the semblance of a forested surround, thousands of trees were planted. Often laborers had to dynamite a hole before planting could even take place.

Hearst was known to have spent $18,000 (a truly exorbitant sum at the time) to move a revered old native oak tree to a prominent position. When Morgan suggested planting Mexican fan palms to bring a soaring, picturesque quality to the setting, her employer, who was already fifty-six years old, decided to purchase 25-foot specimens rather than wait for smaller trees to grow.

In contrast with the commanding mature trees, note the charming cascades of jasmine mingling with pink polyantha roses, delightful purple lantana spilling over retaining walls, and heritage varieties of old-fashioned annuals. Hearst had a penchant for hollyhocks and sweet peas, and he enjoyed a lush, informal style of planting. Lantana coupled with the blushing, pansylike flowers and trailing foliage of ivy geraniums was one of his favorite combinations.

The garden tour (Tour 4) also offers unforgettable impressions of the landscape's formal framework. The dashing forms of Italian cypresses are particularly striking, as the trees' evenly spaced columnar appearance essentially mirrors the Neptune Pool's breathtaking backdrop—a Greco-Roman temple facade glorified by six dynamic vertical columns. Decorating a circular walk are mixed hedges of clipped boxwood and fragrant myrtle that enclose a collection of roses grown as standards. The Fuchsia Walk, dubbed Lover's Lane by Hearst's friend Cary Grant, displays numerous varieties of ornamental fuchsias with dangling blooms.

After visiting the gardens of Italy, Hearst wrote Julia Morgan that he wanted to expand the terraces. Today walks along the promenade, terraces, and walkways of Hearst's gardens hold the promise of wonderful memories. You'll behold classical sculpture, radiant statuary, and unique fountains ornamenting the artistically arranged flora at Hearst's incomparable La Cuesta Encantada.

❀ **Admission:** Fee.

Garden open: Garden tour (Tour 4) is offered daily from April through October from about 8:20 A.M. to 3:20 P.M. Closed Thanksgiving, Christmas, and New Year's Day. See the Web site for specific hours on specific dates.

Further information: Reservations are strongly recommended to guarantee the specific tour, date, and time you desire. Tours often sell out in advance; limited walk-up tickets may or may not be available. Call or visit the Web site to reserve Tour 4 of the botanical gardens, etc. Gift and museum shops and food concessions are located in the visitor center. To learn about an "accessibly designed tour"—wheelchair accessible, that is—visit the Web site or call well in advance. Outside the United States phone 1 (916) 414–8400, ext. 4100.

Directions: Hearst Castle is located on CA Coast Hwy. 1, approximately midway between San Francisco and Los Angeles, six hours from either city. See the Web site for detailed directions and map.

7. Arboretum of the University of California, Santa Cruz

1156 High Street, **Santa Cruz,** CA 95064; (831) 427–2998; www2.ucsc.edu/arboretum

*L*OCATED on the grounds of the University of California at Santa Cruz, the 135-acre arboretum displays significant and extensive collections of species from the Southern Hemisphere and California. Here you'll find geographically arranged sections devoted to the flora of Australia, New Zealand, South Africa, and South America, plus a section of California natives.

Begun in 1964 with some ninety species of eucalyptus, the arboretum is now a showcase for Australian plants. Important genera such as grevilleas not only flaunt their showy flower clusters but—to the delight of area gardeners—they are some of the few plants deer don't eat. So odd and unlike the shrubs and trees of North America, the plants one sees in the arboretum's Slosson Gardens are a study in botanical contrasts. Look for eye-catching exhibitions of spectacular banksias. These evergreen species often bear countless small flowers that blanket large cone forms. Seek out the grevilleas, too. Varying from low-growing, spreading types to trees 20 feet tall, this large group of sun-loving species sports attractive finely textured foliage. You'll find numerous shrubs in flower all year long in the Elvenia J. Slosson Garden, and in particular from January through April.

Discover one of the arboretum's highlights in the Dean and Jane McHenry Garden, where an outstanding collection of ancient proteas from South Africa astonish visitors with their stunning colors and silky, flosslike textures. Queen proteas are familiar to many who search florist shops for unusual flowers for arrangements. Oleander-leaved proteas, also known as pink minks (*Protea neriifolia*), and ray-flowered proteas (*Protea eximia*) will charm you with their otherworldly beauty. Look also for the colorful, long, dangling blooms and delicate bells of Cape heaths in the fantastic displays of the South Africa section.

In the arboretum, you'll find many more wonderful gardens: the Primitive Flowering Plants, an Aroma Garden, a Cactus and Succulent Garden, and an Eucalyptus Grove. Here, too, Mediterranean regions offer instructive presentations of drought-tolerant plants. Fortunate California gardeners can both appreciate the aesthetic pleasures of the UCSC Arboretum and glean tips for growing attractive species that lend themselves to a regimen of water conservation. Garden lovers from other areas or climes, who cannot hope to grow many of the arboretum's species, will still feel blessed to explore a landscape overflowing with such rare and wondrous flora. Superb vistas of the Pacific Ocean and Monterey Bay are yet another incentive to visit the UCSC Arboretum.

❋ **Admission:** Free, but small donation encouraged.
Garden open: Daily 9:00 A.M. to 5:00 P.M.; closed Thanksgiving and Christmas. Norrie's Gift Shop is open daily 10:00 A.M. to 4:00 P.M.; closed Thanksgiving and from Christmas to New Year's Day.
Further information: Call or visit the Web site for guided tour schedule, a calendar of events, and a map of the garden. Call Norrie's Gift Shop at (831) 423–4977. Norrie's is wheelchair accessible; the gardens vary in accessibility.
Directions: The arboretum is off of CA Coast Hwy. 1, five minutes north of downtown Santa Cruz. From town, follow Bay Street up to the UCSC campus; go left onto High Street and continue about a half mile to the arboretum.

8. Sierra Azul Nursery & Gardens

2660 East Lake Avenue (California Highway 152), **Watsonville**, CA 95076; (831) 763–0939; www.sierraazul.com

*T*HE TWO-AND-A-HALF-ACRE demonstration garden at Sierra Azul is one of the West Coast's best places to learn about trees, shrubs, and perennials that grow well in a Mediterranean climate.

Jeff Rosendale operates Sierra Azul as a retail establishment. He is also the proprietor of Rosendale Nursery, a wholesale enterprise functioning right alongside Sierra Azul's ornamental and educational display gardens.

At this Central Coast destination, you'll find exciting plants propagated for sale, including new species and cultivars. The eye-opening array on view encompasses California flora and fascinating plants from Australia, New Zealand, South Africa, South America, the American Southwest, and Mediterranean countries.

Sierra Azul's harmoniously arranged garden will stimulate ideas for pairing up complementary plants and, on a broader scale, illustrate how to put plants together in expansive compositions of form, texture, and color. Those who garden in summer-dry regions will find here countless drought-tolerant selections.

In talking with Jeff, one thing becomes obvious. Jeff knows plants! From practical guidance to the pursuit of an aesthetic garden plan, he freely shares information based upon years of growing and observing a wealth of plant material.

During my tour of the property, Jeff pointed out various New Zealand flaxes (*Phormium* cultivars) growing in the demonstration garden. As he proceeded to explain the "phormium myth," I was surprised to see how the plants' bold, arching leaves had reverted after a number of years to a yellow-green hue. No evidence remained of the alluring variegation—colorful stripes of cream, deep pink, or apricot—that at first had distinguished them. At the same time, Jeff pointed out that the plants had grown to 6 by 6 feet, or twice the size initially predicted. Engaging in this sort of trial and testing is invaluable for garden enthusiasts, and Jeff is dedicated to the task.

All garden travelers touring the Central Coast are welcome to bring a lunch along. The grounds feature an inviting picnic area.

❀ **Admission:** Free.

Garden open: Daily 9:00 A.M. to 5:30 P.M. Call for seasonal hours or to confirm holiday closures.

Further information: A new gift and garden shop carries hand-painted pottery, gardener's shears, wreaths, sculptural items, and more. Check the Web site for a calendar of events. Garden paths are level and mostly wheelchair accessible.

Directions: The nursery is located 7 miles from the Pacific Ocean, on the eastern edge of the Pajaro Valley near the Santa Cruz Mountains; 90 miles from San Francisco and 40 miles from San Jose.

Santa Barbara Gardenwalks

N

SANTA BARBARA

154

192

Hollister Ave.

Tnpk. Rd.

101

Orchid Dr.

8

225

225

Los Olivos St.

Mission St.

Michelorena St.

State St.

Garden St.

1

7

Montecito St.

Cabrillo Blvd.

5

Alameda Padre Serra

3

144

192

• Montecito

4

101

225

2

6

Pacific Ocean

1. Alice Keck Park Memorial
   Gardens
2. Andrée Clark Bird Refuge
3. Franceschi Park
4. Ganna Walska Lotusland

5. Moreton Bay Fig Tree
6. Santa Barbara Botanic Garden
7. Santa Barbara County
   Courthouse
8. Santa Barbara Orchid Estate

1. Alice Keck Park Memorial Gardens

1500 Santa Barbara Street, **Santa Barbara,** CA 93101;
(805) 564–5418

*D*ONATED TO Santa Barbara by Alice Keck, the land of the memorial gardens that bears the benefactress's name is surely one of the most charming city park settings imaginable. Occupying one square city block in a town recognized for its exuberant gardens, Alice Keck Gardens is a horticultural haven with an imposing collection of trees. The idealized landscape incorporates an inviting pond, complete with a fantasy island and beckoning palms. Low-water gardening is advanced in a series of abundant plantings that demonstrate various types of microclimates found in the semiarid Santa Barbara region.

On my first view of the Alice Keck Memorial Gardens while driving by the corner of Micheltorena and Garden Streets, I was astonished to see a spectacular sprawling Australian tea tree (*Leptospermum laevigatum*).

When I returned to contemplate this fantastic gnarled form, I found a wealth of flowering trees, including Hong Kong orchid (*Bauhinia blakeana*) and Brazilian orchid (*Bauhinia forficata*) trees; sweetshades (*Hymenosporum flavum*); and Natal coral trees (*Erythrina humeana*), a South African native with brilliant orange-red flowers from August through November.

One particularly strange apparition in this garden of arboreal delights is the floss silk tree (*Chorisia speciosa*). A South American species characterized by thorny trunks and branches, the floss silk tree produces vivid flowers resembling hibiscus in fall, with seed pods that contain kapok.

Highlights of the garden include the Dry Creek Bed, where during May, for example, the section sparkles with the foliage and flowers of rockrose and snow-in-summer. Also growing in this alluring area are lamb's ears, salvia, and mounds of heliotrope, which are set off by the contrasting textures of ornamental grasses, yellow trumpet vine, and a graceful gold medallion tree (*Cassia leptophylla*).

The garden's perennial borders exhibit profusely blooming pincushion flowers and Jupiter's beard, intermingled with outrageous angel's trumpet and climbing roses. In another garden section, after the freesias, bluebells, and winter irises die back, a fragrant herbal mélange of catmint, thyme, and lavender follows, enhanced by trailing white gazania and the dainty flowers of ground morning glory.

In another garden realm that celebrates sunny sites, you can admire the pale silvery foliage of artemisia, which appears luminescent against a low-growing form of rosemary. Pindo, triangle, and Mediterranean fan palms add elements of dramatic structure to this garden's visually arresting framework.

❀ **Admission:** Free.

Garden open: Daily sunrise to 10:00 P.M.

Further information: Call the Santa Barbara Parks and Recreation Department at the number above for more details, or write them at P.O. Box 1990, Santa Barbara, CA 93102-1990.

Directions: The garden is located in central Santa Barbara; the property extends from Santa Barbara Street to Garden Street and from Arrellaga Street to Micheltorena Street.

2. Andrée Clark Bird Refuge

1400 East Cabrillo Boulevard, **Santa Barbara,** CA 93108; (805) 564-5418

*B*IRDS OFTEN congregate in, or at least pass through, places of abundant plant life. Originally a tidal marsh, the forty-two-acre Andrée Clark Bird Refuge was originally purchased by the City of Santa Barbara in 1909 for public enjoyment. By 1928 Mrs. Huguette Clark had given the city funds to create an artificial lake as a bird refuge dedicated to the memory of her late sister.

Today the Andrée Clark Bird Refuge is one of Santa Barbara's most agreeable parks, with its sparkling lagoon and inviting footpath that wraps around the water's perimeter. While the south shore of the lagoon emphasizes Santa Barbara's diverse horticulture, the north shore shows a more naturalistic style of landscaping. You'll find that as part of Santa Barbara's Parks Department's revegetation project, north-shore habitats such as a freshwater marsh, a coastal sage scrub, and riparian and oak woodlands have been planted with a variety of native species.

Enjoy the serene setting at the Andrée Clark Bird Refuge, and spend some time observing a variety of freshwater birds. At the city's request, signs have been posted for visitors *not* to feed the ducks or other birds, because it severely degrades the water quality.

❀ **Admission:** Free.
Garden open: Daily sunrise to 10:00 P.M.
Further information: Parking is on the north side of the lagoon. Wheelchair accessibility is limited.
Directions: Located near the intersection of Cabrillo Boulevard and U.S. Highway 101.

3. Franceschi Park

1510 Mission Ridge Road, **Santa Barbara,** CA 93105;
(805) 546–5418

*H*IGH IN THE HILLS of Santa Barbara, a segment of property originally purchased in 1904 by Italian botanist Dr. Francesco Franceschi is now the site of Franceschi Park. Offering breathtaking panoramic views of the pristine coastline, this Santa Barbara city park attracts both horticulture buffs from out of town and locals who appreciate the park's magnificent locale.

The onetime proprietor of a plant nursery, Dr. Franceschi is famous for introducing new plants to the area, and he continues to be celebrated for the botanical collection of rare specimens surviving in the park that carries his name. When you visit, look for signs pointing out the many handsome trees, including Australian species such as the lemon-scented gum tree (*Eucalyptus citriodora*), the grass tree (*Xanthorrhoea arborea*), and Canary Island date palms (*Phoenix canariensis*).

Visitors can enjoy the park's brick patio and use the picnic tables overlooking the city. From here, one sees phenomenal vistas extending from the Colonnade of Palms lining the ocean drive to the surrounding communities and distant Channel Islands.

The glory days of Dr. Franceschi's estate are past, but the Santa Barbara Parks and Recreation Department, along with members of the Santa Barbara Horticultural Society, continue to care for the important flora assembled at the park. One semicircular overlook embellished by a wrought-iron railing can still transport a garden traveler like myself to an elegant era when the park was an aesthetic proving ground for Dr. Franceschi's experimental plantings.

❀ **Admission:** Free.
  Garden open: Daily sunrise to a half hour after sunset.
  Further information: The park is a pleasant place to have a picnic, but note that picnic areas are subject to advance reservation. If you plan

on picnicking, call the city Parks and Recreation Department at the number listed above to find out whether picnic sites are still available. **Directions:** The park is located in the hills of Santa Barbara. Take Mission Street. Turn left onto Laguna, then right onto Los Olivos, and continue to Alameda Padre Serra; go left on Moreno, which becomes Mission Ridge. The park entrance is on the left.

4. Ganna Walska Lotusland

695 Ashley Road (mailing address), **Santa Barbara,** CA 93108; (805) 969–9990 (tour reservations), (805) 969–3767 (administration); www.lotusland.org

*T*HE IMAGES of a sensual kingdom invoked by the Lotusland name can only pale in comparison to the actual realm created by Madame Ganna Walska. Unquestionably one of the country's great gardens, Lotusland stretches over thirty-seven acres in Montecito, adjacent to Santa Barbara. The origins of the gardens trace back to 1882, when nurseryman R. Kinton Stevens began planting exotic subtropical trees, palms, and rare specimen plants at his nursery and home, known by the early 1890s as Tanglewood.

Subsequent landowners Mr. and Mrs. E. Palmer Gavit called their estate Cuesta Linda. On this property they had Reginald Johnson design a handsome Spanish colonial revival–style residence in 1919. Not long afterward, Santa Barbara architect George Washington Smith remodeled the house and built the estate's swimming pool and pink perimeter wall. The horticultural history of Lotusland recommences with the landscape design efforts of Peter Riedel, the horticulturist engaged by the Gavits to plan the gardens.

Opera singer and world traveler Madame Ganna Walska purchased the estate in 1941, and she devoted the remaining forty-odd years of her life to creating a botanical wonderland. Madame Walska's Lotusland is distinguished by a matchless, dramatic style. Upon her death in 1984, the Ganna Walska Lotusland Foundation (a nonprofit educational institution) was funded by Madame Walska's estate to care for and preserve these uncommonly beautiful gardens and to provide visitors with access to the incredible retreat.

Lotusland's main house and surrounding grounds include a formal parterre garden, the Neptune fountain, and hedged allées. The lemon arbor is designed along straight and axial lines, while the paths weaving through areas devoted to plant collections are pleasingly curvilinear. With her own acute sense of design and enthusiasm for plants, Madame Walska worked at various times with distinguished landscape architects. Lockwood de Forest and Ralph T. Stevens helped to create the intriguing plan that dazzles today's visitors with its surprising transitions and stunning settings. In later years, Ganna Walska called upon horticulturists Charles Glass and Robert Foster, who were instrumental in the renovation of aloe plantings, the cactus garden, succulents, and the installation of a new cycad garden.

Formerly a eucalyptus grove, the parking lot now provides entree to the visitor center, where the Lotusland tour commences. Pass through the Australian Garden, a recent addition, and you'll cross a sweeping gravel entryway. Continue along on the bark paths edged with burnished glass slag, which is used lavishly throughout the gardens. As in Madame Walska's day, the blue-green glass fragments catch the light as you meander through sultry tropical areas planted with gingers and ferns. Forested sections are decorated with blooming begonias and bromeliads, and an epiphyllum garden is draped in hanging orchid cacti.

Lotusland's eccentric character and uniqueness are revealed most notably in an overabundance of bristly, barbed, dramatically jagged vegetation. In the gardens' upper stories, you'll find great masses of the exotic, eye-catching forms, including trees that were planted before the turn of the twentieth century. Among the stunning reminders of the garden's early nursery phase are towering specimens, such as bizarre ancient Australian bunya-bunya trees exhibiting odd protuberances on their elongated trunks. Unexpectedly lovely wine palms (*Jubea chilensis*) of magnificent girth are shrouded in somber, pale bark that resembles rhinoceros hide.

Perhaps best known for its cycad collection, Lotusland contains rare examples of *Encephalartos woodii*, a plant that has vanished from the wild. With their sharp, prickly leaves and imperative, architectural forms, cycads are often mistaken for palms by those who are unfamiliar with the genus. Botanically speaking, cycads date to ancient times and are related to plants that existed 250 million years ago. Adorning the Cycad Garden, a tranquil koi pond makes a wonderful resting point from which you can observe the exciting botanical specimens. The spiky edges of *Encephalartos horridus* aren't "horrible" at all, as its epithet implies, but a compelling, sculptural illustration of a primitive plant form. Bearing leaves of a remarkably cool shade of silvery blue, with each leaf projecting outward at differing angles, this South African cycad can't help but draw attention to itself. *E. trispinosus*, another sinister-appearing species, exhibits leathery leaves in transfixing tones that can vary from light gray-blue to soft blue-green. Although resembling a palm, cycads bear cones and are related to conifers. During one serendipitous visit in early summer, I saw a specimen exhibit a large cone ensconced within its bower of leaves. Another plant alongside had recently dropped a cone of hefty proportions, which splintered, strewing hundreds of bright red and yellow-orange seeds on the ground in bewitching disarray.

Madame Walska's Blue Garden and the impressive Succulent Collection are worthy of their legend. Picture the impact made by combining all sorts of plants with bluish foliage. From blue Atlas cedars to whimsical tufts of blue fescue grass planted to form a ground-covering carpet, Lotusland's Blue Garden creates a resounding impression with its diversity of glaucous specimens. If upon hearing the term *succulent* you conjure up the image of a small, common houseplant, the array of specimens found in the area devoted to this group of plants will amaze you. Distinguished by their fleshy leaves and stems that hold water, and likewise by their ability to survive in arid conditions, the succulents at Lotusland have been artistically arranged so that the bold beauty of these unusual forms is displayed in an optimum situation.

Contrary to Lotusland's reputation for outright eccentricity, you'll find lovely traditional elements in the midst of unconventional displays. Laid out in geometric motifs, beautiful redbrick paths from the 1920s follow around the peripheries of garden areas and lead through the plantings. Observe how in Madame Walska's magnificent Water Garden the path follows the contour of a lushly planted lotus pond. Here brilliantly patterned ceramic tiles adorn the benches, while crimson flowering canna lilies light up the boggy plantings nearby. Creating an alluring focal point in the midst of the pond, a stand of papyrus inhabits a crisp circular shape.

When you arrive at the courtyard of Lotusland's residence (where the foundation's offices are now ensconced), you'll find a conspicuous demonstration of cacti and euphorbias—an expression of the departed diva's outlandish temperament. Married six times to a succession of colorful characters, Madame Ganna Walska had a penchant for such bizarre botanical species as *Euphorbia ingens*. The gangly forms and pendulous parts of this tropical plant decorate the house's pink stucco facade.

Prominent among Lotusland's extensive plant collections are more than one hundred types of aloes. As they flower, aloes are oddly striking: Fantastical flower clusters appear atop tottering unbranched spikes, creating candelabra-like forms and peculiar forked stems. Many aloes bloom throughout the year, but they are particularly superb in February. You'll find one of Lotusland's most extravagant water features in the Aloe Garden. Ornamented by two triple-tiered fountains of giant clam shells, the garden's organically shaped pristine pool is a transcendent baby blue, and its rim is decorated with abalone shells. In this elaborate setting, the precious glimmering seashells offset the animated architecture of the aloe grove for a stunning pictorial effect.

A horticultural adventure of uncommon rapture, Ganna Walska Lotusland is certain to be a thrilling destination on your itinerary of California's Central Coast.

❀ **Admission:** Fee.

Garden open: Mid-February to mid-November.

Further information: Docent-led tours for adults and children, ages ten and older, are available Wednesday through Saturday at 10:00 A.M. and 1:30 P.M. Children under ten may accompany their families on tours on Thursday and the second Saturday of each month. Advance reservations are necessary and may be made by calling (805) 969–9990 between 9:00 A.M. and noon year-round. If you need special assistance to participate in a tour, inform the visitor services office when you call. Most of the gardens at Lotusland are wheelchair accessible; however, wheelchairs are not provided.

Directions: Specific directions to Lotusland are provided once reservations have been confirmed.

5. Moreton Bay Fig Tree

Montecito and Chapala Streets, **Santa Barbara,** CA 93101;
(805) 564–5418

𝒫LANTED IN 1874 in Santa Barbara, this gigantic example of a native fig tree from Moreton Bay in Australia stakes a claim as the largest tree of its kind in the United States.

After having survived transplanting from a Santa Barbara location 1 block to the east, the Moreton Bay fig tree (*Ficus macrophylla*) has been ensconced in its current position for some 125 years.

Officially designated as a "tree of notable historic interest," the spectacular colossus has been granted protected status by the City of Santa Barbara. A protective post and anchor chain barrier around the tree canopy and accompanying signs inform the public of how to fully appreciate and preserve this arboreal gem for future generations.

❀ Admission: Free.

Garden open: Sunrise to a half hour after sunset.

Further information: The area is partially wheelchair accessible, with improvements soon to come.

Directions: The area is located a few blocks from the ocean, where U.S. 101 crosses Chapala Street.

6. Santa Barbara Botanic Garden

1212 Mission Canyon Road, **Santa Barbara,** CA 93105; (805) 682–4726; www.sbbg.org

*T*HE SANTA BARBARA BOTANIC GARDEN was established in 1926 by Mrs. Anna Dorinda Blaksley Bliss to honor the memory of her father, Henry Blaksley. Dedicated to the study of California's native plants, the seventy-eight-acre property features more than 5½ miles of lovely walking trails winding through the garden's regional planting schemes. Here you'll find sections of manzanita, arroyo, desert, ceanothus, chaparral, meadow, island, and redwood.

It would be difficult to fathom a setting more pleasing to the eye or a more thriving collection of the state's vast range of flora. The Santa Ynez Mountains provide a stirring backdrop, and Santa Barbara's splendid climate endows the garden with conditions similar to those of the Mediterranean. The botanic garden's landscape encompasses naturalistic meadowlands and craggy canyons; a redwood forest; a historic Mission Dam; and lofty ridgetops from where you can gaze down upon the Channel Islands.

The Desert Section is positioned just beyond the entrance to the garden. Representing countless examples of the agave and cactus families, these plants of dramatic form and texture are presided

over by imposing California fan palms (*Washingtonia filifera*), the state's only native palm tree. Formidable boulders rise along the section's paths. Look for the eye-catching Joshua tree, Shaw's agave, and the coast prickly pear, admired for its colorful springtime display of fruit that emerges along the edges of the plant's paddle-shaped stems. After a wet winter, ephemeral species often burst forth with colorful blossoms among the densely arranged spiny specimens. The rewards of the rainy season include such delicate compatriots as dune evening primrose and thistle sage.

Every month of the year suggests special incentives to visit the botanic garden. From February through March, the Ceanothus Section is in bloom. At this time garden sojourners take to hiking along the Porter Trail to a place where it begins to ascend the ridge. Here one encounters an especially admirable variety of ceanothus species and cultivars. You'll see ground-covering forms to sizable shrubs and smallish trees. All reveal beautiful blue-hued and white flowers that brighten the rugged surroundings. The Campbell Trail provides another scenic walk, with steep earthen pathways passing through chaparral plantings and leading down to the canyon floor. Here you'll discover the rustic Campbell Bridge that crosses Mission Creek. Where the Campbell Trail meets the Pritchett Trail, you'll observe a transition into oak woodlands and an area of leathery-leaved chaparral vegetation.

Spring brings a bonanza of butterflies drawn to the garden's bounty of blooming flowers. By May the Meadow Section is awash with ornamental perennial bunchgrasses and radiant annual wild-flowers; California poppies; and the myriad blues of lupines, gilias, phacelias, and blue-eyed grass. Along the Meadow Walk, age-old coast live oaks provide tranquil sanctuary. Nearby, sunbathing frogs revel in the Sellar and Bessie Bullard brook and pond area, where bright scarlet, water-loving monkey flowers, azure blue lobelias, and yellow pond lilies add colorful accents. Observe how the weathered branches used to create low fencing along the edge of the path are structural elements of understated beauty. Such features endow the garden's landscape with a wonderful aesthetic integrity.

The botanic garden's Island Section is of particular interest for its display of rare examples of live-forevers. Scientifically classified as *Dudleya*, this distinctive genus is characterized by small gray-leaved and green succulents restricted to western North America, but found mainly on the offshore islands of Southern California and Baja. June is prime bloom season for *Dudleyas*, as well as for sages and desert willows. Once August rolls around, you'll find the garden aglow with the colors of goldenrods, asters, and California fuchsias. In the fall, the delightfully colored leaves of maples, sycamores, and cottonwoods catch the eye, and migratory and resident birds seem to be everywhere you look.

Another garden area worth seeking out is the Home Demonstration Garden. What makes it so instructive is the way it showcases water-conserving California natives growing in a residential landscape.

Whichever path you follow, whatever time of year you stop over, the Santa Barbara Botanic Garden will charm you with its stimulating walks through diverse communities of native vegetation that are interspersed with noteworthy cultivars.

✿ **Admission:** Fee

Garden open: November through February: daily 9:00 A.M. to 4:00 P.M. March through October: daily 9:00 A.M. to 5:00 P.M. Open one hour later on weekends. Closed Thanksgiving, Christmas Eve, Christmas Day, and New Year's Day. Retail nursery and garden shop are open during garden hours.

Further information: With a paid admission, you receive a map of the gardens for a self-guided visit. Check the Web site or call for information on guided tours or news of special events. The nursery offers a fine selection of native California and Mediterranean plants for sale. The garden shop is excellent, with many unique gift items and a wonderful atmosphere. The garden may close during some events. Wheelchair access is limited.

Directions: To reach the Santa Barbara Botanic Garden, located in the foothills above the city, proceed from downtown Santa Barbara, driving past Santa Barbara Mission and continuing north to Foothill Road (California Highway 192). Turn right and follow signs to the botanic garden.

7. Santa Barbara County Courthouse

1100 Anacapa Street, **Santa Barbara,** CA 93101; (805) 962–6464

*A*s you explore Santa Barbara's city center, you'll discover this exemplary public building, with its gleaming white facade, ornamental archways, wrought-iron decoration, and expansive, low-pitched red tile roof. Santa Barbara County Courthouse is further enhanced by sweeping lawns and the exuberant plantings that surround it.

To call the courthouse a stunning architectural accomplishment is in no way a hyperbole. The now-classic edifice was designed by William Mooser after a severe earthquake in 1925 destroyed a great deal of Santa Barbara's downtown. Mooser used a studied mix of Spanish colonial and Mediterranean design themes, combined with rich decorative embellishments that make reference to Moorish and Islamic influences. Today the Santa Barbara County Courthouse building can be looked upon as a definitive example of Southern Californian architecture, representing all that we have come to equate with that alluring style.

Locate the docent's booth just inside the building and purchase a pamphlet entitled *Discover the Botanical Treasures of the Santa Barbara County Courthouse*. On the courthouse grounds, you'll find an amazing collection of exotic palms and trees. This veritable botanical extravaganza represents specimens gathered from twenty-five countries and six continents.

Ample signs will help in identifying rarities such as paradise and umbrella palms, which are found only on one small South Pacific island. Now extinct in its native habitat, the Franceschi palm appears here among more than forty other varieties of extraordinary palms.

Hearkening back to the days when missionaries first introduced Canary Island date palms to our shores, these auspicious trees once provided fronds for Palm Sunday services. Now, however, they stand as symbols of Southern California's cloudless skies and relaxed lifestyle.

Admission: Free; small fee for pamphlet.

Garden open: Grounds are always open. The courthouse building is open to the public weekdays 8:00 A.M. to 4:45 P.M., Saturday, Sunday, and holidays 10:00 A.M. to 4:45 P.M.; closed Christmas.

Further information: *Discover the Botanical Treasures of the Santa Barbara Courthouse* provides descriptions of the courthouse building and landscaped grounds. The grounds are level; a sunken garden can be viewed at street level.

Directions: The courthouse is located in downtown Santa Barbara on the city block bordered by Anapamu, Santa Barbara, Figueroa, and Anacapa Streets.

8. Santa Barbara Orchid Estate

1250 Orchid Drive, **Santa Barbara,** CA 93111; (805) 967–1284, (800) 553–3387; www.sborchid.com

*T*HE LUSH PLANTINGS along the driveway and the palm-lined walkways of Santa Barbara Orchid Estate announce the glorious flora that attracts legions of orchid lovers.

Two acres of orchids await your discovery here, with one acre of plants displayed outdoors and an acre of exotic orchids found under glass. An approachable staff gladly answers questions to dispel some of the mystique surrounding these gorgeous blooms, the cultivation of which has intimidated many gardeners.

Santa Barbara Orchid Estate specializes in cool-growing varieties of orchids; 50 percent are varieties of the genus *Cymbidium*. As you walk through the establishment's aisles, you'll see an abundance of orchids growing in various cultural conditions. Signs explain key points about the different types of orchids and provide information on how to care for them in your home, or in an outdoor environment such as that of Southern California, or during the summer season in other parts of the country.

Orchids are always blooming at Santa Barbara Orchid Estate, but note that in March 90 percent of the cymbidium plants are simultaneously in bloom, creating an extraordinary exhibition. Try if possible to plan your visit at this time, so that you can behold this incredible sight.

Cut flowers, as well as plants, are available for purchase at

Santa Barbara Orchid Estate. A variety of orchid gifts and blooming plants can be shipped.

❀ **Admission:** Free.

Garden open: Monday through Saturday 8:00 A.M. to 4:30 P.M., Sunday 11:00 A.M. to 4:00 P.M.; closed most major holidays.

Further information: Check the Web site for details on holiday closings. Aisles are not fully wheelchair accessible.

Directions: Coming from either the north or south, take U.S. 101, then turn toward the ocean onto Patterson Avenue, which dead-ends at Orchid Drive.

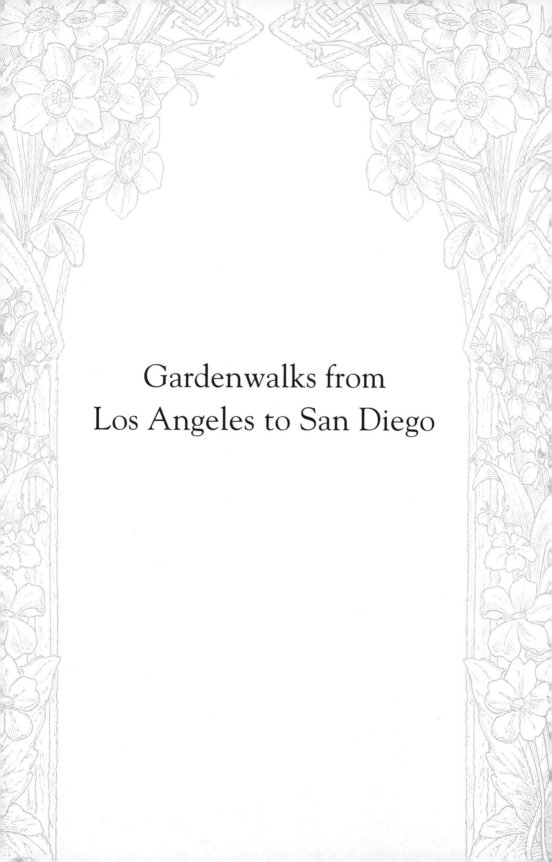

Gardenwalks from
Los Angeles to San Diego

Los Angeles and Vicinity
Gardenwalks

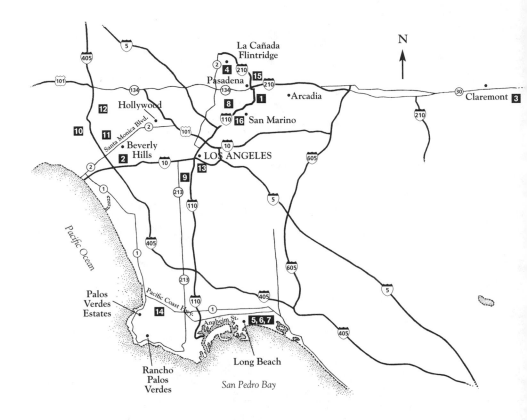

1. Arcadia: Los Angeles County Arboretum & Botanic Garden
2. Beverly Hills: Virginia Robinson Gardens
3. Claremont: Rancho Santa Ana Botanic Garden
4. La Cañada Flintridge: Descanso Gardens
5. Long Beach: Earl Burns Miller Japanese Garden
6. Long Beach: Rancho Los Alamitos Historic Ranch and Gardens
7. Long Beach: Rancho Los Cerritos
8. Los Angeles: Charles F. Lummis Home and Garden—El Alisal
9. Los Angeles: Exposition Park Rose Garden
10. Los Angeles: The Getty Center Central Garden
11. Los Angeles: Mildred E. Mathias Botanical Garden
12. Los Angeles: UCLA Hannah Carter Japanese Garden
13. Los Angeles: Walt Disney Concert Hall Community Park
14. Palos Verdes Peninsula: South Coast Botanic Garden
15. Pasadena: Norton Simon Museum Sculpture Garden
16. San Marino: The Huntington Botanical Gardens

1. Los Angeles County Arboretum & Botanic Garden

301 North Baldwin Avenue, **Arcadia,** CA 91007; (626) 821–3222;
www.arboretum.org

A JEWEL AMONG Southern California gardens, the L.A.
County Arboretum & Botanic Garden offers plant lovers a
panoply of demonstration gardens, educational exhibits, and special
events throughout the year. Operated jointly by the Los Angeles
County Department of Parks and Recreation and the California
Arboretum Foundation, the lovely landscape covers 127 acres.

The arboretum is divided into sections arranged according to
the geographic origins of species. The Tropical Forest, Redwood and
Native Oak Groves, and Australian, South American, and African
Sections highlight rare and unusual flora from around the globe.
Magnolias, ancient cycads, and acacias are represented in significant
plant collections. The arboretum nurtures an assembly of such
Australian native trees and shrubs as eucalyptus, leptospermum
(commonly known as tea tree), and melaleuca. The considerable
presence of these species reflects how well they thrive in the balmy
Southern California climate.

The peaceful Baldwin Lake provides a protected refuge for
wildlife, affording a pleasing environment for garden travelers. Surrounded by the silhouettes of lofty palms and the dense foliage of
innumerable trees, the lake invites repose. Visitors can observe
colorful peafowl, migrating ducks, and many other birds that congregate here by the lake with the rabbits and turtles living in the
sanctuary of the arboretum.

If visiting time is limited, set your sights upon the Meyberg Waterfall, one of the garden's most popular attractions. Locate Baldwin Lake and Circle Road on the visitor map, then proceed past Tule Pond, following Waterfall Walk into the North American/ Asiatic Section. Head toward the Herb Garden, and from there just up the road to the right is the waterfall, situated on the arboretum's western border. The lovely views here are uplifting.

Both of historic appeal, the Hugo Reid Adobe and the gingerbread-embellished Queen Anne Cottage are state and national landmarks, respectively. Native Gabrieleno-style Indian wickiups (a type of dwelling) and other restored structures like the Santa Anita Depot provide wonderful glimpses of the region's historical heritage. For history buffs, these buildings offer satisfying encounters with California's bygone days.

The arboretum also boasts the new Sunset Demonstration Gardens. The one-and-one-half acre design plan includes eight small gardens: the Water Retreat, the Nostalgia Garden, Gardening under the Oaks, and the Courtyard Garden, to name a few. On the visitor map, you'll find them on the way to the Tropical Greenhouse. Other additional attractions at the arboretum include the Water Conservation Garden and the Tropical and Begonia Greenhouses.

🏵 **Admission:** Fee; the third Tuesday of each month is free.

Garden open: Daily 9:00 A.M. to 4:30 P.M.; closed Christmas Day. Check Web site or call for extended summer hours.

Further information: The Web site features information on tours, classes, special happenings, and updates on what's in bloom. Phone (626) 447–8751 for gift shop information. Facilities include a reference library, and ADA accessible shuttle tram. Fee charged for the tram; call to verify tram operation schedule. Some areas of rough terrain are not wheelchair accessible, but most walkways and tram roads can be accessed by wheelchair users.

Directions: The arboretum is approximately forty-five minutes northeast of downtown Los Angeles, just east of Pasadena, and south of the Baldwin Avenue exit of Interstate 210.

2. Virginia Robinson Gardens

Beverly Hills, CA 90210; (310) 276-5367;
http://parks.co.la.ca.us/virginia_gardens.html

*T*HE 1911 Mediterranean revival mansion of Mr. and Mrs. Harry Winchester Robinson and the surrounding Italian terraced gardens are one of the earliest homes and landscapes built in this Southern California Eden. Cloistered within luxurious Beverly Hills, the Virginia Robinson Gardens exemplifies a graciousness and elegance associated with both its locale and architectural period.

Extending over more than six acres of picturesque hillside, the gardens are divided into five specific garden areas, including the Italian Terrace, the Mall, the Rose, and the Kitchen Gardens. Exuberant flower borders, mature cycads, and a stunning patio with decorative balustrades enliven the atmosphere of the formal Mall Garden. In the Italian Terrace Garden, under the shade of sheltering magnolias and handsome trees, camellias, azaleas, hydrangeas, and bevies of exotics burst forth with their beautiful blooms. Here also, charming brick paths lead garden wanderers to admire the aged patina of stone fountains and elevated ponds.

Mrs. Robinson left her lovely home and beguiling grounds to Los Angeles County. Visitors have continued to admire the unique landscaping, especially the unrivaled grove of Australian king palm trees, planted at the suggestion of well-known landscape architect Charles Gibbs Adams. Among the gardens' many water features, an ornate pool with exceptional mosaic work is impressive. Accentuated by regal Roman arches, a Renaissance revival pavilion rises above the serene pool. This ornamental building takes its inspiration from Italy's Villa Pisani.

A visit to the Virginia Robinson Gardens allows contemporary garden lovers to experience a noble manifestation of wealth as expressed in horticultural abundance.

❁ **Admission:** Fee.

Garden open: Tours offered Tuesday through Friday by appointment only.

Further information: Call for reservations and to confirm times for docent-led tours. Limited parking available. Wheelchair accessibility is limited; call for details.

Directions: The gardens are just north of Los Angeles, in the center of Beverly Hills. Directions are provided once reservations are confirmed.

3. Rancho Santa Ana Botanic Garden

1500 North College Avenue, **Claremont**, CA 91711-3157;
(909) 625–8767; www.rsabg.org

*R*ANCHO SANTA ANA Botanic Garden's eighty-three-acre site deserves exploration for its exceptional collections of native flora, including 2,800 plant species and hundreds of rare and endangered plants.

Three distinctive areas within the garden feature plants that thrive in the following types of environments: dense clay (in the Indian Hill Mesa); sedimentary, rocky soils (in the East Alluvial Gardens); and a combination of sand, gravel, rock, and alluvial deposits that form the basis of the impressive fifty-five-acre expanse of the California Plant Communities.

The Indian Hill Mesa exhibits numerous types of manzanitas (*Arctostaphylos*), in flower from late November through early March. These winter-blooming western natives are characterized by lovely red bark, a sculptural interplay of branches, and charming flowers that dangle like bells. The mesa section is especially delightful during March and April when masses of California wild lilacs (*Ceanothus*) are blooming.

In the East Alluvial Gardens, you'll find groupings of desert, coastal, and Channel Island plants, and the wonderful Palm Oasis, which features an arrangement of handsome fan palms (*Washingtonia filifera*), the only palm tree native to the state of California. The California Plant Communities, the expansive area devoted to the state's plants, includes among its rich offerings big berry manzanitas, California flannel bushes, and *Nolina parryi*, which is related to the yuccas. Commonly called Parry nolina, the plants display their stunning flower rosettes on phenomenal stalks 10 feet tall in early spring.

Look also for the California Cultivar Garden, showcasing cultivated varieties of plants, and the Riparian Woodland, located along the banks between the garden's upper and lower pond. You can consult the *Garden Map and Guide for Visitors* to locate any gardens. Remember, although springtime wildflower displays are lovely and colorful, visitors can enjoy this haven on any given day of the year.

❀ **Admission:** Free; donations encouraged.

Garden open: Daily 8:00 A.M. to 5:00 P.M.; closed July Fourth, Thanksgiving, Christmas, and New Year's Day. The California Garden Shop is open 9:00 A.M. to 5:00 P.M. The research library is open Monday through Friday 9:00 A.M. to 3:00 P.M.

Further information: Log on to the Web site for a calendar of special events. The shop features a host of books, gift items, and a selection of educational toys for children. To visit the library, call extension 236 for an appointment. Several of the garden pathways are wheelchair accessible; an accessibility guide is available in the garden shop free of charge. Visitors may make advance reservations for a guided tram tour by calling the garden; the tram will accommodate a wheelchair. Advance reservations are required and a nominal fee is charged.

Directions: The garden is about one hour and fifteen minutes northeast of downtown Los Angeles. From I–210, take the Towne Avenue exit south approximately 1 mile to Foothill Boulevard. At Foothill Boulevard, turn left (east) and proceed about 1 mile and turn onto College Avenue, then proceed to the parking lot. Printable directions are available on the Web site.

4. Descanso Gardens

1418 Descanso Drive, **La Cañada Flintridge,** CA 91011;
(818) 949–4200; www.descansogardens.org

*I*N 1937 E. Manchester Boddy, businessman and publisher of the
Los Angeles Daily News, purchased property in the San Rafael
Hills north of Los Angeles. He named this land Rancho del Descanso. The enchanting woodland setting endures today as Descanso
Gardens, comprising a 160-acre garden with 80 planted acres.
Recognized as part of Boddy's extraordinary horticultural legacy,
Descanso Gardens features a magnificent camellia forest—one of
the largest in North America—that draws visitors from far and near.

Boddy's passion for camellias began early on, when he realized
that the mature coast live oak trees growing on the land would provide the perfect filtered shade habitat for the beautiful flowering
shrubs. Planting began immediately after Boddy optioned the property, and as the saying goes, the rest is history. The camellia forest
consists of an estimated 50,000 plants, with more than 400 varieties
of camellias represented, including many unique varieties developed
at Descanso. Some specimens are more than 30 feet tall. You'll see
the large-flowered *Camellia reticulata,* brought to Rancho del Descanso in 1948, and in October an impressive display of the C. *sasanqua* species. From January throughout March, and October through
December, the gardens' serene woodland paths are punctuated with
the extravagant flowers of early- and late-blooming types of camellias. A refreshing host of annuals, planted among the flower beds,
add continual color and good cheer.

Visitors and garden members look forward to the informal style
and peaceful setting of the Descanso Gardens. Here people can take
lovely morning walks along the Nature Trail or explore the restrained beauty of the Fern Canyon. Occasional visitors to the Los
Angeles area can also take refuge in these tranquil gardens, which

are not far from the city center yet provide a dramatic contrast to L.A.'s unceasing activity.

In the spring you can enjoy expansive borders chock-full of tulips and daffodils or stroll beneath stately magnolias sheltering fine displays of azaleas. Descanso's Iris Garden displays California's largest collection of breathtaking bearded irises. During April 1,500 named varieties create a dazzling show. Roses and wildflowers also exhibit their finery at this time, while Descanso's famous Lilac Grove highlights shrubs that were specifically developed to bloom in Southern California's mild climate. These fragrant, radiant lilacs are a surprising delight.

Eight acres at Descanso Gardens are devoted to a native plant collection, with areas of chaparral representing the spirit of a Southern Californian landscape. Devoted bird lovers head for a lake on the property that features a bird sanctuary. An observation station built in conjunction with the Audubon Society provides a restful spot to study the many migrating and permanent species that nest or seek shelter within the sanctuary of Descanso.

The International Rosarium enchants rose lovers, with twenty different theme gardens that commemorate various types of roses from antique to modern. Opened in 1994, the rosarium provides particularly helpful signs that explain different types of flower forms, specific plant traits, origins of plants, and derivations of hybrid roses. A Victorian gazebo, a handsome walled mission garden, a lengthy arbor dubbed Noisette Tunnelle, and *Rosa wichuraiana* arches are a few examples of how garden ornamentation and hardscaping combine to provide wonderful environments for the display of rose collections. Embellishing the rosarium are exuberant companion plantings of perennials and shrubs, spilling over onto grassy paths.

Not surprisingly, Descanso Gardens features an admirable Japanese Tea House and Garden, inspired by the Asian origins of camellias.

Explore the discreet loveliness of the setting with an unhurried stroll through the landscape. The alluring flora—azaleas that bloom in April, Japanese maples ablaze in the fall, and elegant bamboo year-round—encourages a considered awareness of the garden's symbolic elements. Philosophical concepts, such as how the element of moving water suggests one's journey through life, can enrich the garden experience. However, the sensory delights provided by the pool and waterfalls here are admirable in their own right.

During open hours the public is invited to enjoy art exhibits and the wood-paneled Boddy Library, located in Boddy's former home. Should you choose to amble around the exterior of the twenty-two-room mansion Boddy built in 1938, you'll soon discover a secret garden niche. Here, adjoining the Boddy House and Art Gallery, is a hidden Chinese Garden, established by Boddy years ago.

What a revelation this intimate garden space proves to be, with age-old relief sculptures from China installed around the upper perimeter of the garden's walls. Note the amazingly vivid glazes that decorate these reliefs, and the skilled craftsmanship reflected in the vigorous modeling of their figures. In this exquisite walled garden, my curiosity was stirred. I found myself pondering both the rarefied setting and the narrative revealed by the sculptural relics. Moreover, I wondered what story they might tell about the man who was inspired to build such a secluded garden amid the grand scope of his own Rancho del Descanso.

❀ **Admission:** Fee; parking is free.

Garden open: Daily 9:00 A.M. to 5:00 P.M.; closed Christmas Day. Cafe is open daily 10:00 A.M. to 3:00 P.M. Gift shop is open weekdays 10:00 A.M. to 4:00 P.M.; Saturday and Sunday 10:00 A.M. to 4:45 P.M.

Further information: Check the Web site to learn about special events, what's blooming, and the schedule of tram tours. Trams do not run on Monday. The gift shop features a fine selection of books, garden accessories, and gift items with garden themes. Call the information center at the number above with any questions about the gardens. Paved roads and restrooms are wheelchair accessible.

Directions: Descanso is twenty minutes north of downtown Los Angeles, just south of I–210, off California Highway 2 (Glendale Freeway). Detailed directions and a map can be found on the Web site.

5. Earl Burns Miller Japanese Garden

California State University at Long Beach, Earl Warren Drive, **Long Beach,** CA 90840; (562) 985–8885; www.csulb.edu/~jgarden

COLORFUL AZALEAS light up a hillside during a springtime visit to this traditional Japanese garden, located on the campus of California State University at Long Beach. The 1.3-acre Earl Burns Miller Japanese Garden represents a dream that became a reality for Mrs. Loraine Miller Collins, who wished to create a place that offers rejuvenation to the weary and aesthetic inspiration for those seeking beauty.

Dedicated in 1981 to her late husband, Earl Burns Miller, the garden is full of fragrant magnolias that provide color in summer and chrysanthemums and liquidambar trees that light up autumn days in golden tones. Designed by landscape architect Edward R. Lovell, the Earl Burns Miller Garden offers a lovely setting to enjoy diverse flora, with landscaping punctuated by the potent forms of significant objects. Note the exemplary proportions of an arched bridge, the three-tiered pagoda, and stone lanterns. If you stop to regard these important garden elements, your attention will be drawn to the sculpted shapes of trees and the textural interplay of shrubbery. Stroll the garden's paths and enjoy the emblematic streambed of black pebbles. Note as well the poetic rustle when you approach the Chinese willow's cascading drapery.

In this Japanese garden, amid the jade green, pale chartreuse, and emerald tones of evergreen specimens, you'll find a peaceful feeling and quietude.

❀ **Admission:** Free; fee charged on days when a public program is offered. **Garden open:** Tuesday through Friday 8:00 A.M. to 3:30 P.M., Sunday noon to 4:00 P.M.; closed Monday and Saturday. Dates vary; call ahead to confirm holiday and seasonal closures taking place throughout the year. General details are listed on the Web site.

Further information: Visit the Web site for a listing of garden events. Pathways and restrooms are wheelchair accessible.

Directions: The garden is approximately one hour south of downtown Los Angeles. Take Interstate 405 to the Bellflower exit south to State University Drive; turn left onto Earl Warren Drive. Go left on Earl Warren to parking lot 16. The garden is located across the street.

6. Rancho Los Alamitos Historic Ranch and Gardens

6400 Bixby Hill Road, **Long Beach,** CA 90815;
(562) 431–3541

*O*N A HISTORIC seven-and-a-half-acre setting, you'll find a ranch house, barns, and four acres of gardens now restored and preserved for the public's benefit. One of the two adobe homes situated on this ranch land (see the next entry, Rancho Los Cerritos) was once owned by members of the Bixby family.

Landscape architect Florence Yoch is still celebrated today for the Oleander Walk she originally designed in the 1920s for a relation of the Bixby clan. Plantings highlight cacti and citrus trees. Among a number of theme gardens, the friendship garden stands out. The Rancho Los Alamitos landscaping is enhanced by a charming fountain and courtyard that resonate with Spanish colonial influence, while venerable trees of considerable girth add to the site's historical appeal.

Admission: Free.

Garden open: Wednesday through Sunday 1:00 to 5:00 P.M.

Further information: Tell the staff you wish to look at the gardens and you can spend as long as you like exploring them. You can also request a tour of the gardens. Tours are required for the house and barnyard areas, but reservations are not required. House and barnyard are wheelchair accessible. The gardens are partially accessible.

Directions: The ranch is in Long Beach; enter through the gate at the intersection of Anaheim Road and Palo Verde Avenue. To see a map, log on to www.longbeach.gov and search for Rancho Los Alamitos.

7. Rancho Los Cerritos

4600 Virginia Road, **Long Beach,** CA 90807; (562) 570–1755; www.rancholoscerritos.org

*T*HIS HISTORIC two-story adobe, circa 1844, features interiors that represent late-nineteenth-century life. The grounds stretch over approximately five acres of land once used to raise cattle and sheep. The lovely formal gardens are attributed to Ralph D. Cornell, a prominent Southern California landscape architect associated with Cook, Hall & Cornell. An enclosed courtyard garden and another spacious area of inviting lawns and charming old brick walkways enhance the restored adobe home. Here, as at Rancho Los Alamitos, towering trees contribute to the atmosphere of a bygone epoch.

❀ **Admission:** Free; donations welcome.

Garden open: Wednesday through Sunday 1:00 to 5:00 P.M.; closed major holidays.

Further information: Self-guided tours are available Wednesday through Friday. Call to confirm times for guided tours on Saturday and Sunday. The first floor of the adobe is wheelchair accessible. Most of the main garden is accessible; the landscaped inner courtyard and the orchard are also accessible.

Directions: Rancho Los Cerritos is 1 block west of Long Beach Boulevard at San Antonio Drive. Log on to the Web site for detailed driving directions or to see a map.

8. Charles F. Lummis Home and Garden— El Alisal

200 East Avenue 43, Los Angeles, CA 90031; (323) 222-0546

*T*HE HISTORICAL SOCIETY of Southern California maintains its headquarters at the Charles Lummis Home, known also as El Alisal. Celebrated as a city of Los Angeles and state of California Historical Monument, and included on the National Register of Historic Places, El Alisal was once home to the unconventional, multitalented author, journalist, and founder of the Southwest Museum, Charles Lummis. The property is now owned and maintained by the Los Angeles Department of Recreation and Parks.

Lummis chose the location for his home in 1895. Over a span of some twelve years, the resourceful individualist proceeded to construct a rocky citadel for himself. Deriving inspiration from a majestic sycamore with four huge trunks, Lummis named his new abode El Alisal. The impressive thirteen-room building possesses a steadfast character and eye-catching appeal.

Visitors to the Charles F. Lummis Home find a noteworthy two-acre garden that illustrates the uses and attractions of drought-tolerant plants. Designed in 1985 by landscape architect Robert Perry, the Lummis garden plan highlights a low-maintenance approach. Composed of five distinct sections, the design includes citrus and desert gardens, a regional plant garden incorporating Mediterranean species, a lovely yarrow meadow, and a California native garden. A dry streambed complements the design. You'll find the landscaping educational in its selections of plants and siting— a vibrant, aesthetic showcase of interesting indigenous species and cultivated varieties that prosper with lesser amounts of water.

In front of the entry court, the yarrow meadow serves as a creative substitute for a lawn. Among the selection of regional plants are toyon and California lilac, with their seasonal show of blooms and berries. Scent is another important element in the overall garden plan. Lavender, thyme, and sage provide lovely aromas as one walks along the garden's paths of decomposed granite. In early summer, the tall flowering spikes of Pride of Madeira appear, while lovely shade trees like the western redbud add color in the fall.

When touring the Lummis Home, you can explore its museum exhibit of archaeological artifacts that once belonged to Charles Lummis. Among the interior's fascinating decorative pieces, look for the dining room sideboard, with carved doors dating to 1776. You'll also view framed photographs of writers, singers, artists, and other celebrities that Lummis played host to at one time or another.

❋ **Admission:** Free.

Garden open: The house is open Friday, Saturday, and Sunday noon to 4:00 P.M., except certain holidays. To walk through the garden at hours other than when the Lummis Home is open, call ahead Monday through Friday 8:30 A.M. to 5:00 P.M. to speak with someone in the historical society office.

Further information: Pathways in garden are flat and mostly wheelchair accessible.

Directions: El Alisal is located in Los Angeles' Highland Park neighborhood at the intersection of Avenue 43 and California Highway 110 (Pasadena Freeway). Take the Avenue 43 exit.

9. Exposition Park Rose Garden

701 State Drive, between Figueroa Street and Menlo Avenue,
Los Angeles, CA 90037; (213) 765–5397;
www.laparks.org/exporosegarden/rosegarden.htm

*B*EFORE THE CITY of Los Angeles leased the land in 1911, Exposition Park was an agricultural area affiliated with the State of California's Agricultural Association. At that time, the park was given its current name, and a sunken garden, measuring 800 by 300 feet, was installed and enclosed by a masonry wall. The advent of World War I slowed down progress on Exposition Park's formal seven-acre garden. It was 1928 before the rose garden itself was actually completed.

On a gardenwalk today through Exposition Park Rose Garden, you will enjoy some 200 varieties of roses. On view here are 20,000 plants, arranged in 30-by-30-foot beds and embellished with a circular fountain, statuary, and sculptures. The garden is awash with blooms from April into December. Visitors to the garden can relax here before continuing their tour of Los Angeles.

❀ **Admission:** Free.
   Garden open: Daily 9:00 A.M. to sunset. Closed January 1 through March 15 for maintenance.
   Further information: Partially wheelchair accessible from the State Drive entrance.
   Directions: The garden is located by the Los Angeles Coliseum, just south of downtown Los Angeles.

10. The Getty Center Central Garden

1200 Getty Center Drive, **Los Angeles,** CA 90049-1681; (310) 440–7300; www.getty.edu

*B*REATHTAKING in its entirety, at a cost of approximately $1 billion, the Getty Center is the awe-inspiring legacy of one man and the private foundation he established to support and sustain art and culture. After thirteen years of planning, the Getty opened its doors to the public in December 1997. Larger than life, the center consists of an amalgamation of buildings, including the formidable J. Paul Getty Museum that exhibits Getty's superb art collection, together with institutes devoted to research and conservation, arts education, museum management, and a grant program. The center's triumphant design incorporates water features, a tram system, cafes, and a restaurant—all of which elaborate on the incandescent architecture. But it is artist Robert Irwin's ravishing Central Garden that functions as the icing on the cake.

The Getty Center is the culmination of the visionary ideas of architect Richard Meier in association with the J. Paul Getty Trust. With its remarkable synthesis of design, place, and purpose, the Getty salutes the new millennium from its magnificent site in the Santa Monica Mountains.

Situated on a 110-acre hillside, the Getty's campus is strikingly modernist yet visitor friendly. Spectacular terraces offer vistas encompassing the Los Angeles city skyline and sprawling labyrinth of streets, and extending to the San Gabriel Mountains, Santa Catalina Island, and the Pacific Ocean. While the view may evoke a euphoric response among visitors, the building material used also provides a satisfying aesthetic experience. Note the exciting tactile qualities of prominent fossilized remains on the surfaces of the Roman classic travertine covering the 1.2 million square feet of the center's walls and pavement.

Major hillsides of the Getty Center are the landscape design work of Emet L. Wemple & Associates Landscape Architects, while other gardens on the campus have been designed by Olin Partnership of Philadelphia. The Getty Center commissioned Robert Irwin to design the 134,000-square-foot Central Garden as a work of art. Important art commissions often generate conflicting opinions. In the case of the Central Garden, the idea was controversial to be sure. Although his previous expertise was not horticultural, Irwin's skillful touch and satisfying command of space are apparent in the visually engaging Central Garden. His garden scheme is made up of well-chosen elements: a tree-lined walkway, a streambed strewn with boulders, a plaza, a cascading waterfall, and a reflecting pool featuring a maze laid out with azaleas.

Begun in the spring of 1996 and completed in December 1997, the plan of the Central Garden echoes a natural ravine within the existing topography. With the passing of time and the changing seasons, the lush plantings are expected to reveal varying arrangements of plant material. By constantly introducing new plant combinations and schemes, the garden's dominant theme is to surprise and give pleasure to visitors. In the garden, you'll find carved in stone Robert Irwin's statement: EVER PRESENT NEVER TWICE THE SAME/ EVER CHANGING NEVER LESS THAN WHOLE.

Arriving at the Central Garden on my inaugural visit, I found the rocky watercourse decked out in tall scarlet canna lilies accompanied by a profusion of herbs and grasses. This exquisite tapestry, woven primarily of deep claret and silvery hues, had distinct accents of grays and greens. Zigzag walkways, traversing the hillside's gentle descent, lead through the luscious arrangements of plants. Once you reach the plaza, cascading water spills over a stone wall, directing the focus down toward the reflecting pool. Here you'll see the configuration of the azalea maze apparently floating within the pool's encircling water. Despite this captivating illusion, the azaleas are planted in soil.

The Central Garden's plaza readily accommodates the bustling, ebullient crowds as well as solitary pilgrims drawn to the Getty Center. To underscore the exciting dimensions of the plaza landing, Irwin created a number of soaring, splayed sculptural constructions, fabricated of industrial rebar and festooned in bougainvillea. In addition to supporting the colorful vines, the volumetric steel bowers suggest places where you may wish to stop and rest.

I found the horticultural vignettes located around the pool area wildly romantic and totally intoxicating. Curving swaths of steel function as the garden's contoured retaining walls. From one of many benches nestled in secluded niches, I could appreciate the metal's rusty patina, a stunning contrast to the extravagant sensory delight offered by masses of bright blooms and luscious leaf forms thriving in the raised beds. Overall, more than 500 types of plants are found in the Central Garden.

The pool area's terraced gardens create an amphitheater-like setting. In this central space, a cool impression is made by the clipped green shrubbery maze, with its circular frame of gray sedum. In a striking juxtaposition, countless varieties of plants are showcased around the staggered levels above the pool. In one instance, the bold swords of variegated phormiums played off immense and flamboyant dahlias. Arranged according to special themes, the color combinations often go beyond exuberant. If you look in another direction, rose standards, purple coneflowers, and uncommon tropical vines work their magic, while everywhere bees and burnished butterflies hover over the fragrant flowers.

After completing your tour of the Central Garden, locate the south promontory on the Getty Center map. The cactus garden planted here offers its own pleasures. The exalted scale and use of space at the Getty Center simply dazzles. Glistening in the Southern California sun, the center is a haven for art and garden lovers alike. Don't miss the opportunity to enjoy the beauty of its buildings and priceless artworks, its panoramic views, and its enthralling gardens.

✿ **Admission:** Free; parking fee charged per car.
Garden open: Tuesday through Thursday 10:00 A.M. to 6:00 P.M., Friday and Saturday 10:00 A.M. to 9:00 P.M., Sunday 10:00 A.M. to 6:00 P.M.; closed Monday and major holidays (call for holiday closures).
Further information: The Getty Center is entirely wheelchair accessible.
Directions: The center is just off I–405 in Los Angeles; take the Getty Center Drive exit and follow signs to the entrance. Visit the user-friendly Web site to see a map or for details on taking public transportation.

11. Mildred E. Mathias Botanical Garden

University of California at Los Angeles, Hilgard and Le Conte Avenues, Box 951606, **Los Angeles,** CA 90095-1606; (310) 825-1260; www.botgard.ucla.edu/bg-home.htm

$\mathcal{S}$ITUATED ON THE campus of the University of California at Los Angeles, the Mildred E. Mathias Botanical Garden boasts one of the country's largest gatherings of tropical and subtropical plants. The garden's seven frost-free acres display botanical collections of uncommon trees and flora from around the world.

Named for the garden's director from 1956 to 1974, Dr. Mildred Mathias, the garden features more than 5,000 species representing 225 plant families. Special collections include bromeliads, Malesian rhododendrons, ferns, cycads, palms, and the newest one devoted to plants native to the Hawaiian Islands. Another distinctive collection, the lily alliance, highlights the order Liliales. Incorporated here are a wide spectrum of related plants—from trees and vines to species demonstrating long periods of dormancy.

A monumental, endangered Torrey pine and two giant rose gum (*Eucalyptus grandis*) exemplify the exceptional tree specimens you'll encounter here. In addition to numerous species of eucalyptus and ficus, the garden's collections include a particularly intriguing array of spectacular flowering trees. Look for many members of the bignon family of plants, particularly the African tulip tree (*Spathodea campanulata*), growing near the corner of South Tiverton Avenue and Charles E. Young Drive. Given suitable conditions, the tree produces huge, rounded red flowers from March through November. The Malesian rhododendrons also produce an exhilarating exhibition of blossoms all year-round. Some fine specimens are in flower every day, January through December.

Consult the Mathias Botanical Garden map to locate the hillside section (number 5), where you'll observe a satisfying collection of palm trees native to both Northern and Southern Hemispheres. In the Hawaiian Island section (number 12 on the map), look for colorful, showy species of hibiscus. Lovers of flora will find endless marvels to contemplate and admire at UCLA's Mildred E. Mathias Botanical Garden.

❀ **Admission:** Free.

Garden open: Monday through Friday 8:00 A.M. to 5:00 P.M. (winter closing 4:00 P.M.), Saturday and Sunday 8:00 A.M. to 4:00 P.M.; closed on university holidays.

Further information: The main entrance is on Tiverton Avenue; north entrance is opposite the Patio, behind the Botany Building. For tour information call (310) 206–6707; the garden sometimes closes due to bad weather. Parking is limited; to park on campus, you must purchase a parking pass at an information kiosk. Or you can use public parking lots in nearby Westwood. About half the garden paths are wheelchair accessible, and plans are in the works to make the path on the south end accessible.

Directions: The garden is located at the southeastern corner of the UCLA campus, in the Westwood section of Los Angeles. Log on to the Web site for maps and detailed directions.

12. UCLA Hannah Carter Japanese Garden

Los Angeles, CA 90077; (310) 825–4574;
www.japanesegarden.ucla.edu

*A*FFILIATED WITH the University of California at Los Angeles, the Hannah Carter Japanese Garden features a lovely pond with animated koi and a notable 1,000-year-old stone carving. As stated in a pamphlet, the garden's design signifies the cycle from unrestrained youthfulness to sedate maturity, presented in a counterclockwise progression. You'll find a more buoyant spirit in garden areas around the main entrance, while sections to the right reveal a controlled character.

❀ **Admission:** Free.

Garden open: Visits by reservation only, Tuesday, Wednesday, and Friday 10:00 A.M. to 3:00 P.M. Check the Web site for an up-to-date listing of holiday and seasonal closures.

Further information: The address will be provided when you call to make a reservation for either a self-guided tour of the Kyoto-style Japanese Garden or to schedule a docent tour. Note that the garden may close due to inclement weather. Parking is limited and reservations are required. The garden's hillside terrain is not accessible to wheelchairs; its steep paths, stairways and ungated ponds make it unsuitable for young children. Sensible shoes are recommended.

Directions: The garden is 1 mile north of the UCLA campus in Bel-Air.

13. Walt Disney Concert Hall Community Park

111 South Grand Avenue, **Los Angeles,** CA 90012;
(213) 972–7211; www.wdch.org

A FABULOUS new public garden wraps around the voluptuous stainless-steel facade of the Walt Disney Concert Hall in Los Angeles, architect Frank Gehry's recently unveiled tour de force. The building's gleaming curves energize the urban setting and simultaneously cosset the horticultural oasis positioned atop the 3.6-acre site in the Bunker Hill neighborhood.

Two separate gardens, in fact, make up the layout created by designer Melinda Taylor and landscape architect Lawrence Moline, the founding principal of LRM, Ltd.

A main garden 34 feet in the air runs the length of the project's west boundary, above Hope Street between First and Second, while a smaller Founders' Garden is located at the corner of First and Hope Streets.

Signature design elements come into play as soon as you enter the garden. Notice the prominently placed planting beds filled with perennials and shrubs. Their organic contours flow in tandem with an arrangement of mature ornamental trees.

Designer Taylor knits together plants that are pleasing to the touch, from downy *Salvia officinalis* 'Berggarten' and the woolly leaves of variegated helichrysum to aromatic herbs such as rosemary, Russian sage, and scented pelargoniums. Airy grasses and sedges serve as allies, along with roses pegged to clamber up and over a wall facing the street. *Montanoa grandiflora,* the daisy tree, is among specimens providing multiseasonal interest for areas of dappled shade.

A sense of tradition rather than trendiness governs the flora, while the inclusion of small, semiprivate spaces results in a welcoming, intimate atmosphere unusual for a public park. Taylor told me she intended the trees to provide a counterpoint to the building's size, thus creating a space that is human in scale.

Rather than use plants that appear frequently in civic settings, like strelitzia and star jasmine, Taylor creates a plant palette with milkweed and salvias, demonstrating her interest in attracting birds, bees, and butterflies.

A popular gathering spot, the Blue Ribbon Garden emerges at the center of the garden. Gehry designed a fountain here to emulate a many-petaled flower, and he dedicated it to the late Lillian Disney. "A Rose For Lilly" features a mosaic surface composed of Royal Delft shards, calling to mind Mrs. Disney's fondness for the blue and white porcelain.

Venerable trees lend backbone and artistry to the garden plan. Their rhythmical placement seems to advance the movement of visitors through the curving travertine walkways.

Each tree has a distinct personality. Taken together, they display a fascinating diversity of forms. Yet their skillful positioning illustrates the designer's sensitivity in responding to the sculptural forms of the building itself.

Observe how the tree canopy is orchestrated to achieve seasonal complexity. Taking its cue from the Los Angeles Philharmonic's concert season, the color scheme ushers forth displays of vivid blooms and perfumed flower clusters, shapely foliage, and brilliant leaf hues.

A show of autumn leaves accents Chinese pistache trees, while flamboyant flowers appear on the Hong Kong orchid trees through the fall into wintertime.

Broad leaves cloak the pink snowball tree from crown to ground plane. In January, flowers marked by a scent likened to butter and sugar are added ornamentation.

Lilac pink inflorescences adorn pink trumpet trees to announce the arrival of spring. And from March through May, the entire scene is enlivened by the fiery red flowers of naked coral trees, *Erythrina coralloides*. The candlelike blossoms of these deciduous trees find their match in winter, when the strikingly sculptural branches are exposed.

One particular naked coral tree stands out as a scene-stealer: Taylor gave it the nickname Venus. You'll find it looming at the top of the stairway at Grand near Second Street. Perhaps its shape will remind you of the Venus de Milo sculpture.

In early summer tipu trees bloom in hues of apricot to yellow. A cool green perspective reigns by high summer, but when the tipu trees are encircled by ocher carpets made up of fallen flowers, the philharmonic's season comes to an end.

Located 1 block from the Museum of Contemporary Art and the Cathedral of Our Lady of Angels, the concert hall and its unique gardens offer you a fresh vantage point to view Los Angeles landmarks and the outlying terrain.

When the days and hours of light are long, the garden appears to bask in the large amount of direct light it receives. Taylor emphasizes the low, golden light of the sun as it sets in the late afternoon and early evening. You'll find the garden to be a particularly wonderful place to sit or stroll or gather then.

❀ **Admission:** Free.

Garden open: Daily 5:00 A.M. to 11:00 P.M.; call or visit the Web site to confirm. The Los Angeles Philharmonic Store is open daily 9:30 A.M. to 5:30 P.M. and postperformance on concert evenings. The Patina Restaurant is open Monday through Friday 11:30 A.M. to 2:00 P.M. for lunch; daily 5:00 to 11:00 P.M. for preconcert seating, dinner, and late-night suppers.

Further information: Check the Web site to see the current schedule of guided tours for groups. Audio tours are available to individuals or groups, including a self-guided tour that includes the garden, and are offered daily 9:00 A.M. to 3:00 P.M. on nonmatinee days, 9:00 to 10:30 A.M. on matinee days; fee charged. Call or visit the Web site to find out if a matinee is scheduled: Tours are not available during performances. The Concert Hall Cafe provides food on a casual, "grab and go" basis; call (213) 972–3550 for information. For an elegant meal, call the Patina Restaurant at (213) 972–3331 for lunch, dinner or late-night supper reservations. The concert hall and its gardens are fully wheelchair accessible via ramps and elevators; call guest services at (213) 972–0777 for details.

Directions: The concert hall and garden are located in downtown Los Angeles. Information on public transit and detailed directions can be found on the Web site. Stairways and elevators provide entry to the garden at Grand Avenue and First and Hope Streets.

14. South Coast Botanic Garden

26300 Crenshaw Boulevard, **Palos Verdes Peninsula,** CA 90274; (310) 544–6815; http://parks.co.la.ca.us/south_coast_botanic.html

*H*ERE YOU'LL FIND an inspiring eighty-seven-acre garden built on a sanitary landfill. Visit the successful reclamation project and discover a cultural center, lake, and stream, along with some 2,000 plant species.

❀ **Admission:** Fee.

Garden open: Daily 9:00 A.M. to 4:30 P.M.; closed December 25.

Further information: Call the South Coast Botanic Garden Foundation at (310) 544–1948 to learn more. Areas of rolling terrain are not wheelchair accessible. Much of the garden is ADA compliant, although many pathways are unpaved.

Directions: The garden is located on the Palos Verdes Peninsula, about one hour south of downtown Los Angeles.

15. Norton Simon Museum Sculpture Garden

411 West Colorado Boulevard, **Pasadena,** CA 91105;
(626) 449–6840; www.nortonsimon.org

HEN THE Norton Simon Museum reopened in 1999, the beautifully renovated galleries boasted the unmistakable panache of the architect responsible for the project, Frank Gehry. The museum unveiled a breathtaking redesign of the Sculpture Garden at the same time, created by Nancy Goslee Power & Associates.

A rich sense of history imbues the Norton Simon setting with distinction. The property dates to the 1870s, when Dr. Ezra and Jeanne Carr created a garden here known as Carmelita. In its heyday, the Carrs' beautiful landscape stood out from all others in Pasadena, with expansive plantings encompassing a wealth of species from near and far.

In its contemporary manifestation, the refreshed two-acre Norton Simon Sculpture Garden is a radiant oasis that looks to Monet's Giverny for inspiration.

The former actress and Academy Award–winner Jennifer Jones Simon, widow of Norton Simon, is credited with rousing the museum's board and its art department to go forward with the renovation of the museum and garden.

As you begin your tour of the garden from inside the lobby of the museum, gaze beyond the broad glass doors, and you'll discover beautiful views of the grounds revealed beyond.

In addition to the magnificent collection of sculptures that grace the Norton Simon garden, a convivial pond ornamented by water lilies emerges as a sparkling centerpiece.

Where concrete and angular water elements once dominated the scene, Power's flowing garden plan now lures visitors to explore curving pathways softened by fragrant lavender, the bright blooms of hibiscus, and billowy fountain grass.

The overall effect of the landscaping softens the surroundings, while the watery refuge invites the vitality of birds and the beguiling presence of dragonflies.

Notice the countless trees that animate the grounds, from the commanding form of a mature Moreton Bay fig to cheerful displays of flowers produced by tulip trees. Textural sago palms decorate the pond's discrete waterfall, while the elegant demeanor of weeping Kashmir cypresses enhances the pond itself.

Power designed eight compartmentalized plantings as an integral part of the garden scheme. Each of the sections is ascribed an appealing character defined by a specific color.

The Spring Walk, for instance, presents exuberant yellow trumpet flowers, daylilies, and the tipu tree, *Tipuana tipu*, with clusters of apricot to golden blooms. Continue all the way around the pond in a counterclockwise movement, and you'll arrive at the Grove, where the yellow theme continues with an impressive display of tulip trees (*Liriodendron*).

To span the areas accented with yellow, a palette of colors transitions from orange hues to pinks to blues to lavender. The area dubbed the Moon Garden is most impressive, with giant bamboo, Australian tree ferns, and Chinese flame tree. Here, too, appear the amazing spine-covered trunks of the floss silk tree, *Chorisia speciosa*, with showy flowers similar to hibiscus blooms.

Amid a trove of scented and evergreen shrubs, perennials, and grasses, structural plants like bird of paradise are interplanted throughout. The rich vegetation creates a backdrop, linking all together as you proceed along the garden's decomposed granite paths.

Wander through the naturalistic atmosphere of the Norton Simon garden, coming upon important works by artists such as Henry Moore, Aristide Maillol, and Barbara Hepworth, and you'll see how the alluring placement of the sculptures serves to elevate this very special milieu.

❀ **Admission:** Fee (garden free with museum admission).

Garden open: Wednesday through Monday noon to 6:00 P.M., Friday noon to 9:00 P.M.; closed Tuesday. Closed Thanksgiving, Christmas, and New Year's Day. The museum store closes fifteen minutes early. The cafe is open daily, except Tuesday, noon to 6:00 P.M., and Friday noon to 7:00 P.M.

Further information: Plan to enjoy lunch or a snack in the expanded and relocated Garden Café. Nestled under a grove of tulip trees in the Sculpture Garden, the cafe blends harmoniously with the landscape; call (626) 844–6992. The museum store features art books and unique gift items; call (626) 844–6942. The Sculpture Garden is fully ADA accessible.

Directions: The garden is in Pasadena, on the corner of Orange Grove and Colorado Boulevards, intersection of I–210 (Foothill Freeway) and California Highway 134 (Ventura Freeway). You'll find detailed directions and a map on the Web site.

16. The Huntington Botanical Gardens

The Huntington Library, Art Collections, and Botanical Gardens, 1151 Oxford Road; **San Marino,** CA 91108; (626) 405–2100; www.huntington.org

J. E. HUNTINGTON, creator of Southern California's interurban railway system, and his second wife, Arabella, set up a nonprofit trust to care for their exceptional library of books, fabulous art treasures, and extraordinary gardens. Opened in 1928, the Huntington Library, Art Collections, and Botanical Gardens extended to the public the rare opportunity to view the architectural and horticultural riches of the Huntingtons' San Marino property.

Truly one of the nation's most inspiring landscapes, the Huntington Botanical Gardens make a wonderful stopover for garden lovers and should be included in any itinerary planned for the Los Angeles area. Once ranch land planted with citrus and fruit trees, grain, and other crops, the vast property of nearly 600 acres Henry E. Huntington purchased in 1903 has been remarkably transformed. Today the Huntington occupies a parcel of some 200 acres.

Encompassing 150 landscaped acres, the Huntington Botanical Gardens include the renowned Desert and Palm Gardens, a refined three-acre Rose Garden, and a wonderfully untamed Subtropical Garden. Camellias are highlighted in the Japanese Garden and North Vista areas, while the Shakespeare Garden features some of the oldest roses in cultivation, along with such specimens as violets, pomegranates, columbines, and pansies, which the English bard alluded to in his writings. An informative booklet is available to facilitate a self-guided tour of the Huntington's principal gardens.

Distinguished by an elegant formality, the Huntington Botanical Gardens are set amidst imposing classical buildings and statuary, expanses of lawn, and aristocratic trees. Rose lover that I am, I was enchanted by the irresistibly opulent exhibition of roses. The lush area devoted to David Austin's English roses, in particular, reveals a marvelous display of the hybridizer's many-petaled, exquisitely fragrant flowers. Bordered by luxuriant azure *Agapanthus orientalis* 'Huntington Blue', the rose arbor is an admirable landmark to seek out, as is an eighteenth-century stone temple featuring the heavenly statue *Love, the Captive of Youth.*

Dramatic topography, a grand scale, and fascinating faux wood arbors are some of the striking characteristics of the Japanese Garden. Here the Japanese House displays and illuminates the Japanese art of flower arranging. Stroll on the camellia-lined walkways and wander through towering bamboo groves, enjoying shady havens. Note the intriguingly designed, cast-concrete arbors that are known to fool the eye with their skillful emulation of tree trunks and branches.

To discover the Zen Garden, which was completed in 1968,

you need to follow the pathway to the left after leaving the Japanese House. In this contemplative courtyard setting, you'll find a garden where the essence of flowing water is suggested by the raked pattern of sand and rock. Just beyond the Zen Garden, you'll find the bonsai court, with its specimens of dwarf trees.

Forty-five full-time gardeners lavish attention on the Huntington Botanical Gardens, helping to maintain the Huntington's eminent position worldwide. In the twelve-acre Desert Garden, displays of cacti and succulents offer a thrilling experience to aficionados of rare flora. Handsome coast live oaks indigenous to the property stand watch over more than 5,000 species of plants native to desert regions. Here are handsome aloe trees and a congregation of barrel-type cactus plants, the roly-poly *Echinocactus grusonii*. When numbers of these robust forms are planted together, passersby are inclined to stop and admire the beautiful, rhythmic composition the plants create.

The Desert Garden features a wealth of thorny plants, including such exotic specimens as the crown of thorns plant (*Euphorbia milii*), with its showy colorful red bracts. Many species found within the succulents and cacti display spectacular spiny protrusions, but they are famous also for the bountiful blossoms and brilliant flowers they produce throughout winter, spring, summer, and fall. A walk through the Desert Garden underscores the remarkable contrast between the alluring blooms and the bizarre appearance of these thorny plants.

In the second formal garden that H. E. Huntington created, the Palm Garden, you'll find more than 100 species of one of the founder's favorite trees. In a landscape brimming with so many types and specimens of palms, you'll find fishtail (*Caryota* species) and jelly palms (*Butia capitata*). With graceful arching fronds that sway in the breeze, thin elegant trunks reaching skyward, and huge clusters of brightly colored fruit, the dramatic, tropical palms have an extraordinary presence. Don't miss the Jungle Garden, the waterfall, and lily ponds. In these areas you'll encounter delightful displays of gingers, bromeliads, water lilies, bamboos, and calla lilies scattered throughout. Look for the magnificent giant ombú with its impressive gnarled trunk. This Argentinean native has unusual spongy wood that conserves water during periods of drought.

For overall impact, the grandeur of the North Vista is unequaled. Here the perfectly proportioned design brings together such elements as a Renaissance fountain, a seventeenth-century sculpture allée, ornamental shrubbery, an elaborate lawn, and a view of the San Gabriel Mountains. Visiting this stately formal garden is like entering a fine seventeenth-century European landscape. Although often reproduced, the garden is even more lovely than the image portrayed in photographs.

New areas at the Huntington include the Helen and Peter Bing Children's Garden. This expansive, unparalleled wonderland offers children a chance to participate in exciting sensory experiences, with features such as the Fog Grotto, Sonic Pool, Rainbow Room, and Prism Tunnel. Kinetic sculptures are creative elements designed to delight and inform kids from two to seven years of age.

A project in the planning stage is a traditional Chinese Garden. The first phase encompasses a three-acre landscape with a woodland backdrop and a large lake. Featuring authentic construction techniques and materials, it promises a stimulating experience that combines aesthetic and educational aspects of classical Chinese culture.

The glorious grounds of the Huntington Botanical Gardens will inspire you to return again and again to visit the art galleries, the open-air collection of sculptural masterworks, and more than 14,000 types of impeccably maintained plants.

❁ **Admission:** Fee; members free. First Thursday of every month is free to all visitors.

Garden open: Tuesday through Friday noon to 4:30 P.M., Saturday and Sunday 10:30 A.M. to 4:30 P.M.; closed Monday and most major holidays. Call or check the Web site for summer hours.

Further information: The bookstore carries an excellent selection of gift items and books. Reservations are required if you wish to have English tea in the Rose Garden Tea Room: Call (626) 683–8131 Tuesday through Sunday. The cafe is another agreeable option for lunch or a snack, and no reservation is necessary. You'll find a trove of information on the Web site, from details on tours to listings of special events and exhibits. All buildings are wheelchair accessible, and most major areas of the gardens are at least partially accessible to wheelchairs: Refer to the general brochure for a color-coded map of the grounds that indicates the best routes, as well as steep areas to be avoided. Wheelchairs are available at the visitor center, but you are advised to call (626) 405–2125 in advance to reserve one.

Directions: The Huntington is approximately thirty minutes north of downtown Los Angeles, east of California Highway 110 (Pasadena Freeway) and just south of the city of Pasadena and I–210 (Foothill Freeway).

Orange County Gardenwalks

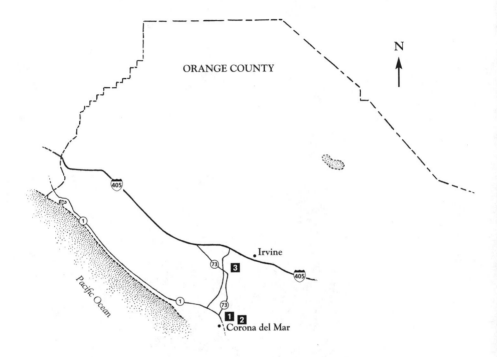

N

ORANGE COUNTY

Pacific Ocean

• Irvine

• Corona del Mar

1. Corona del Mar: Roger's
   Gardens
2. Corona del Mar: Sherman
   Library and Gardens

3. Irvine: University of California
   at Irvine Arboretum

1. Roger's Gardens

2301 San Joaquin Hills Road, **Corona del Mar,** CA 92625;
(949) 640–5800, (800) 647–2356; www.rogersgardens.com

*R*OGER'S GARDENS occupies a prime hilltop site overlooking the Pacific Ocean. Dubbed the Disneyland of nurseries, its seven-and-a-half acres of shops and gardens offer a welcoming oasis of horticultural beauty amid the hustle and bustle of busy Orange County. Arboretum-quality display plantings and thousands of the nursery's signature hanging baskets provide brilliant flower color year-round.

Whether your interest lies in heirloom or gourmet vegetables, colorful annuals, flowering vines, or distinctive and unusual perennials, Roger's has them all. Ramble through artful plantings of perennial color, drink in the fragrance of David Austin English roses, or admire a pair of leaping topiary dolphins as you make your way through the various sections of the nursery grounds.

Cooks and herb gardeners will find no fewer than twenty-four different varieties of basil in the herb garden section, while flower gardeners looking for inspiration need only visit the color bank of triangular display plots alongside the lower walkway to get a score of ideas on how to combine different seasonal plantings.

Roger's isn't just limited to outdoor plantings, though; there's a whole indoor world to explore as well. Stop in at one of the many garden rooms scattered along the pathway leading through the grounds. Each of these separate retail areas has something different to offer, from basic fertilizers and seed packets to garden gifts and one-of-a-kind pieces of garden art. Don't miss the gallery at the nursery's entrance, which features antique garden furniture, decorative garden items, seasonal and holiday collections, and a definitive selection of garden books.

❁ **Admission:** Free.

Garden open: Daily; hours vary by season so it's best to call ahead.

Further information: Check the Web site to get a calendar of special events and seminars or to take a virtual tour through the gardens. Paths are level and wheelchair accessible.

Directions: From Los Angeles, take Interstate 405 south to the Jamboree Road exit west. Follow Jamboree to San Joaquin Hills Road, turn left, and go about 3 blocks. Roger's Gardens will be on your right, just past the intersection of MacArthur Boulevard.

2. Sherman Library and Gardens

2647 East Pacific Coast Highway, **Corona del Mar,** CA 92625; (949) 673–2261; www.slgardens.org

*I*N CONTRAST to the cornucopia of botanical gardens found in nearby Los Angeles, there are but a handful of public gardens to visit in Orange County. The lack of quantity, however, is more than made up for by the quality of the gardens in this area.

The Sherman Library and Gardens is a case in point. Located in the center of downtown Corona del Mar, the two-acre landscape offers proof that good things come in small packages. Residential in both scale and design, the garden capitalizes on its superb growing climate to offer a near-perfect example of the indoor/outdoor living that California is famous for.

An emphasis on floral color, coupled with a liberal use of garden structures, unite the disparate parts of the garden. Flowering vines, including various colorful bougainvillea, cup-of-gold, and *Mandevilla* 'Alice Dupont', clamber up walls and trellises. Sturdy wisteria cloaks the arbor-covered walkways connecting the tropical conservatory and shaded lath house areas to the tiled patio and courtyard gardens that flow out from the main house, which is now home to the research library and gift shop.

The overall result is an effortless intermingling of garden rooms, each with a distinctive theme that highlights its particular group of plantings. Fountains, statuary, hanging baskets, and beds brimming with annual flower color offset the various botanical collections to great effect.

There is a progression to the plantings as well. The pots of colorful cyclamen and begonias that line the covered path leading away from the lath house shade gardens, for example, gradually give way to a display of tropical orchid cacti (*Epiphyllum*) that reside in the protective shade of an ancient California pepper tree (*Schinus molle*). These, in turn, ingeniously set the scene for the display of rare desert cacti and succulents that follows.

This dry garden of mostly desert plants from the arid regions of the American Southwest and Latin America is among the garden's most notable plant collections. The small but choice display includes such specimens as the Mexican grass tree (*Dasylirion longissima*); the so-called Madagascar palm (*Pachypodium lamieri*), which is not a palm at all but a relative of the common oleander; and a stupendous 6-foot-tall example of *Pedilanthus* sp., an unusual-looking succulent with smooth, pencil-thin stems, and reddish, bractlike tips.

Established in 1966, Sherman Gardens also offers remarkable collections of cycads, orchids, and tropical foliage plants, the latter two of which are housed inside a conservatory. Entering this tropical greenhouse, one is greeted by an explosion of foliar color: burgundy-leafed *Irisine*; purple-stemmed torch ginger; fiery red and orange bromeliads; cream, rose, and maroon-splotched leaves of giant fancy-leafed caladiums.

It is this consistent attention to detail that elevates Sherman Gardens to a level of excellence unmatched by similar botanical institutions. Any serious lover of horticulture must visit this garden.

❀ **Admission:** Fee.

Garden open: Daily 10:30 A.M. to 4:00 P.M.; closed on holidays. Gift shop hours are the same.

Further information: Amenities include a courtyard cafe where lunch is served Monday through Friday; call (949) 673–0033 for reservations. Phone the gift shop at (949) 673–0920. Check the Web site to learn about special events or to get a schedule of classes. Wide brick walkways are wheelchair accessible.

Directions: From Los Angeles, take I–405 to the Jamboree Road exit. Head west on Jamboree to California Highway 1 (Pacific Coast Highway), turn left (south), and follow for 1½ blocks. The gardens will be on your right.

3. University of California at Irvine Arboretum

Campus Drive at Jamboree Road, **Irvine,** CA 92697;
(949) 824–5833

LOCATED off one of Irvine's busiest thoroughfares, the UCI Arboretum's thirteen pristine acres offer a refreshing slice of natural beauty in an area better known for its tract-home developments and concrete-and-steel business parks.

As a working research facility attached to a university, the arboretum lacks the frills of an independently financed botanical garden: There's no gift shop, nor even so much as a public information booth. Maps of the grounds are available from a bulletin board at the arboretum's entrance, although the day I went, the supply was exhausted. If that's the case, you're pretty much on your own.

That's less of a drawback than it sounds. The plants are, for the most part, clearly labeled with their botanical name, common name, and place of origin, while the plant collections of interest to the public are confined to an area bordering the long, sloping lawn just past the arboretum's entrance.

Visit on a weekday afternoon and you may have the place to yourself, which makes for a pleasant sort of private-estate-garden atmosphere. Take in the plantings at a leisurely pace, and experience and appreciate the landscape as a whole much better without the human distraction.

Despite its name, the arboretum specializes primarily in South African bulbs, corms, and tubers. Its collection, which contains

more than 200 endangered species, rates as the largest institutional collection outside of South Africa. Many of the delicate bulb beauties are featured in the planting beds that ring the large sloped lawn area leading down to the San Joaquin Marsh Wildlife Preserve. Stroll on the circular path to explore these beauties.

The delicate flowers of *Gladiolus tristis*, the winter-hardy gladiolus, were among the only bulbs in bloom during a late fall visit, along with some early-blooming freesias. It is in spring that the arboretum reaches its full flowering glory, and undoubtedly that is the best time to visit.

While the focus of the arboretum is primarily on South African flowering bulbs, you'll also find here an outstanding aloe collection, probably one of the most extensive anywhere in the world. These large specimen plants make a dramatic display at the top of the sloped site; their large, spiky silhouettes are like punctuation marks in the clear blue sky.

❖ **Admission:** Free; parking meters require quarters.

Garden open: Monday through Saturday 9:00 A.M. to 3:00 P.M.; closed Sunday.

Further information: Most paths are accessible, although some sloped areas are not recommended for wheelchairs.

Directions: From Los Angeles, take I–405 south to the Jamboree Road exit west. Follow Jamboree for about a mile to Campus Drive, then turn left. The arboretum will be immediately on your right.

San Diego and Vicinity
Gardenwalks

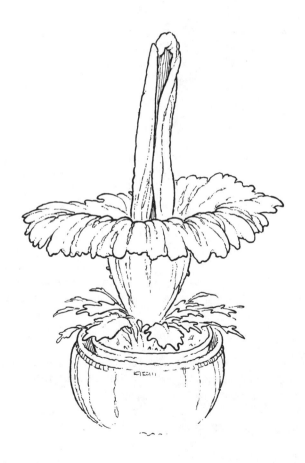

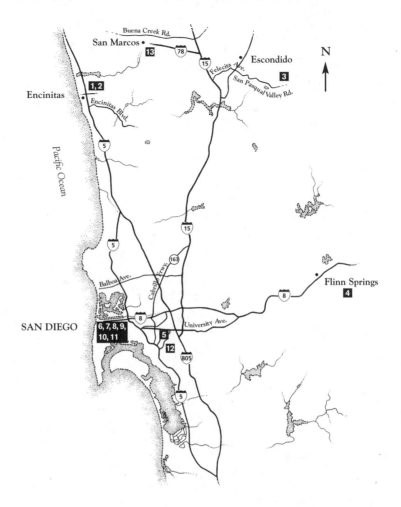

1. Encinitas: Quail Botanical Gardens
2. Encinitas: Weidners' Gardens
3. Escondido: San Diego Wild Animal Park
4. Flinn Springs: Summers Past Farms
5. San Diego: Balboa Park
6. San Diego: Balboa Park Botanical Building
7. San Diego: Desert Garden, Balboa Park
8. San Diego: Inez Grant Parker Memorial Rose Garden, Balboa Park
9. San Diego: Japanese Friendship Garden, Balboa Park
10. San Diego: Marston House and Gardens, Balboa Park
11. San Diego: Palm Canyon, Balboa Park
12. San Diego: San Diego Zoo Botanical Collection at Balboa Park
13. San Marcos: Buena Creek Gardens

1. Quail Botanical Gardens

230 Quail Gardens Drive, **Encinitas,** CA 92024; (760) 436–3036;
www.qbgardens.org

*S*ITTING ATOP a coastal bluff overlooking the Pacific, this 32-acre plant paradise was first established in the 1940s as the private residence of Ruth Baird Larabee, who filled the garden with collections of rare and unusual plants gathered during her extensive world travels. Cycads, aloes, subtropical fruit trees, and several rare dragon trees (*Dracaena draco*) are just some of the original plants that remain on the site today.

Open to the public since 1971, the gardens today are home to more than 10,000 plants representing more than 5,000 species, including some 75 species of bamboo, which make Quail one of the largest and most diverse collections in the country.

Quail's plant collections from all over the globe are grouped by climatic region, with a total of fifteen phytogeographic zones, as these groupings are called, represented. The fifteen zoned displays—encompassing tropical and dry Australia, tropical and dry South America, the Canary Islands, Madagascar, Southeast Asia, the Himalayas, Southeast Africa, Southwest Africa, South Africa, Central America, Baja California, Oceania, and the Mediterranean—form the backbone of the garden layout. Smaller horticultural and demonstration garden areas add thematic displays to diversify the mix.

With less stringent parameters, these thematic display gardens offer a cornucopia of botanical delights, from the spare, dramatic plant forms found in the New World Desert Garden to the exotic Subtropical Fruit Garden, with its more than seventy-five types of fruit-bearing plants like cherimoya, sapote, macadamia, star fruit, and rose apple.

The landscape potential of the region's indigenous flora is the focus of the California Native Plant Display Garden, while the Firescape Demonstration Garden offers homeowners a lesson in wildfire protection through the use of appropriate plant materials and landscaping techniques. Future plans call for the addition of an educational children's garden and a Native plants/Native people exhibit that will focus on plants used by indigenous Indian tribes, such as the Kumeyaay.

The Bamboo Display Garden, along the gardens' western edge, is home to Quail's first (and, so far, only) commissioned work of art—an organic sculpture/water feature created by well-known local artist James Hubbell.

The Walled Garden, part of the original Larabee estate, displays shade-tolerant plants, including some of the original cycads that were first planted there. Beyond it lies the Herb Garden, with medicinal and culinary herbs, and the Horticulture Display Garden, with old-fashioned roses, perennials, and flowering annuals. Fronting the original residence is a large, sloping lawn area graced by mature shade trees, flowering shrubs, and a Victorian gazebo that is popular for weddings.

From the lawn area, a path makes its way through Monterey cypress and Australian dammar pines toward the sound of water, eventually arriving at a deck overlooking the rocky watercourse and falls that mark the start of the gardens' new Tropical Rain Forest exhibit.

Thanks to its wonderfully mild coastal climate, Quail can create a rain forest experience outside, rather than in a conservatory, as most other botanical gardens must. Here you will find plants from the higher rainfall areas of the tropical and subtropical areas of the world: lush green tree ferns, elephant's ear, philodendron, aroids, king palms, epiphytes such as orchids and bromeliads, and a stunning Kashmir cypress whose weeping habit is beautifully offset by the adjacent large-leaf foliage plants.

✿ **Admission:** Fee.

Garden open: Daily 9:00 A.M. to 5:00 P.M.; closed Thanksgiving, Christmas, and New Year's Day. Gift shop and nursery is open daily 10:00 A.M. to 4:00 P.M.

Further information: Check the Web site to review a schedule of events and classes, to take a virtual tour of the garden, or to peruse the *Quail Tracks* newsletter. Call the gift shop at (760) 436–3036 for tour details; tours are free with admission. It should be noted that there are a number of steep inclines to navigate as you make your way through the gardens; partially wheelchair accessible.

Directions: From San Diego take Interstate 5 north about 20 miles to the Encinitas Boulevard exit. Head east for two blocks, then turn left onto Quail Gardens Drive. The garden entrance is a short ways up on the left. Check the Web site to see a map.

2. Weidners' Gardens

695 Normandy Road, **Encinitas,** CA 92024; (760) 436–2194; www.weidners.com

OWNER Evelyn Weidner and her late husband, Bob, initially opened this specialty flower nursery as a "temporary retirement project" back in 1973. But Weidners' Gardens quickly gained fame with its novel "dig your own fields" concept, which allows customers to dig their plants straight out of the nursery's growing fields. Now twenty-five years old, Weidners' boasts a mailing list of more than 8,500 customers for its newsletter.

The nursery maintains a seasonal business schedule based on the bloom cycle of its primary field offerings: rainbow-hued, giant-flower tuberous begonias during the spring and summer months; followed by velvet-petaled pansies and violas in the late fall. A selection of choice potted holiday poinsettias from the nearby Paul

Ecke Poinsettia Ranch round out its fall and winter selection.

While the dig-your-own stock fields remain the core of the business, Weidners' has expanded its inventory over the past few years to include a selection of Proven Winners–brand flowering perennials. Proven Winners plants are made up of a select group of unusual new hybrids developed by a group of individual plant breeders based in Israel, Germany, Japan, Australia, and the United States. Proven Winners plants are bred to be fast-growing, vigorous, and easy to maintain in the home garden.

Perhaps the best-known plant in the Proven Winners line is the "Supertunia," a vigorous-growing (up to an inch a day at the height of the growing season), everblooming petunia that took retail nurseries by storm a few years ago. More recent introductions include a verbena-like ground cover called 'Temari', and 'Million Bells' *Calibrachoa*, a type of cascading miniature petunia.

✳ **Admission:** Free.

Garden open: Seasonally March 1 to Labor Day, and November 1 to December 22, daily 9:30 A.M. to 4:30 P.M. Closed Tuesday; closed Thanksgiving Day. Call ahead to confirm open hours.

Further information: Partial wheelchair access.

Directions: From San Diego take I–5 north to the Leucadia Boulevard exit. Make an immediate left onto the eastern frontage road (Piraeus Street). The nursery is located at the corner of Piraeus Street and Normandy Road. Detailed driving directions and a map can be found on the Web site.

3. San Diego Wild Animal Park

15500 San Pasqual Valley Road, **Escondido,** CA 92027;
(760) 480–0100; www.sandiegozoo.org

*T*WENTY TIMES LARGER than its sister institution, the San
Diego Zoo, the San Diego Wild Animal Park offers a com-
pletely different experience from that of its urban sibling.

Largely barren when it opened to the public in 1972, the
grounds of the 2,200-acre wildlife preserve today showcase some of
the most diverse and unusual plant specimens found anywhere in
the United States. An accredited botanical garden since 1993, the
park's plant collections encompass some 4,000 species and 1,750,000
individual specimens—including more than 260 endangered species
of aloe, cactus, euphorbia, cycad, protea, palm, and agave.

The park's transformation from virtual desert to botanical paradise is the result of a long-term plan known as the Greening of the
Field. Developed by the park's horticulture department, the aim of
the plan is "to plant and improve [its] botanical collection for the
benefit of its animal collection and visitors alike." The project has
resulted in the planting of several thousands of trees as well as in
the naturalistic landscaping of the massive field enclosure to mimic
the native habitats of the animals that roam within.

The department's most ambitious project to date was the landscaping of the park's recently opened Heart of Africa exhibit, a
thirty-acre "walking safari" that allows visitors to get closer than
ever before to the featured wildlife. Horticulturists used plants primarily from central and southern Africa to re-create the many
diverse habitats represented in the exhibit.

Traveling by foot, visitors progress from dense forest to flourishing wetlands, sprawling savannas and, finally, open plains. In
addition to protea, *Pennisetum* (fountain grass), aloes, rocket pin-
cushions, and corn lilies (*Ixia*), the exhibit includes eight different

varieties of acacia trees, including *Acacia abyssinica*, *A. robusta*, *A. caffra*, and *A. xantophloea*, the beautiful fever tree.

In addition to the landscaped enclosures and other portions of the vast grounds, the park features ten specialty display gardens, including several unique single-species ones, such as protea, bonsai, fuchsia, and conifer. Most of these gardens are maintained, and some were even established, by local plant societies, whose members donate both their time and expertise to the projects.

Clustered together at the northern end of the park, behind the administration building, the first specialty garden encountered is the Epiphyllum (or "Epi") House which, with more than 600 specimens, is one of the most comprehensive exhibits of epiphytic cacti in the world. This particular collection is best viewed during the plants' bloom season, from March through early fall.

From the Epi House, visitors proceed to the Bonsai Pavilion, which houses about thirty specimens, and then to the Fuchsia House, following a pathway bordered by a small, gurgling stream that wends its way through the lath-covered structure. Numerous hanging baskets and inground plantings display the wide-ranging varieties that make up the fuchsia collection.

From here, the path leads to the Kupanda Falls Botanical Center, where the 1¼-mile, self-guided tour of the rest of the display gardens begins. The circular hiking trail leads visitors through the Old World Succulent Garden; the Baja (California) Garden, which has the largest global collection of native Baja plants outside of Baja itself; and the extensive, eight-plant-community display of native flora in the California Nativescapes Garden; and then back to the center.

From the center, the path descends through the Conifer Arboretum, which boasts more than 1,000 plants representing 400 species, including one of the last twelve North African cypresses left in the world. You'll also traverse the Protea Garden before the path wends its way back to the main section of the park.

Display gardens located elsewhere on the grounds include the Herb Garden, with more than 400 varieties of herbs, and the Water-Wise Demonstration Garden, an educational display developed in cooperation with the San Diego Xeriscape Council. Nearby, a recently added Compost Demonstration Site features the latest in composting techniques and equipment.

✿ **Admission:** Fee.

Garden open: Daily 9:00 A.M. to 4:00 P.M. Call or visit the Web site for extended summer hours.

Further information: Most of the areas in the park open to guests are wheelchair accessible.

Directions: From San Diego, take Interstate 15 north to the Via Rancho Parkway exit, then follow the signs to the Wild Animal Park.

4. Summers Past Farms

15602 Olde Highway 80, **Flinn Springs,** CA 92021; (619) 390–1523; www.summerspastfarms.com

*L*OCATED ON four rural acres in San Diego's East County, this highly successful retail herb-and-perennial nursery, which today grows in excess of 30,000 plants, started as a small herb plot intended only to satisfy the culinary needs of owner Sheryl Lozier. As Sheryl's interest in gardening grew, so did the plot, until seven years ago she and her husband, Marshall, decided to quit their jobs and devote themselves full-time to their plant-growing endeavor.

The couple set about converting Marshall's longtime family homestead into a retail nursery operation. Today, the former barn houses a gift shop and classroom space for Sheryl's wreath-making and culinary classes, while the former tractor shed has become a full-fledged soap-making factory.

The front yard is now a lath-covered retail area displaying assorted pots of herbs and flowers for sale. Beyond this, a vine-covered arbor houses a small cappuccino bar and a selection of chairs and tables for customers who want to linger a while.

Featured display plantings on the grounds include a potpourri demonstration garden; a flowering perennial garden; a children's garden; a "secret" walled garden of sweet peas, hollyhocks, and other cottage garden flowers; and of course an extensive patch filled with fragrant herbs.

❀ **Admission:** Free.

Garden open: Wednesday through Saturday 9:00 A.M. to 5:00 P.M., Sunday 10:00 A.M. to 5:00 P.M.; closed Monday and Tuesday. Call for holiday hours.

Further information: Check the Web site for special events and classes. A ramp provides wheelchair access to the barn.

Directions: From San Diego, take Interstate 8 east to the Harbison Canyon/Dunbar Lane exit. Turn left onto Dunbar Lane, then left again onto Old Highway 80. The nursery is located a half mile down on the right. Visit the Web site to see a map.

5. Balboa Park

1549 El Prado, **San Diego,** CA 92101; (619) 235–1100; www.balboapark.org or www.sannet.gov/park-and-recreation

*S*ITUATED ON some 1,400 acres in the city's urban core, Balboa Park is one of the most lushly planted city parks in the nation. Given its inauspicious beginnings, that's quite an achievement.

Although land was set aside in 1868 for the establishment of City Park, as it was then known, several early attempts to develop the rocky, arid, inhospitable terrain foundered, and it wasn't until the close of the nineteenth century that work got under way in earnest.

Pioneering nurserywoman Kate Sessions is largely credited with landscaping the northwestern portion of the park under a novel lease agreement with the city. In exchange for leasing land for a nursery on the park's northwestern edge, Sessions agreed to plant one hundred trees a year throughout the park for the duration of her lease.

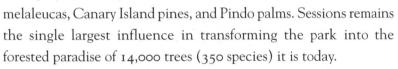

She far exceeded that quota, however, planting several thousand specimens in the park during the decade that she operated there. Many of the largest trees on the park's west mesa are her legacy, including the cork oaks, melaleucas, Canary Island pines, and Pindo palms. Sessions remains the single largest influence in transforming the park into the forested paradise of 14,000 trees (350 species) it is today.

Planting intensified as the city prepared to host the 1915 Panama-California Exposition, and the park was renamed Balboa, after the Spanish explorer. The Spanish colonial architecture from which the park gets its old-world charm is a legacy of the later California Pacific International Exposition, held 1935–36.

Today Balboa Park serves as the cultural heart of the city, housing museums, galleries, and performing arts sites, as well as several notable botanical gardens that offer a cornucopia of horticultural pleasures. Because each of these gardens offers a unique experience, they are detailed separately below.

❀ **Admission:** Free.

Garden open: Daily around the clock.

Further information: Call the visitor center at (619) 239–0512 or log on to either Web site to learn about the park's many gardens and facilities. Portions are wheelchair accessible.

Directions: Located in downtown San Diego, the park's western entrance is at Laurel Street and Sixth Avenue, and its eastern entrance at Park Boulevard and President's Way. Web sites provide maps and detailed directions.

6. Balboa Park Botanical Building

The Prado, Balboa Park, **San Diego,** CA 92101; (619) 235–1100

*D*ESIGNED BY well-known architect Carlton Winslow, this impressive domed building ranked as the largest lath structure in the world when it was built in 1915, and it remains among the largest ones today. The building measures 250 feet long, 75 feet wide, and 60 feet tall. It took more than 70,000 linear feet of redwood to construct it.

The interior of the Balboa Park Botanical Building houses 2,100 permanent plantings representing more than 350 different species of tropical plants, including an outstanding collection of ferns. Its many niches invite discovery, with a variety of plants chosen to accommodate a broad range of botanical interests. The plantings are augmented by seasonal floral exhibits, making for an ever-changing display of botanical beauty.

Winslow also designed the Lily Pond in front of the Botanical Building, which is actually two ponds separated by a balustrade bridge. The smaller upper lily pond, closest to the Botanical Building, is planted with a selection of popular water lilies (*Nymphaea* sp.), as well as a variety of bog plants, including papyrus (*Cyperus papyrus*), Japanese arrowhead, primrose creeper, and water iris.

The lower lily pond, the larger of the two at 193 feet long and 42 feet wide, was designed in the manner of a reflecting pool, but its formal lines are broken up by the colorful water lilies and spectacular Indian lotus plants (*Nelumbo lucifera*) that bloom on the water's surface. Brilliant orange Japanese koi, sun-basking turtles, and splashing ducks add a realistic touch of movement to the idyllic scene.

✾ **Admission:** Free.
Garden open: Friday through Wednesday 10:00 A.M. to 4:00 P.M.; closed Thursday and city holidays.
Further information: The building is mostly wheelchair accessible.
Directions: The Botanical Building is located on the Prado, to the west of the Museum of Art.

7. Desert Garden, Balboa Park

Park Boulevard, **San Diego**, CA 92101; (619) 235–1100

*T*HE DESERT GARDEN, which dates from 1935, moved to its present location on the east side of Park Boulevard in 1977. Encompassing two-and-a-half acres, this garden showcases some 1,300 drought-resistant cacti and succulents representing more than 150 species from around the world. Plantings include several coral trees (*Erythrina*), giant tree aloes, and surrealistic-looking boojum trees from Baja California.

> ❀ **Admission:** Free.
> **Garden open:** Daily around the clock.
> **Further information:** This garden is only partially wheelchair accessible.
> **Directions:** The garden is north of the footbridge at Park Boulevard, by the Natural History Museum.

8. Inez Grant Parker Memorial Rose Garden, Balboa Park

Off Park Boulevard, **San Diego**, CA 92101; (619) 235–1100

*L*YING ADJACENT to the Desert Garden, the three-acre Inez Grant Parker Memorial Rose Garden contains more than 2,500 roses representing more than 200 varieties, including hybrid teas, grandifloras, floribundas, ramblers, shrubs, and old garden roses.

Established in 1975, the rose garden is an officially designated All-America Rose Selections Display Garden. It boasts a simple but effective design, with tiered rose beds forming concentric rings around a circular arbor covered with climbing white *Rosa* x *fortuniana*. Stone benches in the shade of the pergola offer an ideal spot to enjoy a sack lunch or relax. Thanks to San Diego's mild, Mediterranean climate, visitors will find roses in bloom from March through December, with peak bloom occurring from April through early June.

❀ **Admission:** Free.

Garden open: Daily around the clock.

Further information: The garden is mostly wheelchair accessible.

Directions: The rose garden is located south of the footbridge at Park Boulevard, by the Natural History Museum.

9. Japanese Friendship Garden, Balboa Park

2125 Park Boulevard (mailing address), **San Diego,** CA 92101; (619) 232–2780; www.niwa.org

*S*ITUATED NEAR the Spreckels Organ Pavilion in the park's center, the eleven-and-a-half-acre Japanese Friendship Garden will be the largest Japanese garden in the United States when it is completed.

The garden is named San-Kei-En, or Three Scenery Garden, for the water, pastoral, and mountain landscape themes it encompasses. The master plan calls for the garden to be built in three phases. During the first phase, a small entry garden, an exhibit house, a traditional sand and stone garden, and a viewing platform overlooking a small canyon were completed.

Designed by Japanese architect Takeshi Nakajima, this part of the garden and its structures are distinguished by simple materials and economical design. A wisteria-covered arbor graces the viewing platform, while in the sand and stone garden, the sand is raked in simple patterns of lines and concentric circles around the spare monuments of stone.

Restrained plantings in the entry garden include pines, azaleas, sunburst locust, Japanese maple, saucer magnolia, purple-leaf plum, ginkgo, camphor, and variegated mock orange. Several varieties of bamboo fences serve to connect the disparate parts of the garden.

The second phase of development, currently under way, encompasses the canyon portion of the garden. No date for the final phase of development has been set, since funding has yet to be secured.

✿ **Admission:** Fee.

Garden open: Memorial Day through Labor Day: Monday through Friday 10:00 A.M. to 5:00 P.M., Saturday and Sunday 10:00 A.M. to 4:00 P.M. Call to confirm other seasonal hours.

Further information: Call (619) 231–0048 to confirm open hours for the Tea Pavilion, serving food and specialty teas. Call the office at (619) 232–2721 or check the Web site to learn more about expansion plans for this wonderful garden. Partially wheelchair accessible.

Directions: The garden is located near the Spreckels Organ Pavilion; log on to the Web site to see a detailed map and directions to the garden.

10. Marston House and Gardens, Balboa Park

3525 Seventh Avenue, **San Diego,** CA 92101; (619) 298–3142

*D*ESIGNED BY renowned turn-of-the-twentieth-century architect Irving Gill, the historic Marston House is located on Seventh Avenue along Balboa Park's western edge. Completed in 1905, the Craftsman-style home served as the residence of the city founding father George W. Marston and his family.

The expansive gardens that surround the house are landscaped, for the most part, in the English romantic style with California overtones. San Diego horticulture pioneer Kate Sessions was responsible for much of the gardens' design, including most of the mature tree specimens found on the site. Some of the more distinctive of these include the lemon-scented gums (*Eucalyptus citriodora*), deodar cedars, and Canary Island pines.

Sessions also planted the perennial beds that border the long sloping lawn on the southeastern side of the property, and the cactus and succulent garden that descends down the side of the canyon at the rear.

By contrast, the garden areas on the north side of the house are much more formal in look; they are the work of a succession of various nationally known landscape architects, among them John Nolen and William Templeton Johnson. Here roses and other flowering plants are confined within geometrically formal planting beds, while a stone balustrade separates the entire area from the wilder landscape beyond.

The concept works best in the semienclosed walled patio garden, largely because of the beauty of the tile mural that covers the rear wall. The decorative pattern of the tile recalls the Islamic-style garden, much admired by prominent San Diegans at the time.

A registered historic site, the Marston House and Gardens are managed by the San Diego Historical Society, with the grounds maintained as a public historic garden by the city's Park and Recreation Department.

�֎ **Admission:** Free for self-guided tours of gardens and grounds.
Garden open: Daily.
Further information: Guided tours of the house and gardens are offered Friday, Saturday, and Sunday noon to 4:00 P.M.; fee charged for the one-hour tour of the house or the one-and-a-half-hour tour, which also takes in the rose and herb gardens of the four-and-a-half-acre estate. Partially wheelchair accessible.
Directions: The Marston House and Gardens are located in the northwest corner of Balboa Park, at Upas Street and Seventh Avenue.

11. Palm Canyon, Balboa Park

San Diego, CA 92101; (619) 235–1100

*P*ALM CANYON lies in the center of Balboa Park, just west of the Spreckels Organ Pavilion. A wooden footbridge crosses over the canyon, weaving between queen palms, blue fan palms (*Brahea armata*), and bamboolike *Chamaedorea* underplanted with clusters of crinum lilies, ginger, and other subtropicals.

The canyon itself contains 450 palms (58 species) within its two acres, including a prominent group of Mexican fan palms (*Washingtonia robusta*) that date to the early 1900s. A wooden staircase to the south of the House of Charm leads to a narrow path that wends its way along the canyon floor, flanked on either side by towering palms that eclipse the sky, creating moist, cool conditions for plants like clivia, philodendron, and elephant's ear to thrive in. The dominant palm within the canyon is the pendulous paradise palm, *Howea fosterana*. Sentry palms, pygmy date palms, and the graceful feather palms are also in abundance.

The point where the plantings end and the natural canyon continues down toward California Highway 163, is a good place to turn around and head back; the only way out is to retrace your steps the way you came.

✿ **Admission:** Free.
Garden open: Daily around the clock.
Further information: Palm Canyon is not wheelchair accessible.
Directions: The canyon is located south of the House of Charm and opposite the Japanese Friendship Garden.

12. San Diego Zoo Botanical Collection at Balboa Park

2920 Zoo Drive, **San Diego**, CA 92101; (619) 234–3153; www.sandiegozoo.org

ALTHOUGH best known for its animals, the San Diego Zoo has been an accredited botanical garden since 1993. Thanks to San Diego's mild climate, the grounds are filled with a variety of colorful blooms year-round.

Located in the northeast corner of Balboa Park, the zoo grounds encompass one hundred acres and incorporate ten bioclimatic zones in which more than 6,500 different species of plants are showcased.

Included among its several notable botanical collections are more than 400 species of palms, 150 aloe species, and more than 800 types of orchids, as well as 49 coral tree taxa and cultivars. Its cycad collection, which totals some 80 species, contains such unusual examples as *Encephalartos munchii*, the munch cycad, and *E. natalensis*, the Natal giant cycad.

Some plants in the zoo's collection are grown as feed for specific animals. Several of its thirty-one varieties of bamboo, for example, are integral to the diet of the two giant pandas on loan to the zoo from China, while foliage from its many eucalyptus trees satisfy the appetites of its resident koalas. And its thirty-one ficus species include those necessary to the survival of the zoo's Sumatran rhino population.

Although some of the plant collections, such as the palms and cycads, are grouped together in a specific area of the park—in the case of the cycads, it's at the top of the trail leading down to Bear Canyon—plants from other collections can be found scattered throughout the grounds. Orchids, for example, can be found throughout the Tiger River exhibit, as well as in Fern Canyon and at the main orchid greenhouse.

Also scattered throughout the grounds are several whimsical topiary animals. The most impressive are the two life-size elephants that grace the zoo's entrance plaza. The ivy-covered beasts incorporate ingenious internal irrigation systems that maintain optimum moisture levels for the growing plant material.

❀ **Admission:** Fee.

Garden open: Daily 9:00 A.M. to 4:00 P.M. Call or check the Web site for extended summer hours.

Further information: Wheelchairs and electric personal scooters are available for rental, on a limited basis, near the front entrance of the zoo. The regular guided bus tour is accessible to guests in wheelchairs.

Directions: The zoo is located on the eastern edge of Balboa Park, at Park Boulevard and Zoo Drive.

13. Buena Creek Gardens

418 Buena Creek Road, **San Marcos**, CA 92069; (760) 744–2810;
www.buenacreekgardens.com

*B*UENA CREEK GARDENS offers the largest selection of flowering trees, shrubs, vines, and perennial plants in Southern California—more than 5,000 varieties altogether. This four-acre retail nursery and its display gardens are a year-round flowering mecca for plant enthusiasts.

Featured display gardens include a half-acre Sun Perennial Garden, a Shade Garden, a Palm Canyon, and a Drought-Tolerant Garden. Of these, the Sun Perennial Garden is the showcase and, as such, is constantly being updated to incorporate the latest and most popular hybrids. Recent additions to the site include several unusual varieties of ornamental grasses—just a small sampling of the more than twenty varieties offered for sale by the nursery.

The nursery is also an officially accredited American Hemerocallis (Daylily) Society Display Garden, with some 2,000 different varieties of daylilies in cultivation year-round. From old classics to the latest modern tetraploids, Buena Creek's daylily selection is geared to both the casual home gardener and the serious hybridizer/collector. Most of the daylilies are grown for sale through the nursery's mail-order division, Cordon Bleu Daylilies, but visitors to the nursery are free to buy any of the selections they find on-site that appeal to them.

While the daylily bloom season begins in May and continues through summer and into fall, the three large growing fields are at their best during the month of June, when the daylily bloom reaches its peak. The crop's bloom time is generally consistent from year to year, but vagaries in the weather can occasionally advance or delay the season. This was the case following the 1997–98 winter weather phenomenon known as El Niño, which delayed the start of the 1998 bloom season by a full month and a half. For this reason, daylily aficionados who plan to visit the nursery during bloom time are encouraged to call ahead for a bloom-status report to avoid possible disappointment.

❀ **Admission:** Free.

Garden open: Thursday through Sunday 10:00 A.M. to 4:00 P.M.; closed Monday through Wednesday. Call to confirm open hours, or check the Web site for special closure dates.

Further information: Most of the gardens are fully wheelchair accessible; assistance provided for restroom accessibility.

Directions: From San Diego take I–15 north about 35 miles to the Deer Springs Road exit. Follow Deer Springs to the Y junction at Twin Oaks Valley Road. Turn left onto Twin Oaks, continue about ¼ mile to Buena Creek Road. Turn right; the nursery will be on your right. Visit the Web site to see a map.

Garden Lodgings

*L*IKE MANY TRAVELERS who maintain full, even jam-packed itineraries, I sometimes yearn for a quiet place to unwind at the end of a heavily scheduled day of trekking from one garden destination to another. It's not the confines of a rented room I seek, but rather a secluded, preferably verdant area for contemplation.

The congenial bed-and-breakfast inns recommended here provide guests with the customary amenities, and then some. In general, you'll find luscious breakfasts and freshly baked snacks, complimentary beverages, private baths, and furnishings intended for your comfort and pleasure.

Criteria for inclusion, however, extend beyond such desirable attributes. In the end, it was a special sort of aesthetic sensibility, perhaps best described as a naturalistic style of garden design, that I found to be the most inviting.

In my attempts to find places that would add an element of enchantment to each day's sojourn, I looked for agreeable proprietors who maintain relaxed settings. Sites range from a tiny village lot to an expansive property with woods, meadows, and gardens.

Whether you like a quiet stroll before breakfast, or require a few minutes to breathe in the night air after an evening meal, serene and private places await.

Please note that cancellation policies vary. Always request details when phoning for reservations.

✿ **Price Code**

The following price code is for two adults.
The codes do not include taxes and other fees.

$ $112 to $145
$$ $146 to $250
$$$ $251 to $399
$$$$ More than $400

NORTHERN CALIFORNIA

Carter House Inns

301 L Street, **Eureka,** CA 95501, (707) 444–8062,
(800) 404–1390; www.carterhouse.com

CELEBRATED for majestic ancient redwoods found both to the north and south, the seaport town of Eureka provides an invigorating rest from a scenic motor tour through the region's forests and seashore.

Overlooking Humboldt Bay, Carter House consists of a group of restored historic buildings; their antique furnishings and luxurious amenities add up to tasteful, unstuffy accommodations. It comes as a surprise that one of these handsome Victorians, the Hotel Carter, was actually constructed not so long ago by Mark Carter. A Eurekan by birth, Carter stayed true to Eureka's vernacular architecture in building this lovely complement to the original Carter

House, located just across the street. The rooms in Bell Cottage and very private Carter Cottage present further choices when booking a room.

The Carter House's highly praised gourmet cuisine draws countless callers to Humboldt's county seat. Weary travelers disembarking in Eureka applaud the mouthwatering repasts of Restaurant 301, with its award-winning wine cellar.

Touring the bountiful organic kitchen gardens, a stone's throw away from the bay itself, is yet another pleasure of a stay here. In this expansive garden with its Mediterranean-style plantings, fresh ingredients are harvested daily to be used by the hotel's chefs. Perusing the imaginative fare on a typical Restaurant 301 menu, you are likely to find an assortment of edible flowers.

More than thirty species are cultivated in the Carter House garden, where an inviting symmetry distinguishes the garden's design. With centrally aligned birdbaths and fountain, the display features a rainbow of edible blooms that includes black pansies and signet marigolds, pinks and rose-scented geraniums, primroses and daylilies. Tubular nasturtiums and runner beans scale the heights of trellises, while jasmine drapes over an arbor. In season, masses of flowers and irrepressible greens overflow their beds. Garden aficionados who are guests of the Carter House may inquire about assisting in harvesting the fruits and vegetables, blossoms, and herbs that are used by the hotel restaurant.

✿ **Rates:** $$–$$$$.
Open: Year-round.
Facilities: Thirty-two rooms and suites with private baths; full breakfast served (small service charge). To arrange a tour of the Carter House garden (April to December), contact Carter House prior to visiting. Two rooms are wheelchair accessible.
Directions: Carter House is located 300 miles north of San Francisco and 75 miles south of the Oregon border. U.S. Highway 101 runs directly through Eureka, so whether journeying north from San Fran-

cisco, or south through Washington and Oregon, you can plan a stopover at the Carter House.

Mill Rose Inn

615 Mill Street, **Half Moon Bay,** CA 94019; (650) 726–8750, (800) 900–7673; www.millroseinn.com

ESTEEMED for its lovely beaches and arty ambience, the seaside town of Half Moon Bay entices garden lovers to its charming main street where frequent flower markets overflow onto the town's walkways. A stay in Half Moon Bay also affords easy access to Woodside and the ravishing estate Filoli, with its grand house and extraordinary gardens.

A visit to the Mill Rose Inn promises fetching flower beds and borders, indoor vases, and outdoor planters filled with a frequently changing array of scented, showy blooms. Rooms are appointed in a romantic style, with a delicious breakfast served in your suite if you so choose. To cap off your day, sumptuously rich desserts are provided in the evening.

✿ **Rates:** $$–$$$.
Open: Year-round.
Facilities: Six rooms and suites with private baths, full breakfasts, feather beds, afternoon wine and cheese, and garden views. Visit the Web site for special rates and additional details.
Directions: The inn is about thirty-five minutes south of San Francisco and twenty-five minutes from San Francisco International Airport. Visit the Web site to see a map and get detailed directions.

Madrona Manor

1001 Westside Road, P.O. Box 818, **Healdsburg,** CA 95448; (707) 433–4231, (800) 258–4003; www.madronamanor.com

MADRONA MANOR is listed as a National Historic District, and as such it offers genteel accommodations in an elegant country atmosphere. The inn consists of the main building—a distinctive Victorian mansion built in 1881—and the adjacent Carriage House, the Garden Cottage, the Meadow Wood Complex, and Schoolhouse Complex.

The garden setting here is irresistible, with eight acres of well-groomed lawns, a palm terrace, formal flower beds decorated with fountains, and dignified woodlands.

Surrounded by a noble balustrade, the manor's swimming pool presents a restful spot from which one can view the landscape's orderly citrus orchard and lively floral displays.

Head gardener Geno Ceccato can be counted on to provide the innkeepers with ample material for indoor arrangements. Continually cultivating new species, Ceccato plants prominent annuals such as cleome and amaranthus to add character, verve, and a rather playful element to flower beds. Scarlet and lavender salvias, multicolored cosmos, morning-glory vines, and impatiens are all used at times to adorn slopes, freestanding fences, and borders.

Appetizing herbs are interspersed with various edibles in a lovely terraced culinary garden, another laboratory of sorts for Ceccato. In season, he cultivates some thirty varieties of tomatoes and, in the fall, fifteen varieties of lettuce to serve at the manor's restaurant. The lovely kitchen garden and grounds are a pleasure to behold regardless of the season.

Madrona Manor presents an excellent vantage point for touring the Korbel Garden located in nearby Guerneville and the stunning Ferrari-Carano Winery landscape in Dry Creek Valley.

✿ **Rates:** $$–$$$$.
   Open: Year-round.
   Facilities: Antique furnishings distinguish the Manor's twenty-three rooms and suites; all with private baths and full buffet breakfast. One room is wheelchair accessible.
   Directions: Madrona Manor is 65 miles north of San Francisco in Sonoma County's wine country; ½ mile west of U.S. 101.

Fetzer Inn at Valley Oaks Ranch

Fetzer Vineyards, 13601 Old River Road, **Hopland,** CA 95449;
(800) 846–8637; www.fetzer.com

As IF the area's stunning coastline and convenient access to the picturesque town of Mendocino are not attraction enough, Fetzer Vineyards presents garden travelers with a chance to experience their renowned organic gardens (see the Winery Gardenwalks chapter), and welcoming accommodations.

A fabulous spot to unwind, the Fetzer Inn at Valley Oaks Ranch offers guests a comfortable, relaxed decor and a pool in season. All rooms have patios from which you can admire the adjacent vineyards. The Fetzer Vineyards' sublime five-acre, organically farmed garden will certainly prove to be a high point of any visit here.

Other delights include sampling Fetzer wines at the nearby tasting room and visitor center, where picnicking on the terrace is the order of the day. Select from luscious gourmet fare available at the Garden Cafe.

Alluring, landscaped grounds are a hallmark of Fetzer Vineyards. Near the tasting room you'll notice plantings of fragrant herbs such as lavenders, rue and artemisia varieties, thyme, marjoram, and oregano, together with olive and fig trees and superb pomegranates cloaked in lime green, burnished oval leaves.

> ❀ **Rates:** $–$$; Haas House $$$$.
> **Open:** Year-round.
> **Facilities:** Book one of the six rooms or suites in the Carriage House, the Valley Oaks Cottage, or roomy Haas House, all with private baths and a wine amenity. A wraparound porch, country kitchen, and dining room add to the charms of Haas House, which can accommodate seven or more: the perfect place for a gathering of friends or family. Rates vary seasonally. The Valley Oaks Cottage is wheelchair accessible.
> **Directions:** The Fetzer Inn is located approximately two hours north of San Francisco's Golden Gate Bridge and 1 mile east of U.S. 101 in the town of Hopland, Mendocino County.

Ten Inverness Way Bed & Breakfast

P.O. Box 63, **Inverness,** CA 94937; (415) 669–1648;
www.teninvernessway.com

DELIGHTFULLY COZY, Ten Inverness Way calls itself the perfect inn
for people who like books, long walks, and cottage gardens. Located
in the enchanting environs of Marin County's village of Inverness,
the inn is a civilized hostelry, which displays a diminutive kitchen
garden in the rear.

For a relaxing soak after a day spent wandering around the
Point Reyes Seashore, try the hot tub found in the garden cottage
located just a few yards up the walkway.

❀ **Rates:** $–$$.
Open: Year-round.
Facilities: Four rooms plus one small suite, all with queen beds and private baths. A full breakfast is served. You'll savor fresh-baked cookies
and tea in the afternoon and complimentary wine and cheese in the
evening. Easy access to beach-combing, hiking, horseback riding, bird-
watching, and wine country gardens a bit farther afield make this an
exceptional base for exploring the Bay Area.
Directions: This B&B is about one hour north of San Francisco.
Detailed directions are on the Web site.

Brookside Vineyard Bed & Breakfast

3194 Redwood Road, **Napa,** CA 94558; (707) 944–1661

TRAVELING Napa roadways often means assuming your place in a
motorcade of pilgrims determined to sample the products of every
winery en route. Given correct directions and an advance reservation, however, you'll find a peaceful respite at this California
mission–style retreat tucked away outside the town of Napa in the
heart of the wine country.

By the time we learned about Brookside Vineyard Bed &
Breakfast, its three rooms were already booked. I had to content myself

with strolling the grounds of the inn's intimate, sequestered setting, and chatting with the owners, Susan and Tom Ridley. (We made certain to reserve a room the next time we passed through the area!)

As you approach the inn along a tree-lined entry road, the home's sprawling form emerges amid regular rows of grapevines in the warmly colored Napa soil. Like a welcoming vision, it is an integral part of the pattern created by the linear plantings.

In their working vineyard, the Ridleys raise fine-quality Syrah grapes that are sold to local wineries and used for their own label. Nestled in this intriguing landscape, Brookside Vineyard B&B offers guests quite a few surprises. Once settled into one of three spacious rooms, wander out back to glimpse the swimming pool area with its terraced gardens and lavish display of roses and lavender.

Lovingly tended grounds here invite repose. Whether you choose to sit by the pool and look out over towering oak and bay trees, or prefer to explore Brookside's grassy lawns, you'll find nothing contrived about Brookside Vineyard's landscape.

A hidden bench may persuade you to pause for a while, but take time to wander through the formidable stand of Douglas fir adjacent to the fruit orchard. The setting is simply wonderful for regrouping from the day's activities. Here you can take pleasure in gazing out over land that reaches back toward a meandering creek planted with native specimens.

The B&B's proximity to nearby garden destinations makes many wonderful day trips feasible.

✿ **Rates:** $–$$.
Open: Year-round.
Facilities: Three comfortable rooms with private baths. One features a fireplace, sauna, and private patio. Full breakfast served.
Directions: Brookside Vineyard is located about one hour north of San Francisco, just north of the town of Napa and west of California Highway 29.

Gerstle Park Inn

34 Grove Street, **San Rafael,** CA 94901; (415) 721–7611;
(800) 726–7611; www.gerstleparkinn.com

A GRACIOUS INN featuring elegant yet unpretentious accommodations, Gerstle Park opened for business in December 1995. Although the one-and-a-half-acre property in Marin County is within walking distance of downtown San Rafael, Gerstle Park's superb setting makes one feel miles away from the bustle of the town. Situated on a quiet cul-de-sac, the historic mansion and carriage house adjoin wooded parklands that are part of Marin County open space.

Built before the turn of the twentieth century, the inn's beautifully restored buildings are surrounded by giant oaks, cedars, and redwoods. The main house, which measures 6,800 square feet, contains eight spacious guest rooms, elegant parlors, a dining area, and a hospitable kitchen where guests will find delicious treats day and night. The appealing, fully equipped one-bedroom suites located in the carriage house are ideal for an extended stay.

In this unexpectedly tranquil setting, brick walkways connect patios to garden areas where you can stroll undisturbed. Many rooms have decks or patio access that open onto the inn's interior gardens and beguiling hillside pasture. Deer are frequently seen in the upper orchard.

What makes Gerstle Park Inn so convenient is that one can retreat from the bustling activity of nearby tourist locales to enjoy this quiet haven, and still take advantage of day trips to coastal destinations, winery gardens, specialty nurseries, and public gardens that may be included in your itinerary. From here, San Francisco is readily accessible by car or ferry, Berkeley's gardens are within easy reach of the Richmond/San Rafael Bridge, and Sonoma's treasures are but a short drive north.

❀ **Rates:** $$.

Open: Year-round.

Facilities: Twelve rooms, including cottages with kitchen facilities for extended stays. All with private bath; full breakfast included.

Directions: The inn is located approximately twenty minutes north of San Francisco's Golden Gate Bridge; take U.S. 101 north to the Central San Rafael exit. Detailed directions are on the Web site.

SANTA CRUZ TO SANTA BARBARA

J. Patrick House Bed & Breakfast

2990 Burton Drive, **Cambria,** CA 93428; (805) 927–3812,
(800) 341–5258; www.jpatrickhouse.com

MEXICAN SAGE, the evergreen blue pea and princess flower shrubs, and countless fuchsias are among the blooming plants that grace J. Patrick House's grounds. Located only several miles from Hearst Castle in charming Cambria, the wooded setting provides a refreshing contrast to the sweeping ocean vistas of California Coast Highway 1 and the rolling hills of nearby Paso Robles Wine Country.

An attractive wooden pergola festooned with enticing jasmine connects the main log cabin to the carriage house. The inn's two buildings provide impeccably maintained accommodations. Guests enjoy breakfast in the garden room and wine and hors d'oeuvres in a cozy living room in the main log cabin.

A fairly recent addition to the landscape is an array of succulents, installed alongside a fenced area next to the pergola. Walking around the inn, you'll find water fountains, statuary, birdbaths, and a gazing globe amid the various plantings around the grounds. When you visit, stroll around and search out colorful flowering maples (*Abutilon*), poor man's rhododendron (*Impatiens oliveri*), and other appealing flora surrounding the inn.

❀ **Rates:** $$.

Open: Year-round.

Facilities: Eight rooms feature wood-burning fireplaces and private baths. Full breakfast served; wine and hors d'oeuvres offered each evening, and freshly baked chocolate chip cookies and milk provided before bed.

Directions: Cambria is located just south of Hearst Castle, San Simeon, on California Coast Highway 1 (Pacific Coast Highway); approximately four hours from either San Francisco or Los Angeles. From U.S. 101, approach the town by following California Highway 46 west.

The Just Inn

Justin Vineyards & Winery, 11680 Chimney Rock Road, **Paso Robles,** CA 93446; (805) 237–4149, (800) 726–0049; www.justinwine.com

ON CALIFORNIA'S Central Coast, the 160-acre family owned and operated Justin Vineyards and Winery runs also the Just Inn bed-and-breakfast suites. An inviting getaway, the inn is located less than 10 miles from the Pacific Ocean, in a rural setting of beautiful hills, imposing oaks, and superb landscaping.

Situated in the wine country region of Paso Robles, the Just Inn gardens combine Mediterranean accents with English-style plantings. Garden elements include a large pergola overgrown with luxuriant vines; stately terracotta planters embellished with lions' heads; and perhaps the garden's most prominent component: warm-toned, orange-tinted stone retaining walls, which delineate the garden's overall framework.

Flower beds overflowing with lavender and herbs, expansive borders filled with roses and flowering specimens, and a water garden that can be viewed from the balcony of each suite are all encircled with this attractive stonework. The flowing lines created by the rough, low retaining walls integrate the garden into the vineyard landscape.

Near the town of Paso Robles, yet worlds away from any sort of stress or noise, the inn provides convenient access to the neighboring

Sycamore Farms, the Hearst Castle Gardens, and the town of Cambria, where you can visit the quaint Heart's Ease Herb Shop & Gardens.

✿ **Rates:** $$$.
Open: Year-round.
Facilities: Four suites feature first-class amenities and comfortably elegant country decor, with fireplaces and private baths; full breakfast served. Staying at the Just Inn is just like luxuriating in a private villa, where you can expect to be pampered. A fine restaurant provides gourmet dinners served in the intimate Deborah's Room.
Directions: The Just Inn is conveniently located midway between San Francisco and Los Angeles. From the intersection of U.S. 101 and CA 46 east, proceed 8 miles west on Twenty-fourth Street, then onto Lake Nacimiento Road. At Chimney Rock Road continue driving west 7 miles to the inn.

Glenborough Inn

1327 Bath Street, **Santa Barbara,** CA 93101; (805) 966–0589, (888) 966–0589; www.glenboroughinn.com

A VIBRANT rose garden bids a cheerful welcome at Glenborough Inn. Lavender and evening primrose, poppies, and innumerable other flowers add to the impressive streetside display. Here also ornamental plum trees enhance and echo the inn's painted trim. This entranceway garden underscores the facade of the main house, a Craftsman-style bungalow. The inn's other three separate buildings are La Casa, a private cottage, which is located right next door; the Victorian Cottage, circa 1886; and the White Farm House, circa 1912, directly across the street.

Offering garden views, private entries, Franklin stoves, and a variety of decor themes, the Glenborough Inn cultivates a gracious, accommodating environment that emphasizes guests' privacy. In keeping with this philosophy, breakfast is delivered to the rooms rather than served in a common area.

Glenborough's relaxed, informal atmosphere makes this inn the perfect getaway.

✿ **Rates:** $–$$$.
Open: Year-round.
Facilities: Choose to book one of six rooms or an entire cottage that sleeps up to six people. Full hot breakfast served.
Directions: The inn is in downtown Santa Barbara. Visit the Web site to see a map and for reservations and information.

Simpson House Inn

121 East Arrellaga Street, **Santa Barbara,** CA 93101;
(800) 676–1280; www.simpsonhouseinn.com

AMONG ITS many accolades, the historic Simpson House Inn has been awarded the American Automobile Association's coveted Five Diamond Award. The first North American bed-and-breakfast inn ever to receive the travel organization's highest rating, Simpson House Inn features displays of unusual orchids in the main house and an acre of formal English gardens. Highlights include fountains, statuary, and lovely trees—from a one hundred-year-old English oak to magnolias, fruit trees, and formidable pittosporums that perfume the air in early spring.

Simpson House Inn has also achieved landmark status. The innkeepers accomplished a fine restoration of the 1874 Eastlake Victorian house, with its beautiful signature veranda. The 1878 barn was also restored. After dismantling the structure in 1992, the owners reconstructed the barn to maintain its architectural integrity while updating it in grand style.

Obviously not your average bed and breakfast, the Simpson House Inn features an atmosphere where guests may expect to be pampered. Luxurious furnishings and orchids adorn each of the inn's rooms. In the early evening, guests are served Mediterranean hors d'oeuvres accompanied by California wines.

This very private retreat is just a short stroll from the delightful botanical collections of Alice Keck Memorial Garden and within easy walking distance of many other attractions.

✿ **Rates:** $$–$$$$.
Open: Year-round.
Facilities: The inn offers fifteen guest rooms and cottages, with private baths and full gourmet breakfast served. Lavish amenities include afternoon tea and spa services (the latter available in the privacy of your guest room). One room is wheelchair accessible.
Directions: The inn is located in the heart of Santa Barbara. Visit the Web site for detailed directions.

LOS ANGELES TO SAN DIEGO

Victoria Rock Bed and Breakfast

2952 Victoria Drive, **Alpine,** CA 91901; (619) 659–5967;
www.victoria-rock-bb.com

LOCATED IN San Diego's rural East County, this former single-family residence opened for business as a bed-and-breakfast in mid-1998. Amiable owners/proprietors Darrel and Helga Doliber (she hails from Germany, home of the bed-and-breakfast) named the establishment after the locally famous rock formation visible from their home, which bears an uncanny likeness to Britain's Queen Victoria in profile.

The Dolibers' sprawling backyard is an officially certified National Wildlife Federation Backyard Wildlife Habitat. Among the more salient features of the three-acre setting are a romantic, oak-enclosed wedding grotto and a butterfly and hummingbird garden that attracts daily visitors, including several different species of hummingbirds. Bird-watchers have identified several dozen other bird species on the property.

✿ **Rates:** $.
Open: Year-round.

Facilities: Four suites; each has a distinctive decorating theme, outside sitting area, and private bath. Full gourmet breakfast served.

Directions: The B&B is 28 miles from downtown San Diego. From San Diego take Interstate 8 east to the Tavern Road exit. Cross over the freeway and make a right onto Victoria Park Terrace. Follow to Victoria Drive and turn left. Continue on Victoria until you reach the 2900 block. You'll find a map of the area on the Web site.

The Bed & Breakfast Inn at La Jolla

7773 Draper Street, **La Jolla,** CA 92037; (858) 456–2066, (800) 582–2466; www.innlajolla.com

BUILT IN 1913 by the well-known Southern California architect Irving Gill, the Inn at La Jolla is a registered historical site. Its lovely, tranquil gardens were originally planted by renowned horticulturist Kate Sessions, who was responsible for much of the early landscaping of San Diego's Balboa Park.

The onetime home of famous American composer John Phillip Sousa and his family, the inn retains many of its original features. Many of the rooms have garden views, and flowers abound inside and out.

❁ **Rates:** $$–$$$.

Open: Year-round.

Facilities: The inn has fifteen rooms: Eight rooms are located in the original house, two rooms are situated around past the dining area, and five are in an annex. A full breakfast is served, and guests can attend a wine and cheese reception in the afternoon or enjoy iced tea and cookies whenever they like.

Directions: From San Diego take Interstate 5 north to the La Jolla Parkway west exit. Detailed directions and a map are found on the Web site.

The Seal Beach Inn & Gardens

212 Fifth Street, **Seal Beach,** CA 90740-6115;
(562) 493–2416, (800) 443–3292;
www.sealbeachinn.com

ONE OF THE country's original tourist courts opened for business in 1923, 25 miles south of Los Angeles. Today that vintage lodging is a beautifully renovated bed-and-breakfast retreat, christened the Seal Beach Inn & Gardens.

Situated just a short stroll from the sea shore, the inn is tucked away in a peaceful coastal town adjacent to Long Beach. An hour's drive from Los Angeles, yet seemingly a million miles away from the frenzied energy of the city's crowded freeways, the Seal Beach Inn & Gardens is an oasis. You'll find here an array of antique furnishings and fascinating architectural elements, from decorative ironwork balcony railings to inviting gates, elegant benches, and cafe tables. Wander through the courtyard and terraces, patio, and pathways, and discover the intimate scale of the inn and the warm and helpful staff—another hallmark of the Seal Beach Inn.

The owner, an avid collector with a wonderful eye for antiques, has decorated indoor rooms and outdoor areas with objects of rare beauty. I was enchanted by an antique Parisian fountain ornamenting the swimming pool and patio area. The fountain was among the many acquisitions that filled seventeen shipping crates bought by the innkeepers on one of their European sojourns.

Garden spaces adorn every secluded nook found throughout the property. Growing in flower beds and containers, vibrant hibiscus and mandevilla with their incandescent blooms commingle with a wonderful scramble of flowering vines—clematis and honeysuckle, wisteria and bougainvillea, among others. Although threatening to camouflage large expanses of exquisitely patterned wrought iron, the vines are a superb embellishment to the architecture of the inn's buildings.

Delightful foxgloves, delphiniums, and a bevy of flowering perennials consort with frilly annuals. Note also the varied shapes and textures of palm trees, delicate ferns, and blooming bushes. The exhilarating sea air combines with scented geraniums, fragrant freesias, and nicotiana, extending a cordial greeting to guests of this charming Southern California inn.

❀ **Rates:** $–$$$.
Open: Year-round.
Facilities: The inn has twenty-three rooms and suites, all with private baths; full gourmet breakfast and afternoon hors d'oeuvres are served.
Directions: Take Interstate 405 to the Seal Beach Boulevard exit. Detailed directions can be found on the Web site. The inn is just off CA Coast Hwy. 1, about one hour south of downtown Los Angeles and the Los Angeles International Airport.

Artists' Inn and Cottage Bed & Breakfast

1038 Magnolia Street, **South Pasadena,** CA 91030;
(626) 799–5668, (888) 799–5668; www.artistsinns.com

THE BEAUTIFUL blooms of mature rose bushes line the entry walk-way and flank the white picket fence surrounding the Artists' Inn. Situated on a spacious corner property in South Pasadena, the inn acquired a second building, expanding from the six rooms located in its original 1895 Victorian home to include an additional four rooms and suites in an adjacent circa-1909 cottage.

An eclectic, artistic touch defines the bed-and-breakfast's general ambience as well as the interior decor of each accommodation. All rooms at the Artists' Inn are either named after individual artists or art movements. The color schemes, furnishings, and fittings reflect the aesthetic sensibilities associated with Degas, Van Gogh, Gauguin, Grandma Moses, and Georgia O'Keeffe. Theme-oriented rooms represent eighteenth-century English, Italian, impressionist, and expressionist painters.

A distinctly vintage appeal distinguishes accommodations in the original building, while the rooms in the newly restored cottage reflect a more contemporary touch.

Descanso Gardens, the Huntington Botanical Gardens, and the Los Angeles County Arboretum & Botanical Garden are a brief drive by car from the Artists' Inn. If you avoid rush-hour traffic, the Getty Center is approximately one hour away.

✿ **Rates:** $–$$.
Open: Year-round.
Facilities: The inn has ten rooms and suites, all with private baths. Full breakfast and afternoon refreshments are served.
Directions: Avoid commuter hours, and the Artists' Inn in South Pasadena is approximately a half hour northeast of downtown Los Angeles, or about forty-five minutes from the Los Angeles International Airport.

Resources for Gardeners

*L*ISTED UNDER this heading you will find distinctive products and services such as uncommon garden ornaments and Internet sites that post up-to-the-minute events. Rare gardening books, aged chicken manure for your roses, and the perfect cultivating tool can be found here.

There are hundreds of fine plant nurseries and garden centers and other laudable establishments I came across in my travels; however, I could not include them all. Don't let that stop you from going farther afield. Allow yourself to wander and you're certain to find additional sites that will stir your particular passions.

PERIODICALS AND WEB SITES

Bay Area Gardens Network

www.ruthbancroftgarden.org/bayareagardens

THE BAY AREA Gardens Network is a consortium of botanical gardens located throughout the San Francisco Bay Area. Member gardens produce a wonderful brochure, *Greater Bay Area Gardens*, containing a guide to dozens of public gardens. The brochure features a map and listings for arboretums, botanical gardens, and garden centers spanning the Monterey Peninsula to Mendocino County.

You can often pick up a copy of the brochure at one of the member gardens or at special events such as the San Francisco Flower & Garden Show. The Bay Area Gardens (BAG) Network plans to have its own Web site, but presently, the Ruth Bancroft Garden hosts a Web page for the BAG Network: www.ruthbancroftgarden .org/bayareagardens. You can download the brochure in a printable format.

The Garden Conservancy's Open Days Directory

P.O. Box 219, Cold Spring, NY 10516; (888) 842–2442, (415) 561–3990 (San Francisco office); www.gardenconservancy.org

THE GARDEN CONSERVANCY is a national organization that works to preserve outstanding American gardens and to generate interest in the country's gardening heritage. Ruth Bancroft's wonderful garden in Northern California is credited with inspiring Frank Cabot to found the Garden Conservancy. In so doing, Cabot spearheaded and inspired others to go forward and create a thriving membership, one that continues to grow and to provide support for gardens from coast to coast.

Akin to England's National Gardens Scheme, the Garden Conservancy's Open Days Program also provides the rare opportunity to visit an array of private gardens. Like the *Yellow Book* produced by the National Gardens Scheme, with its listings of private gardens that open for charity, the Garden Conservancy publishes its yearly *Open Days Directory: The Guide to Visiting America's Best Private Gardens*.

Obtain a copy of the directory to be privy to a schedule of days when you can enjoy self-guided tours of private sanctuaries you might never see under any other circumstance—public gardens are included, too.

If you plan to visit gardens around the country, you may want to purchase the national edition, with listings for nearly two dozen states and British Columbia. Have the regional West edition in hand if you are interested in coordinating visits to gardens while traveling in California; the West edition covers the six western states and British Columbia. Other editions include the Northeast, Midwest, and South.

The national edition can be purchased at bookstores or by visiting www.gardenconservancy.org. Regional editions are available from bookstores, nurseries, or the Garden Conservancy Web site, where you'll also find prices for the various editions, shipping fees, and discount coupons.

Open dates and times vary from year to year, but gardens must pass muster to be included in the program. Be assured that each special landscape will encompass a worthy garden design and inspirational plantings. Gorgeous views are oftentimes an added bonus.

To plan your itinerary, first peruse the directory to glean a listing of open days by date. Go to the California section, where you'll find a chronological listing by county, then by town. The special days that are set aside unfold from spring through fall, with the names of each garden and a description provided to help you make your selections. A nominal fee is collected at each garden when you visit; no reservations are required. You'll find detailed driving directions included in each garden listing. One free admission coupon is included in each book.

Many garden owners open their gates to the public only once, so in any given year, you may have occasion to experience a glorious and surprising gardenscape that will remain hidden to the public ever after.

Mediterranean Garden Society

www.mediterraneangardensociety.org

THIS DELIGHTFULLY informative Web site offers a trove of wisdom for gardeners dealing with Mediterranean climate conditions as well as for visitors who wish to attend a special talk or presentation while spending time in California.

Click on International Branches for a link to the Northern California Branch of the Mediterranean Garden Society (MGS). Here you'll find up-to-date listings of events taking place year-round throughout California, from symposiums to garden tours to meetings of the society held in alluring locales. As I write this entry, for example, an annual general meeting of the MGS is scheduled to take place on the Greek island of Corfu. Application information is available on the Web site.

Founded in 1994, the society draws to its ranks a dynamic group of individuals, with members hailing from Australia, California, Italy, South Africa, and beyond. Dedicated to the study of plants and the implementation of regionally appropriate gardening,

the society provides its membership with an invaluable forum for sharing information.

Peruse *News & Views*, an online magazine presenting a fascinating range of articles. You'll discover personal accounts of the trials other gardeners come up against and their successes. And you'll find images of beautifully cultivated plants and inviting garden settings. Whether you're an armchair traveler, or prone to wanderlust, the inspirational content may cause you to consider booking a flight to some distant clime.

Pacific Horticulture magazine

P.O. Box 680, Berkeley, CA 94701; (510) 849–1627; www.pacifichorticulture.org

A MATCHLESS RESOURCE for the West Coast's garden and plant lovers, *Pacific Horticulture* magazine offers quarterly issues filled with intelligent writing and exquisite photography. Serious gardeners from Vancouver to San Diego can turn to this periodical for stimulating articles on plants, places, and prominent people that inhabit the realms of gardening, horticulture, and botany. *Pacific Horticulture* also updates readers with book reviews, a "Laboratory Report," and calendar listing of events and happenings throughout California and the Northwest.

Count on *Pacific Horticulture* for its dependably incisive and appealing stories. In one issue, editor Richard G. Turner Jr. set a thoughtful tone with insightful musings on the critique of landscape design. Articles included "Trees of Golden Gate Park: Silk Oak and Two Lindens," by Elizabeth McClintock; "Coleus," by Richard W. Hartlage; an ode to seasonal highlights at Matanzas Creek Winery gardens, by Julie Greenberg; and an article on Italy's Landriana Gardens, by Joan Tesei.

Pacific Horticulture is published by the nonprofit Pacific Horticultural Foundation, which is supported by the California

Horticultural Society, the Strybing Arboretum Society, the Western Horticultural Society, the Southern California Horticultural Society, and the Northwest Horticultural Society. Issues appear quarterly in January, April, July, and October.

GARDEN SITES, SHOPS, BOOKSTORES, AND SHOWS

Lompoc Flower Fields

> c/o Lompoc Valley Chamber of Commerce, P.O. Box 626,
> 111 South I Street, Lompoc, CA 93438-0626; (800) 240-0999;
> www.lompoc.com

THE BLOOMS may change from year to year, but if you're planning to travel through the Lompoc Valley during the high season of May through September, you can count upon 19 miles of glowing flower fields. Larkspur, lavender, and lobelia; stock, statice, and sweet peas are some of the luscious flowers you'll most likely behold.

For nearly one hundred years, commercial growers have cultivated colorful blooms in the Lompoc Valley, where crops thrive in the mellow climate with cool, moist summer conditions. Not only are impressive amounts of flower seeds produced in these fields, but also beautiful cut flowers are harvested for sale to florists and for use in dried arrangements across the western United States.

During the annual Lompoc Flower Festival held the last weekend in June, the Alpha Literary and Improvement Club presents its annual flower show. Admission fee is charged. At other times, enjoy your own self-guided tour of the flower fields by contacting the Lompoc Valley Chamber of Commerce and requesting a map. You may wish to call before your visit to find out the status of fields currently in bloom.

❀ **Directions:** Lompoc is located about one hour north of Santa Barbara (three hours north of Los Angeles). Approach the town from U.S. Highway 101, exiting onto California Highway 246 west in the direction of the Pacific Ocean.

San Francisco Flower & Garden Show

(800) 829–9751 (information), (415) 771–6909 (office);
www.gardenshow.com

ONE OF THE country's premier gardening extravaganzas, the San Francisco Flower & Garden Show dazzles showgoers. In the show's thirteenth year it moved from a downtown Fort Mason location to the spacious Cow Palace. This affords visitors freeway access and plenty of parking, and it provides exhibitors with the boundless space they yearned for in the past.

One of the recent shows featured three acres of exhibits, including inspirational vignettes for urban garden settings, an orchid show, botanical art exhibit, a children's garden competition, droves of seminars hosted by Sunset Publishing, a marketplace with 250 booths featuring the latest and best in all sorts of gardening essentials (and nonessentials), a plant market, and of course sensational display gardens to please visitors who possess the fortitude to cover all that ground.

As many as twenty-four beautifully landscaped, full-size display gardens are featured. In addition, the Garden Living area demonstrates how California gardens are enjoyed as living space. An Orchid Pavilion encompasses an impressive 20,000 square feet of exhibition space, to the delight of orchid lovers.

The San Francisco Flower & Garden show is regularly held in springtime, around mid-March. Each year, the show offers visitors more to see and do than in the previous years. Those of us from other climes may visit upcoming shows for the breathtaking rush of ushering in a new gardening year amidst the exceptional sights and spectacles of these events. The show's lovely if fleeting gardenscapes can be counted upon to illustrate imaginative elements appropriate to the numerous microclimates within the greater San Francisco Bay Area, and to lend ideas for designs and plantings that gardeners everywhere will appreciate.

Every year the San Francisco Flower & Garden Show's opening gala (along with a portion of the gate proceeds) benefits the Friends of Recreation and Parks of San Francisco.

❧ **Directions:** To approach the Cow Palace from San Francisco, take U.S. Highway 101 south to the Cow Palace/Third Street exit. Travel south on Bayshore Boulevard, then turn right onto Geneva Avenue.

Sonoma County Farm Trails

P.O. Box 6032, Santa Rosa, CA 95406; (707) 571–8288, (800) 207–9464; www.farmtrails.org

AN ORGANIZATION of family farms, specialty growers, and wineries, Sonoma County Farm Trails produces a yearly map listing dozens of member establishments who invite your visit and certainly will not turn away your commerce. Do fresh raspberries, delectable culinary condiments, and fine wines pique your interest? Maybe you'll be traveling with a child who would enjoy petting a llama or observing an emu up close? By devoting a day to sampling the fresh produce and diverse fare at a few select destinations, you can begin to explore the fertile dominion that is Sonoma.

Surveying participating businesses can be fascinating and fun, especially if the thought of shopping for hand-spun yarns or hand-crafted herbal gifts sounds tempting. Even exotic cats and birds number among the pets available for purchase or adoption. You'll also find Christmas tree farms, places to picnic, and purveyors of fresh and dried flowers.

Gardeners flock to the area to buy manures, worm castings, and mulches from various Farm Trails merchants. So what, you might ask, could top the discovery of serviceable essentials like quality fertilizers? Well, Sonoma lures horticulturally oriented tourists from across the country with a mind-boggling array of specialty nurseries, many of which feature irresistible display gardens filled with rare plant species. Usually there are specimens for sale as well.

In order for a nursery to become a Farm Trails member, the vast majority of plant stock must be propagated on-site, not purchased from other growers. You'll find wonderful varieties of native plants, scented geraniums, bearded iris, orchid hybrids, rhododendron and azaleas, daylilies, camellias, bog plants, Japanese maples, and carnivorous plants. When purchasing plants directly from one of these growers, you'll be able to ask an expert on the premises for advice on what conditions a particular species requires in order to thrive.

Telephone for the *Farm Trails Map & Guide*. You can also view a Farm Trails map online or request a copy from the Web site: www.farmtrails.org. *Note:* Before embarking on a trip, be sure to phone ahead to confirm business hours for each participating member of Sonoma County Farm Trails you wish to visit.

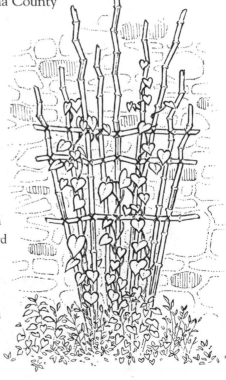

✿ **Directions:** Sonoma County and its countless attractions are located just one hour north of San Francisco and the Golden Gate Bridge. Take U.S. 101 to the California Highway 37 exit, proceeding north on California Highway 121 to the historic town of Sonoma. Or stay on U.S. 101 and travel northward to explore Petaluma, Santa Rosa, Geyserville, and Cloverdale. The Sonoma County Farm Trails map presents a detailed view of the county's streets, back roads, and members' locations.

Smith & Hawken stores

Berkeley: 1330 Tenth Street; (510) 527–1076

Beverly Hills: 370 North Canon Drive; (310) 247–0737

Costa Mesa: South Coast Plaza, 3333 Bristol Street; (714) 437–9526

Los Gatos: 26 Santa Cruz Avenue; (408) 354–6500

Mill Valley: 35 Corte Madera Avenue; (415) 381–1800

Palo Alto: 705 Stanford Center; (650) 321–0403

Pasadena: 519 South Lake Avenue; (626) 584–0644

San Francisco: 2040 Fillmore Street; (415) 776–3424

San Diego: Fashion Valley Center, 7007 Friars Road, Suite 340;
   (619) 298–0441

Walnut Creek: 1365 North Broadway; (925) 280–0015

www.smithandhawken.com

NO OTHER enterprise equals the high visibility and panache associated with Smith & Hawken's ever-expanding line of accoutrements—from useful, well-made tools for maintaining a garden to aesthetic embellishments that tickle one's fancy.

With its classic garden furnishings and comfortably cosmopolitan apparel, Smith & Hawken has been at the forefront of the gardening blitz that's sweeping the country. Whether you wish to create a personal garden sanctuary outdoors or to introduce a decorative botanical theme indoors, you'll find a wealth of furnishings and accessories at Smith & Hawken.

There are a slew of shops in California, so if you find yourself in the neighborhood of any Smith & Hawken store, pay a visit and see if you can resist *not* buying something for yourself or a special friend who gardens.

In Marin County, stop by the original Smith & Hawken Mill Valley nursery located at the foot of Mount Tamalpais, to see where it all began.

❀ **Directions:** Call before visiting any of Smith & Hawken's stores for hours of operation and directions. You'll find detailed driving directions on the Web site.

VLT Gardner Horticultural & Botanical Books

2014 Garden Street, Santa Barbara, CA 93105;
(805) 563–9435

PROPRIETOR Virginia Gardner offers a treasure trove of 6,000 new and vintage books. Specializing in regional gardening—Southern California specifically—Virginia carries a range of books on horticulture, botany, and gardening of all persuasions.

A botany major in college, Virginia also studied art and landscape design. A founding member of the California Garden and Landscape History Society, Virginia has served on the board of the Southern California Horticultural Society and *Pacific Horticulture* magazine, and she conducts docent tours at Ganna Walska Lotusland. In 2003 Virginia was the Southern California Horticultural Society honoree for horticulturist of the year.

Before starting her own enterprise, Virginia sold books as a volunteer for the Southern California Botanists, which was established in the 1920s. Engaging, opinionated, and refreshingly unconventional, Virginia conducts business by appointment only. If you're a book lover or gardening enthusiast and you'd like an opportunity to pore over a marvelous collection of gardening tomes, contact VLT Gardner Books in advance to arrange a date.

VLT Gardner's offerings include a suite of ten selected Mattioli botanical engravings (also sold separately), printed from original 1596 woodblocks. Also available are numbered limited new-edition copies of *California Gardens*, by Winifred Starr Dobyns, and *Lotusland: A Photographic Odyssey*, a colorful chronicle of Ganna Walska's fantastic Santa Barbara gardens, with text by Theodore Roosevelt Gardner II.

Choosing an Outing

ARBORETUMS

Northern California
San Francisco Botanical Garden
    at Strybing Arboretum,
    Golden Gate Park
Villa Montalvo

Santa Cruz to Santa Barbara
Arboretum of the University of
    California, Santa Cruz
Santa Barbara County Courthouse

Los Angeles to San Diego
Los Angeles County Arboretum
Palm Canyon, Balboa Park
University of California at
    Irvine Arboretum

BOTANICAL GARDENS
AND CONSERVATORIES

Northern California
Conservatory of Flowers,
    Golden Gate Park

Marin-Bolinas Botanical Gardens
Mendocino Coast Botanical
    Gardens
Quarryhill Botanical Garden
Regional Parks Botanic Garden,
    Tilden Regional Park
San Francisco Botanical Garden
    at Strybing Arboretum,
    Golden Gate Park
University of California
    Botanical Garden

Santa Cruz to Santa Barbara
San Luis Obispo Botanical Garden
Santa Barbara Botanic Garden

Los Angeles to San Diego
Balboa Park Botanical Building
Descanso Gardens
The Huntington Botanical
    Gardens
Los Angeles County Arboretum
    and Botanical Garden

Mildred E. Mathias Botanical
   Garden
Quail Botanical Gardens
Rancho Santa Ana Botanic
   Garden
San Diego Wild Animal Park
San Diego Zoo Botanical
   Collection, Balboa Park
Sherman Library and Gardens
South Coast Botanic Garden

CONTEMPORARY
AND MODERNIST GARDENS

Northern California
Artesa Winery
Copia, the American Center for
   Wine, Food & the Arts
Cornerstone Festival of Gardens
The Hess Collection Winery
Matanzas Creek Winery Estate
   Gardens

Los Angeles to San Diego
The Getty Center Central Garden
Norton Simon Museum Sculpture
   Garden
Walt Disney Concert Hall
   Community Park

ECCENTRIC AND
ARTISTIC GARDENS

Northern California
Cafe Beaujolais Garden
Our Own Stuff Gallery Garden

Santa Cruz to Santa Barbara
Ganna Walska Lotusland

Los Angeles to San Diego
The Getty Center Central Garden

ESTATE AND
FORMAL GARDENS

Northern California
Blake Garden
Dunsmuir Historic Estate
Filoli
Villa Montalvo

Santa Cruz to Santa Barbara
Hearst Castle Gardens

Los Angeles to San Diego
Virginia Robinson Gardens

GARDENS THAT
CHILDREN WILL
ESPECIALLY ENJOY

Northern California
Marin-Bolinas Botanical Gardens

Santa Cruz to Santa Barbara
Heart's Ease Herb Shop and
   Gardens

Los Angeles to San Diego
The Huntington Botanical
   Gardens' Children's Garden
San Diego Zoo Botanical
   Collection, Balboa Park
San Diego Wild Animal Park

HABITAT AND
THEMATIC GARDENS

Northern California
Copia, the American Center for
   Wine, Food & the Arts
The Garden at Fetzer Vineyards
The Garden at Green Gulch
Kendall-Jackson Wine Center
Korbel Champagne Cellars
Luther Burbank Home & Gardens
Marin Art and Garden Center

Occidental Arts & Ecology Center
Sunset Garden

Santa Cruz to Santa Barbara
Heart's Ease Herb Shop and
    Gardens
Alice Keck Park Memorial
    Gardens

HISTORIC GARDENS

Northern California
Allied Arts Guild
Dunsmuir Historic Estate
Filoli
Luther Burbank
    Home & Gardens

Santa Cruz to Santa Barbara
Dallidet Adobe
Monterey State Historic Park
    and Adobe Gardens

Los Angeles to San Diego
Charles F. Lummis Home and
    Garden—El Alisal
Marston House and Gardens,
    Balboa Park
Rancho Los Alamitos Historic
    Ranch and Gardens
Rancho Los Cerritos

JAPANESE GARDENS

Northern California
Hakone Gardens
Japanese Friendship Garden
    in Kelley Park
Japanese Tea Garden,
    Golden Gate Park

Los Angeles to San Diego
Japanese Friendship Garden,
    Balboa Park
Earl Burns Miller Japanese Garden

PARKS AND
GARDEN CENTERS

Northern California
Elizabeth F. Gamble Garden
Golden Gate Park
Lakeside Park Gardens
Luther Burbank Home & Gardens
Marin Art and Garden Center
Overfelt Gardens
Shoreline at Mountain View and
    Rengstorff House

Santa Cruz to Santa Barbara
Alice Keck Park Memorial
    Gardens
Andrée Clark Bird Refuge
Franceschi Park

Los Angeles to San Diego
Balboa Park
Walt Disney Concert Hall
    Community Park

ROSE GARDENS

Northern California
Berkeley Rose Garden
Garden Valley Ranch
Morcom Rose Garden
Rose Garden, Golden Gate Park
Russian River Rose Company
San Jose Municipal Rose Garden

Los Angeles to San Diego
Inez Grant Parker Memorial Rose
    Garden, Balboa Park

SPECIALTY PLANT NURSERIES
AND
DISPLAY GARDENS

Northern California
California Carnivores
Digging Dog Nursery

Garden Valley Ranch
Geraniaceae Nursery and Gardens
Sonoma Horticultural Nursery
Yerba Buena Nursery

Santa Cruz to Santa Barbara
Santa Barbara Orchid Estate
Sierra Azul Nursery & Gardens
Sycamore Farms

Los Angeles to San Diego
Buena Creek Gardens
Roger's Gardens
Summers Past Farms
Weidners' Gardens

SUCCULENT GARDENS

Northern California
Arizona Garden at Stanford
  University
Marin-Bolinas Botanical Gardens
The Ruth Bancroft Garden

Santa Cruz to Santa Barbara
Ganna Walska Lotusland

Los Angeles to San Diego
Desert Garden, Balboa Park

Glossary

allée: A formal element in garden design such as a long pathway, connecting road, or avenue running between queues of symmetrically planted trees.

arbor: A structure that may serve as an entryway or focal point within the garden, often providing support for climbing vines or roses.

arboretum: A site dedicated to the cultivation and study of trees.

bog: A consistently wet garden area; a habitat specifically designed to remain waterlogged in order to grow plants known to thrive in damp conditions.

bonsai: An art form encompassing venerated techniques for growing dwarf trees or shrubs in ornamental shapes; also refers to a plant pruned and trained in this way.

bromeliad: A large family of primarily tropical plants, many of which grow on trees or rocks in natural settings and derive moisture and nutritional sustenance from the air. Some types of bromeliads grow in terrestrial environments where porous plant matter accumulates, such as the forest floor.

copse: A gathering or small grove of trees or shrubs.

Craftsman style: Spanning the years 1876 to 1916, this style was inspired by nature and craft traditions. The Craftsman bungalow appears to hug the earth, with a distinctly horizontal design: Interiors exhibit a rather open floor plan. Use of local materials is common, such as stone for fireplaces, decorative wrought iron, and simple but abundant woodwork—ceiling beams, built-in shelves, wainscotting, and the like.

cycad: Primitive, cone-bearing evergreen plants; palm or fern-like in appearance.

epiphyte: A type of plant that grows on another plant for support, but not for its nutrients; examples include non-parasitic plants such as certain orchids. Also known as an air plant because it does not grow in soil.

espalier: A method whereby fruit trees, roses, etc., are trained to grow on a single, planar surface, such as a building wall or a fence, using wires to support particular branches. Designs vary from elaborate crisscross patterns to a layout of horizontal or vertical lines.

garden room: A separate, enclosed area within a larger garden, designed to celebrate a unique idea or character. Boundaries may be created with hedges, walls of brick or stone, or changes in elevation.

gazebo: A pavilion-like structure placed for viewing the garden. Early examples were traditionally designed as six-sided buildings, commonly incorpo-rating filigree metalwork as decorative embellishment. Contemporary gazebos often feature airy designs of open latticework.

hardscaping: Refers to hard materials used in a garden plan, adding definition and substance to the landscaping. Examples include decorative garden structures such as arbors, paved brick paths, ornamental fences, stone walls, rock work encircling ponds, and wooden frames surrounding raised beds.

herbaceous: Nonwoody plants differentiated by top growth that generally dies back to the ground in winter.

Italianate gardens: A style inspired by Italian architecture and garden design. It may incorporate elaborate roofing tiles, intricate stonework, classical statuary, lavish urns, or formal plantings of shrubbery clipped into geometric shapes, archways, or windowlike openings framing a particular vista.

knot garden: Herbs and/or low hedges such as box planted in a decorative knot design. This garden style dates to the sixteenth century.

orangery: Citrus trees cultivated in a greenhouse setting, or orange trees planted outdoors in a decorative manner, as in a courtyard where the trees are arranged according to a particular design.

outcropping: A rocky formation that supports alpine types of plants. In a garden setting, it may allude to a rock of outstanding shape or color set in place to achieve a natural appearance.

parterre: Garden beds shaped in pleasing configurations. They may be outlined by shrubs such as boxwood and feature ornamental flowers or herbs planted within.

pergola: A garden structure much like an elongated arbor, with vertical posts and a horizontal framework or latticework overhead to support climbing plants.

peristyle: A type of courtyard surrounded (or enclosed) by columns; an arrangement of evenly spaced columns encircling a building.

pollard: The technique of severely cutting back the branches of a tree to its trunk: either to restrict growth, to promote dense foliage or, more traditionally, to produce straight new shoots for garden usage such as stakes.

rill: A formal water feature, often constructed in concrete or stone. A rill is generally designed as a straight, narrow channel that moves water from one level or terrace, to the next. A rill's function as an element of garden design is to direct the eyes up or down a slope or across an expanse.

riparian: Along the banks of a river or other watercourse.

scree: A garden habitat that has been implemented with a combination of rocks, gravel, and sand to simulate the type of drainage and overall growing conditions found in natural settings where alpine plants thrive; an accumulation of rock and rubble found on a slope, or at the base of a mountain.

secret garden: A secluded area within the overall plan of a garden meant to please and surprise visitors and to function as an intimate retreat.

tableau: A conspicuous garden scene where plants and design components come together to produce an especially delightful scene.

vignette: The successful combination of various garden elements into a unified point of interest or tableau. It may include alluring plant associations and attractive garden structures or take in a picturesque view.

Index of Gardens, Landscapes, and Notable Designers